DAT

Impacts of Hazardous Technology

SUNY Series in Environmental Public Policy
Lester W. Milbrath, Editor

Impacts of Hazardous Technology

The Psycho-Social Effects of Restarting TMI-1

John Sorensen
Jon Soderstrom
Emily Copenhaver
Sam Carnes
Robert Bolin

State University of New York Press

Published by
State University of New York Press, Albany

For information, address State University of New York
Press, State University Plaza, Albany, N.Y., 12246

Library of Congress Cataloging-in-Publication Data

Impacts of hazardous technology.

   (SUNY series in environmental public policy)
   Bibliography: p.
   1. Metropolitan Edison Company.   2. Three Mile
Island Nuclear Power Plant (Pa.)   3. Nuclear power
plants—Accidents—Economic aspects—Pennsylvania.
4. Nuclear power plants—Accidents—Social aspects—
Pennsylvania.   I. Sorensen, John, 1951–   .
II. Title.   III. Series.
HD9698.U54M475   1986   363.1′79   86–1943
ISBN 0–88706–332–2
ISBN 0–88706–333–0 (pbk.)

10 9 8 7 6 5 4 3 2 1

Contents

Figures

Tables

Acknowledgments

This study was funded in part by the Nuclear Regulatory Commission (NRC) with the Department of Energy through an inter-agency agreement with Oak Ridge National Laboratory, Oak Ridge, Tennessee. ORNL is operated by Martin Marietta Energy Systems, Inc. for the U.S. Department of Energy under subcontract no. DE-AC05-840R21400. We thank Donald Cleary and Michael Kaltman of the NRC for their role in overseeing the research. In addition, our colleagues at ORNL, including William Fulkerson, Bud Zittel, Tom Wilbanks, and Robert Braid, have all helped to make this work possible. Cynthia Flynn and Social Impact Research assisted by collecting data for us in the TMI vicinity. We also thank those who reviewed our work and made helpful suggestion, including Dennis Mileti, Colorado State University; George Warheit, University of Florida; Thomas Drabek, University of Denver; Paul Slovic, Perceptronics; and three anonymous reviewers.

About the Authors

John Sorensen is a geographer in the Energy Division at Oak Ridge National Laboratory (ORNL). His areas of specialty include human response to disasters and emergency planning. He has conducted research and published numerous articles and studies on earthquakes, volcanos, floods, landslides, nuclear power emergencies, chemical accidents, warning systems and hazards education.

Jon Soderstrom is a social psychologist in the Energy Division at ORNL and Director of Technology Applications for Martin Marietta Energy Systems. He is an expert on social science research methods and evaluation research. He is the author of *Social Impact Assessment* and has published journal articles on a variety of topics concerning technology and society.

Emily Copenhaver is on the research staff of the Environmental and Occupational Safety Division at ORNL and serves as the technical training coordinator for the division. She has conducted research on a wide variety of environmental issues. She is the coeditor of several books, including *Indoor Air Quality* and *Health Risk Analysis*.

Sam Carnes is a political scientist in the Energy Division at ORNL. He specializes in environmental policy research and is an expert on institutional issues in hazardous waste management. He is lead author of a recently published series of studies concerning the disposal of chemical nerve agents.

Robert Bolin is a professor in the Sociology and Anthropology Department at New Mexico State University. He has done extensive research on family recovery from natural disasters.

Chapter *1*

TMI Restart: Setting the Scene

Since March 28, 1979, TMI has become one of the best known acronyms since FDR. Three Mile Island (TMI), an obscure little island located midstream of the Susquehanna River near Harrisburg (Pennsylvania's state capitol) and site of two nuclear reactors, has become a paradoxical icon of our times—symbol of the worst accident in U.S. commercial nuclear electric power generation and possible showstopper for U.S. nuclear power, living proof of the "accident that couldn't happen," primary test case for including psychological impacts under the National Environmental Policy Act (NEPA), and instant tourist attraction.

Starting with a cooling water pump failure, the TMI Unit 2 (TMI-2) reactor overheated, melting part of its uranium fuel and discharging radiation. The accident took days to bring under control, due to uncertain and conflicting information about what was actually happening inside the reactor vessel. In 1980, a special TMI commission concluded that a substantial portion of the fuel within the reactor core came within 30 to 60 minutes of a meltdown. A *meltdown* occurs when the fuels melt through the reactor vessel, releasing large amounts of radiation into the atmosphere, particularly if it breaches the containment structures. This accident, previously labeled an impossibility, has had profound impacts on the way scientists and the public alike handle technological and social risks when complex technology fails.

Although TMI Unit 1 (TMI-1) was not in operation and remained untouched at the time of the accident, it could not escape the long shadow of the TMI-2 accident any more than could the other 62 operating reactors of the 95 licensed to operate in the United States. To set the scene for the TMI-1 restart issue, the locale of the reactor and the people

1

residing nearby, the reactor itself, the operating utility, the accident, and the aftermath as related to the restart issue are first reviewed.

The Locale and The People

The two TMI nuclear reactors are located midstream of the Susquehanna River (Figures 1, 2) in eastern Pennsylvania. The portion of the 5-mile radius from TMI on the west side of the Susquehanna River is located approximately equidistant between the cities of York on the south and Harrisburg on the north. Interstate 83 runs in a north-south direction through the 5-mile radius and connects Harrisburg and York. The area is predominately rural in nature with many rolling hills and river valleys. Portions of Newberry, Fairview, Conewago, and East Manchester townships are within the 5-mile radius of TMI on the west side of the river. The 5-mile radius includes the boroughs of York Haven and Goldsboro and several large major developments including Newberry Town, Conewago Heights, Grandview Acres, Valley Green Estates, Redland Village, and several other developments and mobile home parks. Major employers in the area include the federal, state, and local governments and family businesses.

Based on a study done for the Nuclear Regulatory Commission (NRC) by Social Impacts Research (SIR), six identifiable groups reside within the 5-mile radius of TMI on the west side of the river: farmers, retirees, other long-time residents, newcomers-Harrisburg suburbanites (Valley Green Estates area), other newcomers, and transients (Flynn *et al.* 1982).

The portion of the 5-mile radius from TMI on the east side of the Susquehanna River extends to Highspire to the north, almost to Elizabethtown to the east, and almost to Bainbridge to the south. The Pennsylvania Turnpike (Interstate 76) and U.S. Highway 283 are the principal traffic corridors within the area, comprised primarily of small towns and farms. Included in the 5-mile radius are the boroughs of Middletown, Royalton, and a portion of Highspire, as well as Londonderry Township. Major employers on this side of the river include a steel mill and a trailer factory as well as federal, state, and local governments.

As with their counterparts on the west side, the area is populated by six distinct functional social groups: Old Middletowners, Blacks,

Figure 1.   Five-Mile Radius at TMI.

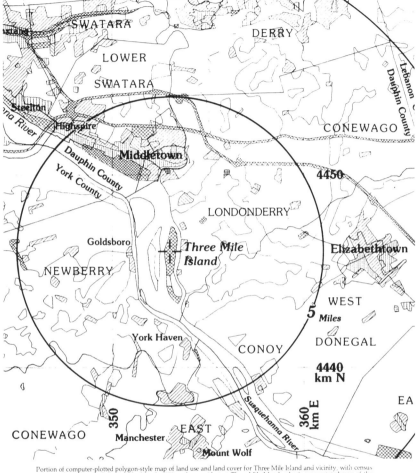

Portion of computer-plotted polygon-style map of land use and land cover for Three Mile Island and vicinity, with census tracts, scale 1:100,000. Following the March 1979 nuclear accident at Three Mile Island, a basic unannotated map of the area was prepared. Because of the use of digital techniques, preparation of the map required only one evening's time.

Source: Interior-Geological Survey, Reston, VA–1982.

Londonderry township long-time residents, Royalton residents, farmers, and residents of newer developments (Flynn *et al.* 1982).

Each of the 12 groups identified in this study (six on each side of the Susquehanna River) has shared characteristics with some of the other groups, but each has certain distinctive characteristics that distinguishes it from the others. Table 1 summarizes some general characteristics of each group according to size, location, length of residency, age, income, and household size. Note, however, that these are general characteristics and may not apply to every group member; more detailed community

Table 1   Summary of general characteristics of the 12 functional social groups identified

| Group | Estimate of TMI population by functional group[a] (%) | Major geographic location | Length of residence | Demographic characteristics | | | Property ownership | Occupation |
				Age	Income	Household size		
East								
• Old Middletowners	42–49	Middletown	Life long	40–65+	Lower middle to upper	2–4	Own	Retired, profes-sional white collar, blue collar
• New-development residents	9–13	Londonderry Township; Middletown suburbs	<15 years	25–45	Low middle to upper middle	2–4	Own and rent	Professionals, white collar, blue collar
• Blacks		Middletown	Most life long, some <10 years	20–65+	Low to middle	4–6	Own and rent	Retired, white collar, blue collar, unemployed
• Royalton residents	14	Royalton	Life long	30–65+	Low to middle	3–5	Own and rent	Retired, blue collar, unemployed
• Farmers		Londonderry Township	Most life long, some <10 years	40–65+	Low middle to upper middle	4–6	Own	Farmer, retired, white collar, blue collar
• Long-term London-derry Township residents		Londonderry Township	Life long	40–65+	Low middle to upper middle	2–5	Own	
Subtotal	~70%							

Table 1 (continued)

Group	Estimate of TMI population by functional group[a] (%)	Major geographic location	Length of residence	Demographic characteristics			Property ownership	Occupation
				Age	Income	Household size		
West								
• Long-time residents	~12	Newberry and Fairview townships, excluding suburban development of North Newberry	>20 years 50% native	50-60	Middle to upper middle	4-5	95%+ own	White collar, blue collar
• Harrisburg suburbanites	6-8	South Fairview townships in suburban development	3-10 years	25-45	Upper middle to upper	4	Own	White collar
• Newcomers	5-6	Goldsboro, York Haven, South Newberry Township	5-14 years	25-45	Low middle to upper middle	4	95%+ own	50% white collar, 50% blue collar
• Retirees	3	Goldsboro, York Haven	Life long	65+	Low middle to middle	2	85%+ own	Retired
• Transients	~1	Goldsboro, York Haven	6 mo-2 years	20-35	Low to low middle	4-6	95%+ rent	70-80% unemployed or on relief; 20-30% blue collar, part-time, seasonal
• Farmers	<1	Newberry and Fairview townships	Life long	50-65	Low middle to upper	5	Own	Farmers
Subtotal	~30%							
Total	~100%							

[a]Estimate by SIA.

Figure 2.   Computer-Plotted Map of Land Use and Land Cover, TMI and Vicinity.

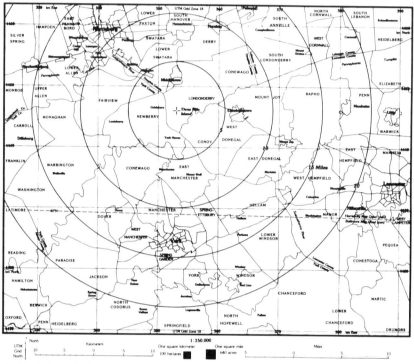

Source: U.S. Geological Survey

profiles can be found in Flynn *et al.* (1982), in an unpublished report documenting data collected for Oak Ridge National Laboratory (ORNL) (Social Impact Research 1982), and in Appendix B which summarizes the two SIR reports. In many cases, the groups identified are true sociological groups that engage in normative, regular face-to-face interaction. In other cases, the profiles characterize aggregates of sociological groups who occupy a similar place in the social structure (e.g., occupational category). The sociological groups can be aggregated in several ways; the criteria for this study are that members of a group occupy a similar place in the social structure and that the effects of a decision made concerning the restart of TMI-1 will be similar for all group members.

The Pennsylvania Department of Health (Goldhaber, Houts and Sabella 1981) has developed a TMI Population Registry comprised of all per-

Table 2   Distribution of TMI population
according to communities[a]

Community	Number	Percent	Side of river
Middletown[b]	9,501	26.75	East
Highspire	1,493	4.20	East
Londonderry Township	4,035	11.36	East
Lower Swatara	4,530	12.75	East
Royalton[b]	945	2.66	East
Conoy Township	1,662	4.68	East
West Donegal Township	2,152	6.06	East
Conewago Township	1,212	3.41	West
East Manchester Township	834	2.34	West
Fairview Township	700	1.97	West
Goldsboro[b]	432	1.21	West
Newberry Township	7,324	20.62	West
York Haven[b]	687	1.93	West
Total	35,507	100.00	

[a]The geographical area is defined by political boundaries of communities which, all or in part, fall with in a 5-mile radius.

[b]100% of the community falls within a 5-mile radius boundary.

Source: M. Goldhaber, 1981.

Table 3   Demographic summary of the TMI population[a]

Number of persons	35,507
Number of households	13,228
Mean number of persons per household	2.7
Median length of residency[b] in same housing unit (years)	5.9
Male/female ratio	1.0
Mean age (years)	33.4
Mean education years (of those 18 and older)	11.7
Percent white	97.0
Percent urban	66.4

[a]The geographical area is defined by political boundaries of communities which, all or in part, fall within a 5-mile radius.

[b]Refers to date first member of the household moved to specified address.

Source: M. Goldhaber, 1981.

sons living within 5 miles of TMI at the time of the accident. The initial report of this registry, approximately 93–95% completed including some townships located within the 5- to 10-mile range, provides some clue to the distribution of the population according to communities (Table 2) and an overall demographic summary of the TMI population (Table 3).

The Utility and the Reactors

General Public Utilities (GPU) is a holding company tying together several utilities such as the Metropolitan Edison Company (Met Ed) (part-owner and operator of TMI), Jersey Central Power and Light, and the Pennsylvania Electric Company (Penelec). Met Ed is a relatively small utility, serving only a portion of the communities included in the 5- to 10-mile impact area described earlier. When TMI-1 was completed in the early 1960s, a second reactor was not envisioned because expected electricity needs of the area could be met by Unit 1 (Stephens 1981:71). However, population and industrial growth patterns did indicate the need for an additional reactor at Jersey Central's Oyster Creek facility. When GPU and Jersey Central encountered labor problems and licensing difficulties in New Jersey (Stephens 1981:71; Gray and Rosen 1982:19), GPU chose to build the Unit 2 at TMI.

TMI-2 [jointly owned by GPU subsidiaries Met Ed (50%), Jersey Central (25%), and Penelec (25%)] was a good example of the 1967 state-of-the-art reactors. It is a *light water reactor* (LWR); that is, it uses enriched uranium fuel, boron control rods, and light water as a moderator and coolant. It is a pressurized water reactor (PWR)—the most common design—in which the water cooling the core transfers heat inside a steam generator to a secondary coolant loop, which drives the turbines for the generation of electricity.

Babcox and Wilcox (B&W) designed and built the TMI reactors. B&W built several of these reactors, but each installation using the PWR reactor may be significantly different. Although B&W supplies the reactor, the structures, control room, turbines, and generators are acquired from other contractors and assembled by yet another contractor known as the architect-engineer. Consequently, even though Units 1 and 2 at TMI are both B&W reactors, they were assembled by different architect-engineers with significant variations in equipment used. As might be expected, the two units also have had very different operating experience records. Unit 1 has had a fairly successful operating history since it went on-line in 1974, but Unit 2 was down for repairs 71% of the time between the time it "went critical" on March 28, 1978, and December 30, 1978 when it went on-line to produce electricity. Between December 30, 1978, and the day of the accident (March 28, 1979), Unit 2 operated at full power less than one-half of the time (Gray and Rosen 1982:54; Stephens 1981:72).

At the time of the accident, Unit 1 was shut down for routine maintenance and refueling. Although untouched by the accident, GPU has spent $95 million refurnishing and improving Unit 1 since the accident, including redesign of the control room, upgraded operator training, better instrumentation, and improved alarms.

The Accident

On March 28, 1979, a pump feeding the cooling water into the reactor core stopped. An emergency core-cooling system, although automatically activated, did not resolve the problem due to a stuck open valve and operator error brought about by conflicting signals from the reactor monitoring systems. Steam forming in the reactor system was superheated by the uncovered, overheated reactor core until superheated, pressurized steam spewed forth from a safety valve. By the time the operators located the malfunctioning valve and restored the coolant, thousands of gallons of radioactive water had spilled onto the floor of the containment building, a general emergency had been declared, and the nation had tuned in on millions of television sets to follow the unfolding story of a potential core meltdown at TMI.

The accident at TMI was characterized by high levels of uncertainty among the nation's nuclear experts and conflicting information regarding the proper way to handle the unfolding accident, especially with regard to the potential explosion of a hydrogen bubble in the containment building, the unknown effects of radiation release, or whether an evacuation was necessary (Stephens 1981; Gray and Rosen 1982). TMI-2 was finally brought to "cold shut-down" after several days but not before part of the reactor core had melted and was reduced to radioactive rubble. Because massive technical documentation is available on the reactor, the accident, and cleanup, no attempt will be made to summarize it further here.

The Aftermath

Prior to the accident, most people in the United States were unaware that two nuclear reactors were located on a small island southwest of Middletown, Pennsylvania. At the time of the Unit 2 accident, Unit

1 was shut down for routine maintenance and refueling. Because of its proximity and nearly identical design, the NRC ordered the reactor to remain down pending further review and investigation.

On September 14, 1979, People Against Nuclear Energy (PANE) of Middletown and seven other groups petitioned the Atomic Safety Licensing Board (ASLB), an independent committee charged with defining issues appropriate for NRC decisionmaking in restoring the operating license for TMI-1, to consider social and psychological impacts as matters of public health and safety under the purview of both the Atomic Energy Act and NEPA. On February 22, 1980, the ASLB ruled out considering the issue under provisions of the Atomic Energy Act. The Board believed, however, that NEPA permitted the NRC to consider community fears, and recommended that they be permitted to include such issues for consideration.

The full Commission twice rejected the contention. PANE petitioned the U.S. Court of Appeals for the District of Columbia seeking to gain a court-ordered assessment of social and psychological impacts of restarting TMI-1. In a decision filed on January 7, 1982, the Court of Appeals voted 2-to-1 in favor of PANE. The NRC was ordered not to allow the restart of Unit 1 until they had prepared such an assessment. The judgment ordered the NRC to make a determination whether "significant new circumstances or information have arisen with respect to the potential psychological health effects of operating the TMI-1 facility." If such circumstances or information did exist, the NRC was directed to prepare a supplemental environmental impact statement considering not only psychological health impacts, but also effects on the well-being of communities surrounding TMI. On April 19, 1983, the Supreme Court overturned the Appeals Court decision and exempted the NRC from preparing an environmental assessment. The basis for the ruling was not that psychological health and well-being are not cognizable under NEPA, but, rather, that the risks of an accident, in essence, are not part of the environment. Risk-induced impacts are not, therefore, appropriate for consideration under NEPA, while impacts resulting from changes in the physical environment are legitimate concerns.

After two more years of hearings and testimony, NRC authorized the restart of TMI-1 by a 4-to-1 vote, effective on June 11, 1985. However, the U.S. Circuit Court of Appeals barred restart on June 7, 1985, pending additional hearing as requested by the State of Pennsylvania, the Union of Concerned Scientists, and Three Mile Island Alert (another community interest group). Finally, NRC gave GPU written permission to restart TMI-1 on October 3, 1985, following the Supreme Court's refusal to block the restart action. On October 4, 1985, Unit 1 restarted after a hiatus of six and one-half years.

In settlement of a class action suit, GPU established a fund paid for by insurers to assist the 600,000 residents of surrounding communities. An Economic Fund of $20 million was set aside to repay business and personal losses, and another $5 million, designated the Public Health Fund, was earmarked for use in studying potential health effects and disseminating the information learned. Administered by Federal Judge Sylvia Rambo, several activities and claims for personal losses have been funded, but little of the total has been committed. These activities include a Public Forum on Nuclear Power, epidemiological studies of possible adverse health effects, payment to local municipalities and school districts within a 25- mile radius of TMI, and payment for personal losses such as lost wages and property damage.

In addition to the $11,000 in settlements from the TMI Economic Fund in February 1983, insurers for GPU in February 1985 reached out-of-court settlements with 280 people who claimed injuries resulting from the TMI-2 accident. The total amount of this settlement was undisclosed, but the County Court in Harrisburg approved settlement for 19 of the 280 cases for $3.9 million, including two cases on behalf of children alleged to have suffered birth defects (Down's Syndrome and cerebral palsy). According to GPU, the settlements represented an economic decision to avoid litigation expenses and were not an admission of liability or that anyone suffered injury from the TMI-2 accident. By August 1985, more than 1,500 lawsuits had been filed by TMI area residents claiming emotional and physical health problems. These plaintiffs claim the accident caused or increased risk of cancer, gallstones, hair loss, infertility, early puberty, vertigo, tumors, birth defects, acquired immune deficiency syndrome (AIDS), and emotional stress.

In the meantime, the cleanup activities at TMI-2 and the management of the utility (GPU/Met Ed) were intermingled with the issue of restarting TMI-1. The credibility of the utility suffered when Met Ed was indicted and convicted on criminal charges of falsifying safety test results, and evidence of cheating on the requalifying examinations for reactor operators was found. Cleanup activities required venting of Krypton gas to the atmosphere (June 29, 1980 to July 12, 1980) and processing thousands of gallons of radioactive water released in the accident; on September 14, 1983, NRC criticized GPU and its cleanup contractor Bechtel North American Power Corporation citing improper procedures and questionable safety of cleanup activities. Whether unavoidable consequences of the accident or ill-advised management practices, these issues affected the restart decisions.

The appended abbreviated chronology (Table 4) attempts to summarize the issues mentioned above and offers a cursory review of the accident's aftermath in the areas with which we are concerned.

This brief review to establish the baseline environment from which the TMI-1 restart issues emerge is followed by discussions of TMI restart and environmental policy, defining the issues from a local perspective, examining the issues from a social science perspective, relating restart to the accident, forecasting the impacts, mitigating the impacts, and projecting implications for environmental management. These later discussions will expand upon the preliminary methodological bases for examining the definition of issues and the measurement of psychological stress related to failure of technology.

Table 4.   Postaccident TMI chronology

10–4–85	TMI-1 restarted.
10–3–85	NRC gives TMI operator, GPU, written permission to restart TMI-1, following the Supreme Court's refusal to block the restart action.
10–2–85	U.S. Supreme Court rules 8-to-1 not to take up the TMI case and lifts the stay.
9–9–85	Electrical fire at TMI-1 damaged switches used to operate nuclear reactor control rods while reactors was on *hot stand-by*.
9–6–85	Pennsylvania State Health Department released report stating that a study of residents living near TMI showed no evidence of increased cancer following the incident.
8–27–85	Third U.S. Circuit Court of Appeals continued stay of TMI-1 restart.
8–18–85	Over 1,500 lawsuits filed by TMI area residents claiming emotional and physical health problems. Plaintiffs claim accident caused or increased risk of cancer, gallstones, hair loss, infertility, early puberty, vertigo, tumors, birth defects, AIDS, and emotional stress.

7–3–85   Federal Judge Sylvia Rambo approved a plan for distribution of $225,000 that owners of TMI have offered 18 local municipalities and school districts within a 25-mile radius of TMI for emergency expenditures incurred during the 1979 accident.

6–15–85   TMI-1 reactor heated to operating temperatures, but reactor not running; condition known as *hot stand-by.*

6–7–85   Judge Collins J. Seitz and two other judges, Third U.S. Circuit Court of Appeals in Philadelphia, barred planned restart of TMI-1 pending hearing. Requested by State of Pennsylvania, Union of Concerned Scientists, and Three Mile Island Alert.

5–29–85   Epidemiologists from Columbia University School of Health began study of possible adverse health effects stemming from TMI-2 accident, financed by $242,000 from TMI Public Health Fund.

5–29–85   NRC authorizes the restart of TMI-1 by 4-to-1 vote. Ruling went into effect June 11, 1985 brought 30 inspectors to monitor around-the-clock the first 3 weeks of operation, and 16 hours per day inspection during the following two months until 100% power production was attained. (Usually one resident inspector.)

3–28–85   150 people participated in rally marking sixth anniversary of TMI-2 accident and demanded a permanent shutdown of TMI.

3–26–85   NRC commissioners decided to reject requests for ouster of ASLB Chairman Ivan Smith.

3–7–85   NRC commissioners asked to decide if their TMI-2 advisory panel could serve as sounding board for area residents' concerns about long-term health effects of the accident. NRC general counsel says this subject outside the group's charter, but panel members listen to residents because no one else in authority would. Need for alternative referral agency such as National Concern Institute. No decision made by NRC.

2–13–85   NRC decided 3-to-2 that the record is complete with respect to safety issues and issues of management competence.

2–8–85   Insurers for GPU reached out-of-court settlements with 280 people who claimed injuries resulting from TMI-2 accident. Total amount of settlement undisclosed but county court in Harrisburg approved settlement of 19 cases for $3.9 million, including two cases on behalf of children alleged to have suffered birth defects from the accident (Downs Syndrome and cerebral palsy). Most claims were for damages from emotional stress or from radiation exposure. According to GPU, the settlements represented an economic decision to avoid litigation expenses and were not an admission of liability or that anyone suffered injury from the accident.

1–11–85   State of Pennsylvania requested that NRC remove Ivan W. Smith from Chair of ASLB presiding over proposal for restart of TMI-1 because he wrote to a federal judge asking for leniency in sentencing of a former TMI supervisor convicted of cheating on an operator licensing test.

6–84   Federal Emergency Mangement Agency (FEMA) told NRC that the November 1983 emergency drill at TMI uncovered four major deficiencies (primarily communications and full participation by one county) and that it had no reasonable assurance that these deficiencies had been corrected. Partial drill in September 1984 to test system.

5–84   Appeal Board decided that ASLB was wrong to conclude that GPU's training program at TMI-1 is adequate for safe restart and ordered licensing board to reopen its hearing on training, including cheating on operator tests and management integrity.

3–84   Met Ed convicted on 7 felony counts stemming from leak rate charges.

11–7–83   Federal Grand Jury at Harrisburg indicted Met Ed on criminal charges of falsifying safety test results before the 1979 accident at TMI, contending that Met Ed attempted to conceal data on the rate of leaking from the reactor's primary cooling system.

9–14–83	NRC Regulatory Panel criticized GPU, owner of TMI, and Bechtel North American Power Corporation (hired by GPU to conduct cleanup of TMI-2) regarding improper procedures and questionable safety of cleanup techniques.
8–31–83	Last of processed waste from the thousands of gallons of radioactive water released in the accident removed from TMI.
4–19–83	Supreme Court ruled that NRC does not have to consider possible psychological harm to nearby residents in deciding whether to reopen TMI-1. In unanimous decision, court held that such an interpretation of NEPA went far beyond the intent of Congress; only consequences that may affect human health by causing changes in water, air, or land are covered. Injunction lifted.
3–28–83	Public Forum on Nuclear Power, three days, Pennsylvania State University, Middletown campus. Sponsored by TMI Public Health Fund.
2–83	TMI Economic Fund disbursed $2.3 million to 11,000 people for personal losses, such as lost wages and property damage. Economic fund has not paid for business losses.
1–24–83	Out-of-court settlement of GPU's $4 billion suit against the builder of the major TMI reactor hardware (B&W) for approximately $37 million. GPU claimed B&W helped cause the TMI-2 accident.
7–82	NRC (and ASLB) recommended restart of Unit 1.
5–18–82	Nonbinding referendum in Pennsylvania state elections; 2-to-1 vote against restart in Dauphin, Cumberland, and Lebanon counties (26% turnout).
1–8–82	The Pennsylvania Public Utility Commission (PUC) awarded Met Ed and Penelec (two components of GPU) a $129 million rate increase. The ruling includes $37.5 million annually from customer rates for cleanup, contingent upon restart of TMI-1.

1–7–82	U.S. Court of Appeals for District of Columbia ruled by 2-to-1 vote that TMI-1 could not be restarted until NRC had considered evidence on psychological effects of the decision on the residents of surrounding communities.
12–14–81	ASLB issued partial initial decision on restart of TMI Unit 1. Voted in favor of restart on technical and emergency planning issues.
8–24–81	Class action suit settlement resulted in fund, paid for by insurers, to benefit the 600,000 people who live within 25 miles of the nuclear plant. Business and personal losses to be repaid from $20 million fund. Potential health effects to be studied and results disseminated with $5 million fund. Administered by Federal Court representative.
7–81	Evidence of operator cheating on Met Ed's requalifying exams.
10–16–80	NRC hearings on restart of TMI-1 began in Harrisburg. Major issues: plant design and hardware, emergency planning, financial capability, and management integrity.
8–8–80	GPU said remaining cleanup work will require an additional five years and $750 million.
7–23–80	Cleanup workers completed first entry into the containment building.
7–12–80	Venting of Krypton gas was completed.
6–29–80	Venting of radioactive Krypton gas from the containment building began.
5–13–80	Jersey Central Power and Light (one of three components of GPU) was awarded a $60 million rate increase by PUC to avoid bankruptcy.
3–80	GPU filed suit against B&W, builder of the reactor vessel. GPU claimed B&W helped cause the accident.
2–22–80	NRC decided that psychological effects were not germane in restart hearings. This decision contested by PANE citizens' group.
2–12–80	Bechtel chosen as prime contractor for the cleanup and rehabilitation of TMI-2.

10–25–79   Cleanup workers decontaminated 300,000 gallons of water in the Auxiliary Fuel Handling Building.

9–14–79   PANE and seven other groups petition ASLB to consider social and psychological impacts as part of public health and safety under NEPA.

8–13–79   GPU unveiled a four-year, $400 million recovery project for TMI Nuclear Station. Company executives expressed hope that government and nuclear industry will help pay for uninsured costs.

8–79   Suspension of GPU's operating license, pending hearings, originally expected to be completed within two years by the ASLB.

7–2–79   NRC ordered TMI-1, the undamaged sister reactor, shut down indefinitely.

3–28–79   Accident at TMI Unit 2, an 843 megawatt nuclear power plant. Reactor's radioactive core overheated and partly melted when the reactor cooling system lost water. Approximately 144,000 persons evacuated the area around TMI. TMI Unit 1 down for refueling at the time.

Chapter *2*

TMI Restart and Environmental Policy

The NRC's May 1985 decision to allow the restart of TMI-1, the U.S. Supreme Court's October 1985 final decision not to upset that order, and the lengthy debate that preceded those decisions have significant implications for environmental policy. In a very real sense, the TMI restart case set a precedent in terms of the breadth of impacts to be considered in decisionmaking and environmental policy. Other issues, such as nuclear power plant emergency response planning, the disposal of chemical nerve agent weapons, and the hazards of operating chemical manufacturing plants, have been broadened in terms of a more fully identified set of decision and action alternatives by the restart debate and its sequenced multiple decisions (see Chapter 1).

The restart controversy also resulted in the proliferation of anticipatory impact assessments. While this situation is not unusual in the context of implementing environmental impact statement (EIS) requirements of the NEPA, it is unusual in its incorporation of psychological impacts of collective decisions and subsequent efforts to refine such concerns for questions about other hazardous technologies. The findings of the research herein and their implications for psycho-social impacts measurement, environmental policy, impact mitigation, and hazard management speak more broadly than simply to the TMI restart controversy. Hazardous technology, or technology that is perceived by many to be hazardous, appears to be a dominant issue of our times. Do we ban such technology (at our peril), do we regulate it (and how do we do so efficiently), do we redesign it (according to what criteria), or do we learn to live (or die) with it? Concerning ourselves with the psycho-social dimensions of contemporary hazardous technology impels us to investigate the prospects and limits of nuclear deterrence (by whatever name), our society's reliance on chemicals, the future of recombinant DNA (deoxyribonucleric acid), hazardous wastes, and the processes and products that generated them, and other complex socio-technical systems. Our investigations must turn to questions of peaceful coexistence, to the design and operation of technology that is environmentally benign, safe, and acceptable.

Alternative Actions

At the very least, the TMI restart case amplifies the multidimensionality of decisionmaking about technology. It validates the notion that technological systems are comprised of a bundle of technical, scientific, social, economic, psychological, and political factors, and are not simply "fixes" with few perturbations outside the realm of technical expertise. Alternative decision processes and products imply a host of impacts. One does not simply throw the switch and determine the direct impacts of that action. Rather, "throw the switch" type decisions are accompanied by decisions about design, information dissemination, decisionmaking, decision implementation, operational monitoring, decommissioning, and, in some cases, perpetual care.

In the case of TMI-1 restart, the types of impacts manifested depend, to no small extent, on which technical restart alternative is chosen, the environment in which the decision is made, and the way it is implemented. Broadly speaking, the two technical alternatives were either to restart or not to restart TMI-1. To restart TMI-1 would, in simplest terms, entail resuming operations at the reactor. The nature of the restart decision environment, in such terms as public access to restart decisionmaking, linkages between TMI-1 restart and TMI-2 cleanup, and media coverage, will affect the kinds of impacts that are manifested. Furthermore, the way operations are resumed is not as simple as turning on a switch and reverting to full power operation. Renewed operations are accompanied by a series of system safety tests as full power is gradually restored over a period of months. Finally, the way information on this process is conveyed to, and accepted by, the public also has implications for the nature and extent of impacts.

Not restarting TMI-1 is a complex endeavor in that it probably requires that the plant also be decommissioned. At present, three technical alternatives exist for decommissioning a plant: mothballing, entombment, and dismantlement. *Mothballing*, the simplest of the three options, means that the plant remains relatively intact, with the removal of only the most easily accessible radioactive materials, but access to the reactor is restricted or prohibited. *Entombment* entails removal of the less radioactive parts, while the parts of the plant where radioactivity is highest are sealed off or covered over, usually with cement. *Dismantlement*, the most extensive decommissioning, requires complete removal of all radioactive materials and demolition of the plant enabling the site to be used for other purposes.

Although all three no-restart options are technically feasible, each option precipitates different kinds of social and psychological impacts. Thus, future operations at TMI are not contingent on a single restart/no-restart decision. Further, the impacts likely to arise are equally complex, depending largely on which of the diverse alternatives is selected and the nature of the environment in which the decision is implemented.

Scope of the Study

Regardless whether TMI-1 is restarted, measurable social and psychological impacts on the surrounding communities and their residents will probably occur. Because the nature and extent of these impacts is impossible to predict with precise accuracy, estimating whether impacts will be significant is difficult. The best way to determine if significant impacts occur is to monitor conditions in the area carefully for a period before and after a decision is made. To assist in ruling out the impacts caused by factors unrelated to a restart decision, monitoring should be instituted at a set of control communities.

Given that this assessment of impacts was made prior to the decision to restart TMI-1, however, a research strategy, based on the principles of social science research, was devised to facilitate projections of impacts. Recognizing that the impacts of restarting a nuclear reactor after an accident are unstudied, the findings from other similar events that have been systematically observed may provide guidance in anticipating impacts. The extent to which it can be shown that the situations are analogous will add confidence to the generalizations and projections.

The objective of the research was to assess the level of similarities between the TMI-1 restart and social and psychological responses to environmental hazards in other areas. In this regard, a number of hypotheses based on the literature of environmental hazards were tested. This research focuses on the determination of the present conditions in the TMI region; whether these conditions were different before the accident; the extent to which these conditions are similar or different from those observed elsewhere; and the extent to which the restart issue is a disruptive event similar to other environmental hazards.

Predicting the Impacts of a TMI-1 Restart Decision

Determining the validity of any generalized understanding of an observed relationship is based on the extent to which a similar pattern of effects is detected at another time, at different places, and with different people. Obviously, one's confidence in the general proposition concerning the presumed causal relationship increases with successive tests under different conditions revealing a similar pattern of evidence.

This confidence in a general proposition allows the analyst to generalize potential effects from one situation to another similar, but untested, situation. The ability to anticipate effects, then, is directly related to the depth of understanding of causal relationships and the extent of similarities between situations. If experience with any given event is high and the conditions for response are well-known, then predictions are facilitated and more likely to be valid. Conversely, if the event is novel and the bases for human response are vague, prediction is rather futile.

While the situation presented by a restart of TMI-1 is unique, the basis for understanding human response to risky and hazardous events is more firmly established. Thus, although predicting the extent of any human behavior or manifestation of psycho-social impacts is not feasible, explaining and predicting why they may or may not occur is.

Even in social situations that have been the focus of much empirical research, predicting human response to a future and seemingly unrecognizable event is not a precise or exact art. While learning from analogous events and extending general findings regarding human behavior in response to disruptive events (e.g., natural hazards) is possible, this type of knowledge can be used only to develop estimates of a range of impacts. To the extent that TMI-1 restart is indeed a unique event, making inferences from any historical base is subject to error. The following discussion of the caveats and inherent weaknesses of prediction defines the limitations of the present effort. Soderstrom (1981) has discussed a number of these problems, including exclusion of variables, changing relationships, and data availability. These problems are discussed briefly below.

Potential Limitations to Prediction

1. EXCLUSION OF VARIABLES

Any given action has, potentially, an infinite number of effects. This is especially true given the complex interactions which are the reality of human response to environmental hazards. Under these circumstances, projections are probably based on an inadequate or inappropriate set of variables. The situation is analogous to the bias introduced using misspecified or underspecified models in econometric forecasting (i.e., including inappropriate variables and/or excluding appropriate variables from equations). Models which are only partially specified, therefore, may be disproportionately dependent on the existence, or nonexistence, of certain variables. Klein (1970) points to the lack of empirical and theoretical clarity as often allowing a great deal of discretion in deciding which variables to include and how to portray their interactions.

Given resource constraints, both human and financial, focusing on a defined set of variables is necessary in order to treat them scientifically. Trade-offs need to be made to arrive at a relevant set of variables. Researchers must balance resource limits against perceived importance. Determination of *importance* is the crucial issue.

Deciding what variables are relevant to study clearly implies value judgments (Cochran 1979). Any appeal to such conceits as *common values* is only a partial solution. Given the complexity and distributional nature of impacts, reaching a consensus on any but the most trivial effects is doubtful. This dissention, which exists not only in the local community but also in the social science community, suggests the need for input from multiple perspectives when guiding the selection of variables. This need is especially critical if the social importance of effects is to guide data collection and analysis rather than mere political expediency (political expediency both in terms of ease of measurement and/or adaptability for the prevailing political climate).

2. CHANGING RELATIONSHIPS

Even if, through some fortuitous set of circumstances, the most relevant and important set of variables has been selected, a further problem exists: changing relationships. As Cronbach (1975) has pointed out, generalizations based on recent studies are not necessarily enduring conclusions; empirical relations change. A relationship observed at one point in time may be quite different when tested years later. Cronbach cites a study that compared middle- and lower-class parenting in which class differences observed in the 1930s were often reversed in the 1950s as a prime example.

Demographers are well aware of the complications this condition can entail for their projections. While the extrapolation of trends can be reasonably accurate as long as the underlying relations remain stable, this accuracy ceases at some "turning point" in the relationships (Johnston 1970; Meidinger 1977). This "failure" is especially discouraging because it occurs at precisely the point where the foresight would be most helpful—where the assumed continuity is broken. In the case of impact projection, this problem is inherently exacerbated, because the projections are based to a significant extent upon the very relationships that stand to be altered (Meidinger 1977).

The complications introduced by changing relationships among variables may be nowhere more challenging than in the study of environmental hazards. The information explosion of recent years regarding DDT (dichloro-diphenyl-trichloro-ethane), saccharin, hazardous wastes (e.g., Love Canal and Times Beach), and other items of daily use and consumption has changed substantially the relationships among key variables. What the public knows, how they know it, who they trust, and who decides, are all questions to which answers are elusive if for no other reason than the need to consider simultaneously a barrage of information that is disseminated to the public and the effects that information transfers on relationships among critical variables. What yesterday was a relatively good understanding about the bases of scientific and political authority may differ substantially when events (e.g., the TMI-2 accident and the chemical accidents in Bhopal, India, and Institute, West Virginia) and government programs (e.g., high-level radioactive waste repository siting and Superfund cleanups of abandoned hazardous waste landfills), and the reporting of such concerns and their interpretation by the public are considered.

3. DATA AVAILABILITY

Johnston (1970) states that the development of a sound forecasting approach demands the fulfillment of at least two fundamental requirements: (1) a theoretical grasp of the relevant processes and interrelationships within the defined system of interest; and (2) a body of information that reflects "the observed operation and mutual influences of the key elements." While a theoretical framework for the TMI-1 restart research on response to environmental threats may be provided in the literature, little empirical evidence is available on the restart. Rather, the majority of the information available on which to base the analysis relates not to the restart but to the TMI-2 accident. In this regard, impacts induced by the restart may be qualitatively and quantitatively different from those induced by the accident. Qualitative differences, for example, may arise because the accident was a transient event inducing acute stress. The restart, on the other hand, although transient in nature, leads to continued operation, a permanent condition potentially capable of causing chronic stress. Quantitative differences may arise either because restart is not perceived to be as threatening as the accident, thereby leading to lower levels of impact, or because the accident and subsequent events have sufficiently sensitized the community such that the additional concern induced by restart will actually lead to higher levels of impact than observed after the accident.

These problems force one to assume a posture of caution and a certain degree of skepticism in developing projections. To the extent that the conditions and interrelationships surrounding TMI-1 restart are reflective of those found in previous research, predictions may be based on a sound empirical foundation. Conversely, the extent to which restart is a unique event, unlike other environmental hazards, may hinder predictions. One purpose of the present research is to determine which of these options is most valid.

Theoretical Assumptions

The research described in this study is largely based on a transactional view of human-environment relations, which maintains that interactions between humans and both the natural and built environments are largely dictated by knowledge, information, and cognitive images of that environment. This interaction, however, is mediated by both situational factors in the environments and individual traits. Consequently, the representation of behavior is one product of complex interactions among biological, personality, sociocultural, environmental, and technological factors. Given this view, separating the individual from the surrounding environment is impossible.

This epistemological position has its roots in Kantian theories of knowledge. Kant essentially argued that the only way to measure reality is through our own cognitive processes. In this sense, no absolute truth or reality exists—merely the products of knowing and thinking. This philosophy has been widely adopted in many modern views of human-environment relations, such as Piaget's and Kaplan's. Their theories hold that a distinction exists between knowledge and behavior. Further, knowledge is acquired through experience, with the self, as well as with the environment; behavior is guided both by knowledge and by environmental experiences.

This line of thinking has had a strong influence on studies of human behavior during times of disaster and human response to hazard and risk. Studies by both sociologists and geographers in those areas have adopted "human ecological" approaches in investigating human response to environmental changes. This research has been guided by the notion that behavior under uncertainty can be characterized only in probabilistic terms: There are no absolutes. Humans cannot control their destinies, nor are they solely at the mercy of natural forces. In adopting this view, decisionmaking is seen largely in the context of Simon's notion of bounded rationality and satisficing behavior. That is, people make decisions without seeking complete knowledge and processing that knowledge in terms of a commonly-shared notion of reality.

The research that follows is largely based on these concepts of human-environment relations and decisionmaking, and seeks to further our understanding of the way humans adapt to new environments and react to new sets of knowledge about those environments. Furthermore, it seeks to identify and articulate the role hazard may play in the process of social change. Scholars have extensively documented the way benefits of technology have impacted social systems. Scant attention, in comparison, has been given to the role externalities of technology have played in shaping humans.

Implications for Environmental Management

The events at TMI, both the accident at Unit 2 and the restart of Unit 1, are unique. We suspect, however, that they are antecedents to major future concerns and may, therefore, provide an indication of generic types of environmental management issues that will be on the public agenda in coming years. In particular, as society confronts itself with (i.e., makes itself aware of) an ever-broadening array of hazardous technologies and the uncertainties and risks associated with the performance of those technologies, their management appears to be coming under heightened scrutiny. Deciding how and under what conditions we veto, allow, or encourage the implementation of potentially hazardous technologies such as nuclear deterrence, recombinant DNA, and hazardous waste disposal, becomes a dominant societal concern.

What is needed first is a recognition of the limits of research. This is well-appreciated by practitioners but not always well understood by decisionmakers. Philosophy of science teaches us all—chemists, physicists, and biologists as well as psychologists, sociologists, geographers, and political scientists, that we cannot know what is true, but rather only what has not yet been ruled as false. We may enhance our understanding of the world around us and reduce the uncertainty of our approximations of reality by using experimental or quasi-experimental research designs where possible or, as is the case of this analysis, by the use of multiple methods and related lines of inquiry and evidence where experimentation is not possible. Many of the important policy questions of our time related to environmental hazards lie between "certainty" or consensual agreement on straightforward concerns (e.g., the infrastructure consequences of high population growth) and widespread disagreement if not overwhelming ignorance on more complex issues (e.g., the relationship between carbon dioxide buildup and long-term climate change). For the in-between cases, using multiple methods and lines of inquiry may enable us to provide guidance on very significant societal problems, including identifying the potential psycho-social impacts of restarting TMI-1, designing decision systems that will permit the resolution of controversial public policy issues, planning emergency response systems for hazardous technologies, and sequentially bounding research on potentially risky endeavors such as recombinant DNA research.

A decisionmaking system sufficiently flexible to permit the pluralistic and evolutionary incorporation of scientific knowledge and a better idea of just what constitutes scientific knowledge is needed. Our imperfect understanding of cognitive processes should perhaps encourage the consideration of information from diverse sources. Thus, the Council on Environmental Quality's (CEQ) regulations (1978) that speak to scoping of environmental impacts suggest consultation with various "experts," including those citizens most affected by the proposed action. A more pragmatic reason is that such an approach constitutes a more efficient use of scarce resources by focusing on issues in conflict rather than on the full array of issues that are potentially interesting. That the scope of concerns may grow simply as expertise increases should also be recognized; what issues are irrelevant today may be so because of our limited understanding rather than because they are inherently ir-relevant. Consequently, the empirical distance between cause and effect can become less and less attenuated and, therefore, the scope of envi-ronmental impacts may become increasingly large, incorporating sec-ondary or indirect effects, as well as primary or direct effects. The scope of the NEPA, which gave rise to our study, can and probably will increase over time, particularly with respect to technologies character-ized by the possibility of low probability/high consequence accidents.

The NEPA also calls for the amelioration or mitigation of adverse impacts. To date, the conventional approach to this requirement has been fairly straightforward because many of the identified impacts have been straightforward. If an aquatic species is endangered by the thermal effects of a nuclear power plant's cooling waters, then restrict the plant's operation; if the educational infrastructure of a community cannot ac-commodate a project-induced influx of school-age children, then hire teachers and provide additional classrooms. Today, however, we are identifying new impacts and encountering more controversial issues for which the design of effective mitigation is more problematic. When this is the case, broadening the evidentiary base by asking those potentially affected to participate not only in the identification of impacts, as is currently called for, but also in the design and implementation of ap-propriate mitigation is particularly important. One indirect—but signif-icant—effect of such an approach should be the realization by the participating public that these issues are very complex and not amenable to easy fixes (and that, by and large, the federal government and its bureaucrats have done a commendable job in the past). The ultimate step in pluralistic participation in the mitigation of adverse impacts may well be the early incorporation of social, cultural, psychological, and political dimensions of technologies during the design phase so that adverse impacts are neutralized before they can occur.

The management of potential environmental hazards has been put under a public microscope as a consequence of numerous discoveries and/or accidents. Hazardous wastes, nuclear power, the chemical in-dustry, and even airplane travel, have all become media stars. In many cases, stardom appears to have been achieved not only because of the "facts" (e.g., contamination of drinking water, acute lethalities from accidents) but also because of a veil of secrecy regarding the manage-ment of such hazardous activities. Scientists and their managers are now required to confess to past sins and, at the same time, admit their uncertainties. This nakedness is terribly uncomfortable for both the emperor and his viewers, and the reacquisition of public trust will probably be a protracted process. Furthermore, there is no guarantee that conventional remedies such as enhanced communications and education will alter the situation substantially, i.e., make believers out of non-believers. At the very least however, such approaches may result in the identification and adoption of adaptive behavior by those affected in the event of an accident; although convincing skeptics that a given technology is safe may be impossible, educating them about what an accident could and could not physically be (e.g., that a nuclear power plant will not explode) and what behaviors are appropriate if an accident occurs is possible. Clearly, public involvement in hazard management is likely to increase regardless.

Conclusion

The relationship between hazardous technologies and social well-being is not well understood. We have attempted, within standard research constraints, to illuminate the relationship as it relates to the restart of TMI–1. Our analysis applies also, however, to a class of analogues, where public controversy prevails concerning hazardous technologies with the possibility of low probability/high consequence events.

Our analysis is confounded by a number of realities. Even though restart will probably have no detectable effects on nearby communities and their residents as social aggregates, certain individuals and groups are at least qualitatively affected by restart and the events surrounding restart. Part of the problem involves the differential distribution of impacts—some people were and are distressed by the situation. We conclude, however, that whether restart, *qua* restart, was and is the cause of their problem is unclear. For these people, the accident and restart of the undamaged reactor affected the quality of their lives, but without restart they may have been similarly affected.

Some affected residents have difficulty distinguishing between accident and restart impacts; concomitantly, unraveling their relationship is also difficult. Although differentiating between the two events and their impacts is feasible from both a conceptual and technical viewpoint, too many people in the impact region associate the two together to make such a distinction viable and relevant. The decision of the U.S. Supreme Court notwithstanding, the accident at Unit 2 is relevant to understanding the psycho-social impacts of restarting Unit 1.

Differentiating the impacts of the TMI-2 accident and TMI-1 restart from other forces that normally affect social and economic change is also difficult. In a very real sense, the external forces that have brought change to Middletown and other communities in the TMI region, including decisions by Met Ed, GPU, the State of Pennsylvania, attention by national media, the NRC, and the U.S. Supreme Court regarding the TMI issue, are all part of a process that makes isolating cause and effect difficult (Greer 1962).

The unanswered question, concerning what will happen as a result of restart, is an empirical one which can only be addressed through additional monitoring and analysis. Unfortunately, however, once a legal decision has been made that an issue is not an issue, following through with additional research is very difficult. The opportunity to develop a scientific basis for identifying and measuring the psycho-social impacts of restarting TMI-1 has been diminished. Our work and the work done by others provides some insight to the issue, but substantial work still must be done in assessing the psycho-social impacts of environmental hazards.

Chapter 3

Defining Relevant Issues: A Local Perspective on Restart

Why Impacts Could Occur

In order to initiate our investigation, a conceptual framework was developed to help guide our analysis by providing a means to identify a range of probable impacts from a restart of TMI-1 and a distribution of these impacts among the populace and social systems. The approach adopted herein assumes that many, but perhaps not all, types of impacts from restarting or not restarting the undamaged reactor are identifiable. Furthermore, it adheres to the notion that the manifestation of impacts are largely explainable in light of current social science theory and knowledge. While the existent research base may not have uncovered all impacts, a systematic application of the theory and knowledge should allow reasonable estimates of the nature and type of many potential impacts. Furthermore, it may be possible to explain with some precision why these impacts will or will not occur.

Social science theories and related empirical research findings can be utilized to suggest a framework that can help explain why impacts will or will not occur as a result of restart. As discussed in the previous chapter, this framework is developed in light of investigations into how people and groups perceive and adjust to hazards in the course of their normal lives (Burton *et al*. 1978; Kates 1977; Mileti 1980; Sorensen and White 1980). It is also framed around research on the way individuals and societies respond to the threat of impending disasters and warnings

(Mileti 1975; Perry *et al.* 1981; Leik *et al.* 1981; Mileti *et al.* 1981). To a lesser extent, it is based on human behavior in and about specific disasters (Quarantelli and Dynes 1977; Quarantelli 1979; Drabek and Key, 1984).

Figure 3 schematically outlines the structure and process by which impacts from restart are hypothesized to occur. The key element in the framework is the manner in which people perceive risks and benefits from restart and continued operation. These perceptions, which are rooted primarily in personal frames of reference (i.e., self and family) and secondarily in more aggregate frames of reference (i.e., groups, community, and society), are a major cause for impacts being manifest or absent. The model (Figure 3) also suggests what types of factors may cause variations in the perception of risk and benefits. Previous research suggests that attitudes towards risk managers, perceptions and attitudes toward nuclear power, information, demographic and individual characteristics, family and group social standards, levels of sensitivity to a disaster, ability to cope, and concern over other issues will shape risk perceptions.

Based on theoretical evidence, the model also suggests how risk perceptions are translated into individual and community impacts. Risk perceptions are translated or encoded through people's general cognitive functioning. Perception may lead to what we call first-order impacts defined as psychological or physiological changes that occur because of the presence of the restart decision. These first-order impacts could lead to further impacts on individuals in the form of coping actions or behavioral manifestations of stress. These can, in turn, lead to group impacts and changes in community well-being.

Before using data collected through discussions with groups in the TMI vicinity to examine the framework in more detail, two hypothetical cases illustrate the processes hypothesized to be at work. These cases represent extremes; others could be postulated which would lead to equally plausible conclusions regarding impacts.

Our first fictitious person, Jane Doe, can be described in terms of the factors in our conceptual framework (Table 5). In general, Jane does not trust TMI's management; she opposes nuclear power in general and is confused by conflicting information about restart. These factors, supported by a difficult experience with evacuation after the 1979 ac-

Figure 3.   A Causal Model of TMI-Restart Impacts.

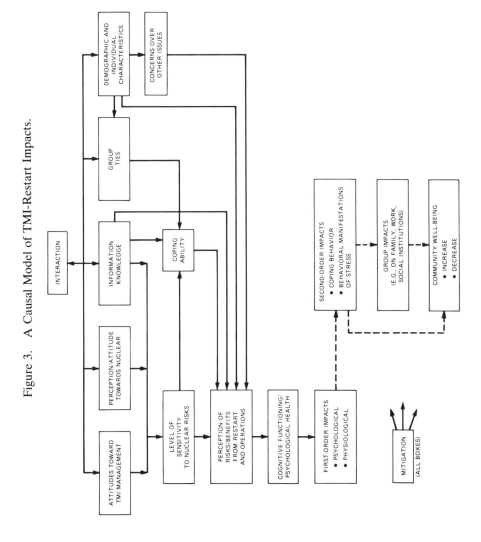

Table 5 Hypothetical values for Jane Doe and Jack Smith

Factor	Jane Doe	Jack Smith
Attitudes toward TMI management	Does not trust Metropolitan Edison; thinks operators	Has faith in ability of the utility
Perception/attitude toward nuclear power	Does not approve of future development of nuclear plants	Feels nuclear power is better than other options
Information/knowledge	Perceives information to be conflicting	Thinks media sensationalizes the issues
Demographic characteristics	Female, 35 years old, 1 child (age 4), married, legal clerk	Male, 35 years old, 1 child (age 4), married, store owner
Level of sensitivity	Feels another accident will occur if TMI is restarted	Has confidence that the reactor will operate safely
Coping ability	Feels that evacuation will not be feasible	Has an evacuation plan for family
Concerns over other issues	Other issues are perceived to be of lesser concern	Feels the economy is a far more serious issue
Family/group ties	Nonsupportive of views about nuclear power	Generally holds shared values and provides support

cident, cause her to be highly sensitive to the possibility of another accident if restart occurs and to believe that she can do little to cope with a future accident. In sum, Jane is very concerned about restart because she perceives it as a significant threat to her own and her family's safety. Her sensitivity is increased by this, and her risk perceptions are constantly reinforced by reading about TMI in the local newspapers, by occasional sirens sounding, and by visual sighting of the cooling towers.

Jane's cognitions of the restart create certain anxieties about her future life in the TMI area, although no observable acute symptoms are manifested. If restart occurs, however, Jane may find her anxiety resulting in withdrawal from her normal social functioning. This detachment would affect her family and marital relationships. She perceives that the likelihood her marriage will fail would increase, and Jane vows to leave the area for good if that happens. Whatever happens to Jane will be the result of several factors, but TMI-1 restart may be the putative cause.

Another hypothetical resident of the area, Jack Smith, illustrates a different outcome to the same causal sequence. Jack basically has trust and confidence in TMI's management. Generally, he favors the development of nuclear power but is somewhat reactive against what he sees as negative and sensationalized media coverage of the restart. If the reactor resumes operations, he feels it will operate safely but is confident he could evacuate if a problem did occur. In part, due to his growing concern with national economic conditions, he does not feel threatened by restart and feels it would be beneficial. His family shares these sentiments, as do his coworkers. If restart occurs, Jack will lead his life as he did before the issue was raised.

These sequences of events and assumptions of causality are illustrative and speculative. The model they purport to describe can be *supported* by previous research findings but can only be *validated* or *tested* by an empirical test of the model through new research.

As the model (Figure 3) outlines, the key reason impacts will occur is that some segment of the population will perceive that they are threatened by the risks of restart and continued operations. The perception of risk will cause psychological and physiological impacts which, through behavior, may affect individual, group, and community structure. We now examine what could happen at TMI as defined by interest groups active in the TMI vicinity.

Focus-Group Discussions

The focus-group discussions were held to elicit concerns regarding the range of potential impacts from the restart of TMI-1. While a comprehensive review of the relevant literature about human responses to environmental hazards provides one means of delineating the range of potential impacts, the uniqueness of the issue indicates a need for an inductive approach to test the relevance and comprehensiveness of the impacts identified by the literature review.

Fundamental to such a strategy is the urgent need for input from multiple perspectives reflecting the range of opinions concerning the potential impacts. These perspectives should represent not only the potential benefits cited by advocates of a project but also the possible costs noted by adversaries. Although each opinion will reflect only a limited subset of possible issues, taken together they form a more comprehensive view of what could potentially happen.

This approach recognizes that few issues are ideologically neutral, and that very few impact categories exist in which the interests of most or all social groups are congruent. Allowing the input of the various factions should, however, facilitate the identification and balancing of the individual biases and improve the value of the impact assessment for subsequent decisionmaking. These discussions permit a characterization of what perceptions these multiple viewpoints reflect and how representatives of groups cluster around common views.

The inclusion of variables relevant to the consensus of individuals by using multiple perspectives helps ensure not only a complete picture of what impacts may arise but also provides information concerning "to whom" these are impacts. Employing multiple perspectives in identifying indicators helps resolve the question of differential impacts, in that it recognizes that different groups will be affected in different ways. This allows the analysts to discover, through research, what the various interest groups are in any given action and how they are affected. Such information is fundamentally important to decisionmakers when determining "adverse" effects and, in the future, when designing mitigation mechanisms responsive to differential impacts.

TMI-Area Meetings

1. PARTICIPANT GROUPS

Several groups were identified as representing a variety of affected interests concerning TMI-1 restart, both in support and opposition. Opposition groups included PANE, TMI Alert, and Newberry Township Steering Committee. Groups favoring restart included Friends and Family of TMI, and area Chambers of Commerce.

The oldest of the opposition groups, TMI Alert, was originally formed in 1977 to resist the proposed opening of TMI-2. Prior to the accident at TMI-2, this Harrisburg-based group was relatively small, but it had gained an activist reputation (Walsh 1981). According to Walsh, the accident caused major changes in the structure and function of TMI Alert. TMI Alert was transformed into the largest protest organization in the area with the goal of becoming the umbrella organization for all area protest groups. To that end, a seven-member steering committee, 30-member planning council, and 12 semiautonomous community group affiliates were formed. While the central administration of TMI Alert is composed primarily of veteran activists, community group leaders tend to be accident-precipitated local activists (Walsh 1981).

After the accident, new anti-TMI protest organizations emerged in Middletown and Newberry Township, small communities within a few miles of the reactors on the east and west shores of the Susquehanna River, respectively. Although each group was aided, to some extent, by TMI Alert in its formative stage, they are currently not affiliated.

The first organization, formed in April 1979, was PANE, whose objectives are to prevent the restart of TMI-1 and to force early cleanup of TMI-2. PANE has approximately 150 families who are dues-paying members, and an additional 600 individuals or families who receive the PANE newsletter. Members reside primarily in the more recently developed areas of Middletown. Differences over appropriate forms of protest and the feeling on the part of PANE that only a truly independent organization could adequately represent the perceived unique risks of their proximity to TMI have kept PANE separate from TMI Alert (Walsh 1981). PANE has become a relatively sophisticated political action group that has successfully lobbied local and state officials to introduce legislation prohibiting restart. PANE's lobbying of the governor and NRC officials helped lead to NRC's August 1979 decision to hold hearings on the TMI-1 restart. Further, PANE successfully brought suit against the NRC and Met Ed to force consideration of social and psychological impacts in the restart decision.

The Newberry Township Steering Committee has also remained autonomous in order to retain a focus on perceived unique "backyard problems." Members of this group come from a primarily rural area and have little history of social protest. They were able to achieve a degree of solidarily through the efforts of 60 members conducting a survey of area residents' attitudes and behavior related to the TMI accident (Walsh 1981).

In support of restart are a group called Friends and Family of TMI (F&F) and the area Chambers of Commerce. F&F was established in Spring 1980. Approximately 700 individuals or families are either F&F members or on its mailing list. F&F is comprised of residents who favor early resumption of operations at TMI-1. F&F excludes TMI employees from its membership, although the spouses of many TMI employees are members of the organization. F&F's objective is to inform community members that TMI-1 can be operated safely and economically.

Two distinguishing factors tend to separate opposition groups from support groups. First, opposition groups are convinced that nuclear power generation is unsafe and that its resultant radiation will cause long-term health problems for everyone. Second, groups in support of restart are equally convinced that nuclear power is safe and that the benefits derived from nuclear power outweigh the associated risks. Support groups are also more likely to benefit economically from the restart of TMI-1 than are opposition groups. For example, the F&F family's major income-earner is more likely to be a TMI employee than is the PANE family's income-earner.

2. Procedure

After an initial contact was made with the leaders of each group, separate meetings were held with a subset of members from each group. Attendees at the meetings were selected by group leaders who were asked to invite a representative cross section of 10 to 15 members.

Meetings were led by a facilitator who controlled the flow of discussion, encouraged participation, and used probes to clarify and maintain continuity in the discussion. An assistant recorded responses on a large pad at the front of the meeting room. To aid in eliciting input from the participants, the facilitator presented sequentially seven topics for discussions:

- What concerns do you have about restart or no-restart?
- Are these different from the concerns about the accident?
- In what ways will restart or no-restart affect you and your family?

- In what ways will restart or no-restart affect your community in general?
- What actions could be taken to reduce or modify your concerns?
- Are there any groups of people expected to be particularly affected?
- What concerns do you have about the present status in which the decision is delayed?

Discussion continued on each topic until the participants felt it had been exhausted before proceeding on to the next topic. All topics were covered at each meeting. Each meeting was concluded with an opportunity to express any other concerns that may have been omitted.

The following is a summary of the TMI-area meetings. It is not an attempt to analyze the strength of concerns or draw conclusions as to what is important. Rather, it identifies the total range of issues and concerns that were raised and attempts to summarize commonalities and differences in the responses. In doing so, responses are reported in terms of the structure of the conceptual model previously discussed. The format of reporting is to list all statements relevant to a given model factor and to highlight the themes running through the statements.

3. RESULTS

Why are people concerned about the decision? The conceptual framework suggests nine general factors (Figure 3) that may play a major role in explaining impacts. A review of the responses to questions in the focus-group meetings substantiates the presence of seven of these factors, but it does not establish their importance or causality; no information was generated concerning group ties and concerns over other issues.

The discussions revealed a number of impacts that were salient to groups either supporting or opposing restart and possible ways of ameliorating their concerns. Following the causal framework noted in Figure 1, we have categorized perceived impacts by type of impact (i.e., individual-level psychological impacts, individual manifestations of stress, group-level psychosocial impacts, or community-level well-being impacts) and by types of groups (i.e., either in support of or opposed to restart). Impact themes are summarized accordingly in Table 6. Impacts are grouped in this manner because it reflects a plausible causal model

Table 6   Perceived Impacts of Restart

Impact Category	Group View	
	Support Restart	Oppose Restart
Individual-level Psychological Impacts	• None	• Fear • "Psychic numbing" • Anxiety • Paranoia - "Trapped feeling" • Loss of control • Hopelessness
Individual Manifestations of Stress	• None	• Disease (cancer, heart) • Medical problems • Lack of rest, sleep • Lethargy • Loss of jobs
Group-level Psychosocial Impacts	• Families will prosper • Will be harrassed by "outsiders"	• Security of home has been lost • Neighborhood vitality/identity has been lost • Families will move • Anxiety on part of relatives • Social stigma of living near plant
Community-level Well-being Impacts	• Taxes won't increase • Population will remain stable • Lower utility bills • Economic growth • Speed clean-up of Unit 2	• Higher taxes • Population decline • Protest/conflict/ violence • Property values decline • Loss of community aesthetics • Decline in residential development

of the manner in which psychological stress associated with risk can be manifested and eventually can result in detectable social change at the group and community level.

Distinct differences in perceived impacts between groups supporting or opposing restart are demonstrated in Table 6. Groups in favor of restart were adamant about not experiencing any negative psychological impacts from the accident and perceived none would result from restart. Conversely, anti-restart groups felt a number of adverse affects had occurred and would be heightened by restart. These impacts included feelings of fear, anxiety, hopelessness, loss of control, and entrapment. While these were not clinically determined, they are common symptoms of threat-induced stress.

Similarily, pro-restart groups did not mention any anticipated individual-level psychological consequences of restart. On the other hand, a number of stress-related problems were anticipated by opposition groups. Attributed to restart are the potential problems of increased disease, restlessness, loss of sleep, loss of jobs, lethargic behavior, and other minor medical problems.

At a group level, both sets anticipated impacts. Pro-restart groups dwelled on various aspects of how they would benefit by restart because of the associated economic benefits. One negative consequence they saw was harrassment by anti-nuclear groups from outside the region if TMI-1 is restarted. Anti-restart groups exhibited a different set of concerns. They felt that since the accident the security of their homes had been lost, and this feeling would be reinforced by restart. Similarly, they thought neighborhoods would lose their vitality and identity, ceasing to be functional social units. The only way to avoid impacts would be to move from their homes, which some would do. These groups also mentioned that living near TMI caused anxiety for their families living elsewhere. Overall they felt burdened by the "stigma" of living near an operating reactor after having experienced an accident.

Both sets of groups saw community change associated with restart. For pro-restart groups, it meant stable population and taxes, lower energy costs, and economic growth, and they saw restart as a prerequisite for cleaning up Unit 2. Anti-restart groups keyed in to similar subjects, but not the same direction of change. To them, restart meant higher taxes. Rather than growth, they foresaw population, real estate, and development declining. They predicted protest and violence if restart was attempted, and, overall, they thought the area would no longer be a good place to live.

As noted in our conceptual framework and addressed in our focus-group discussions, a variety of mechanisms might be implemented to ameliorate or overcome anticipated adverse impacts associated with alternative restart decisions. Table 7 represents a summary of mitigative actions identified by focus-group participants, subsequently organized around eight general categories of mitigation. Interestingly, although the two sets of groups did identify some substantially different mitigative measures, they also identified some common ones. For instance, as

Table 7   Potential Mitigation Measures

Mitigation Category	Group View	
	Support Restart	Oppose Restart
Improve communications between resdients, NRC, and Met Ed	• Publication of weekly radiation levels • Central credible information facility accessible to public & media • Information on economic benefits	• Publication of weekly radiation levels • Central credible information accessible to public media Purchase anti-restart ads to balance pro-restart ads
Decisionmaking	• Cleanup TMI-2 • Change decisionmaking process-roles of NRC, state/local, licensee • Isolate area and decision from national antinuclear groups	• Cleanup TMI-2 • Change decisionmaking process-roles of NRC, state/local, licensee • Increased local input
Public education programs	• Tours of TMI facilities • Integrate local people w/facilities & employees	• Tours of TMI facilties
Emergency preparedness	• Better alert system • Advanced warning on planned abnormal events (e.g., venting)	• Better alert system • Advanced warning on planned abnormal events (e.g., venting) • Better evacuation plan for schools, institutions, handicapped, low income
Relocation assistance		• Short-term relocation assistance to residents
Job training	• for displaced TMI employees (no restart) • for residents (no restart)	
Land use	• Intensify efforts to attract industry (no restart)	
Subsidies	• Rebate on electric utility cost (no restart)	• Purchase houses at pre-accident values • Subsidize home improvement loans to help stabilize

shown in Table 7, groups opposing and supporting restart agreed that weekly publication of local radiation levels, substantial progress on cleaning up TMI-2, and a better alert system would help make a restart decision more acceptable and result in lessened adverse impacts on local individuals and their communities.

Even though both sets of groups suggested some of the same measures, they may have done so for different reasons—weekly publication of radiation levels for those favoring restart would corroborate the safety of the plant, while for those opposing restart it would alert the population to radiation dangers. Similarly, changes in the decisionmaking process for those supporting restart would include isolating the area and the decision from nonlocal antinuclear groups, while for those opposing restart it would include enhanced local input into decisionmaking.

The two sets of groups did diverge more substantially on other potential mitigative mechanisms. For instance, those favoring restart felt that the adverse economic impacts associated with a no-restart decision might be ameliorated through job training, attracting new industry, and rebates on electric utility costs. Members of groups opposing restart wanted to protect the economic security of their homes (i.e., the equity in their investments) through property value guarantees (i.e., purchase at preaccident values) and/or stabilization of property values through the subsidization of home improvement loans. Their concerns over health and safety might be ameliorated through better evacuation plans and other activities.

While Table 6 presents two dramatically divergent views, Table 7 presents divergence and commonality. It is impossible to predict on the basis of their perceptions, of course, what will occur or who may be correct. However, attempting to understand how the groups arrived at their differing perceptions is helpful.

Cognitive Models Associated with Group Views

Our group discussions revealed some clues about the way groups arrived at their conclusions concerning the psycho-social impacts of restart. In this section, those clues are arranged in order to arrive at an approximation of how broader sets of cognitions may relate to perceived impacts. To structure the analysis, eight different dimensions of beliefs are used, as shown in Figure 3, related to the restart issue which may explain why impacts could occur. These include:

1. attitudes towards TMI managers;
2. attitudes towards nuclear power;
3. attitudes towards information about TMI;
4. sensitivity to nuclear risks;
5. perceived coping ability;
6. concerns over other issues;
7. perceived risks of restart; and
8. perceived benefits of restart.

Table 8 summarizes the nature of group views regarding these eight issues.

1. PRO-RESTART COGNITIVE MODEL

Generally, groups favoring the restart of TMI-1 had faith in the utilities operating nuclear power plants and felt that they employ nuclear experts skilled in operating reactors safely. In contrast, they resented the government's involvement in nuclear power generation and felt that the government's inability to make decisions and overregulation hamper the ability of utilities to perform their management tasks. As expected, they generally favor nuclear power, basing their attitudes on perceptions of lower costs and risks when compared to alternatives.

Pro-restart groups expressed a general attitude that the accident was blown out of proportion and that the media sensationalized all the negative aspects of TMI. Furthermore, they felt that a nuclear power plant can operate safely. These groups were not concerned about radiation risks of routine operations, and they denigrated the likelihood of another accident.

Of much greater concern to them was the current state of the economy, unemployment, cost of living, and the lack of economic growth in the area. Such issues shadowed concern for nuclear risks. Overall, they did not associate restart with increased risks to their safety or to the well-being of the area. On the contrary, they emphasized the benefits of restart in terms of regional economic development and lower electricity rates.

2. ANTI-RESTART COGNITIVE MODEL

At the other extreme, anti-restart groups had a different view of the nuclear world. At a basic level, they had a complete lack of faith

Table 8   Beliefs Held by Groups Supporting and Opposing Restart

Dimension of Beliefs	Group View	
	Support Restart	Oppose Restart
Attitude toward TMI managers	Faith in plant operators and managers, but no faith or trust in ability of NRC	Lack of faith in plant management, government and NRC
Attitudes toward nuclear power developed	Nuclear power is safer than other sources and should be used	Favor shut down of nuclear industry
Attitudes toward information about TMI	Accident has been blown out of proportion and information has been biased against nuclear power	Information is conflicting and not available to everyone
Sensitivity to nuclear risks	Plant can be safely operated	Fear another accident, sensitive to signals of re-occurrence (e.g., sirens)
Coping ability	Feel there will be nothing to cope with	Feel helpless despite any preparations
Concern over other local issues	Area economic conditions	TMI is dominant issue area
Perceived risks TMI-1 restart	None; restart risks are not due to Unit 2 accident	General concern about of radiation effects, likelihood of another accident, waste disposal
Perceived benefits of TMI-1 restart	Lower utility bills, economic development	None

in anyone associated with nuclear power. While this held strongest for Met Ed, it was also true for state and local governments and the NRC. This was accompanied by the generally negative attitudes toward the entire nuclear industry—and not solely TMI. A common group position is that the nuclear industry should be shut down permanently, or, at least, until safety issues could be resolved.

Anti-restart groups felt that not enough information is given to the public about nuclear power and its risks. Moreover, they felt information is conflicting and only selectively distributed. The media was often thought to be pronuclear as demonstrated by their airing of pro-restart commercials and advertisements. Members appeared to place TMI high on their agendas of concerns.

In general, group members feared the risks and potential consequences of TMI-1 continuing operations and functioning normally. The major concern, however, anchored to the possibility of a repeat of their experience with the TMI-2 accident and living with that uncertainty daily.

Discussion

The accident at TMI was characterized by high levels of uncertainty among the nation's nuclear experts and conflicting information regarding the way to deal with the unfolding accident, especially the potential explosion of a hydrogen bubble in the containment building, the unknown effects of radiation releases, and whether an evacuation was necessary. This uncertainty has continued in the aftermath of the accident. Disagreements over the way to proceed with the cleanup of TMI-2, the discovery of corrosion and leaks in the steam generator tubes in Unit 1, and NRC's questioning the management capabilities of Met Ed concerning such issues as reactor operators' cheating on the licensing examination have all contributed to the uneasiness some residents have concerning whether TMI-1 could operate safely.

According to Festinger (1957), when physical reality becomes increasingly uncertain, people rely more and more on *social reality*. People are more likely to conform to what other people are doing, not because they fear punishment from other people, but because others' behavior supplies them with cues and valuable information about what is expected of them.

People seek social reinforcement of beliefs about issues which cannot be definitely answered through selective interactions with other people and with issue-oriented groups. Groups, just as interpersonal relationships, play an important role in helping people reduce their cognitive dissonance. For instance, believing that one's self and family may be in danger is at odds (dissonant) with the behavior of remaining in the area. Membership and participation in groups, then, offer a mechanism for rationalizing the decision to remain in an area perceived as dangerous. For example, members can discuss common concerns, review attempts to cope with those concerns, and plan and implement actions to resolve the concerns. People living in flood-prone areas, for example, have been observed to remove the threatening aspects of their environments by denying the existence of the hazard or by denying the possibility of reoccurrence. Our work suggests that group membership and participation facilitates this process by reinforcement of the dissonance-reducing attitude.

On the other hand, these groups may also arouse fear. While Prasad (1935), in the aftermath of an earthquake, observed rumors of additional pending hazards circulating among persons residing some distance from the actual destruction, Sinha (1952) found few of these rumors discussed by residents of an area which had actually suffered heavy physical damage. Festinger (1957) suggests that these rumors may function to justify the arousal of fear by persons inhabiting undamaged disaster areas. Fear can be aroused in a person who has not experienced any actual danger. To eliminate this dissonant state, rumors creating fear were generated by those unhurt by the earthquake but were unnecessary for those in the path of the destruction.

The accident at TMI was unique in many ways. In one respect, there is a lack of concurrence that a major catastrophe with life- and health-threatening potential occurred. Furthermore, restarting TMI-1 posed a renewed risk that a future accident could happen, no matter how small the probability. Since the major consequence of an accident was the release of radiation which is undetectable without special equipment, few observable cues would appear if another accident occurred, just as there was little physical evidence that such an accident took place with TMI-2 in 1979. Given this situation, it is not surprising that both *fear-mongering* as well as *risk denial* were observed among the discussion groups. The results of the focus-group discussions support these deductions.

Groups favoring restart tended to deny the potential for life-threatening danger from restarting TMI-1. Such risk-denials are based on several factors. First, these groups did not believe that another accident is probable. In fact, they viewed the accident and restart as independent events. They contended that the accident had actually reduced the likelihood of reoccurrence due to the added precautions taken in the interim.

Second, pro-restart groups discussed restart only in terms of the positive economic benefits the area would receive. The only negative consequence was the temporary harrassment from "outsiders" during the resumption of operations. This condition, they felt, would eventually dissipate. For these groups, the risks were the economic consequences of *not* restarting TMI-1.

Finally, groups supporting restart tended to dismiss the contentions of the opposition groups as being uninformed or based on negatively-biased information. The accident was actually a demonstration of the reliability of nuclear power. As proof that the system worked, they pointed to the fact that the incident had been contained by the safety systems without any major offsite radiation releases.

While groups supporting restart reduced the potential risks of re-starting to near zero, groups opposing restart tended to accentuate them. Contrary to the belief of pro-restart groups, opposition groups contended that a future accident at TMI-1 is a virtual certainty. They pointed to the similarity of design and the problems uncovered in Unit 1 since the accident as proof that restart would result in another accident.

Anti-restart groups indicated that they were often sensitized to problems at the plant site and were concerned about health threats due to radiation exposure and their perceived inability to respond if another emergency arose. Unintentional or trial soundings of emergency sirens and declarations of unusual events at the plant were constant sources of apprehension. While encouraging better evacuation planning, they doubted emergency planning efforts would ever be adequate to handle another evacuation. Feelings of helplessness in the event of another accident persisted in spite of individual efforts such as keeping the family automobile's gas tank full and a suitcase packed.

Yet, even if one accepts the explanation that dissonance reduction processes may be at work in the perceptions expressed by the various groups, one is struck by the fact that such divergent views grew out of a common physical event. Two explanations of this apparent paradox appear reasonable. On the one hand, Aronson (1972) suggests that the key may lie in a person's degree of commitment to a particular action or belief through selective perceptions and choice of information. At the same time, perceptions and attitudes might be a function of the distribution of benefits associated with a particular activity.

Evidence from the focus group discussions lends credence to these explanations. One would expect the members of F&F and the area Chamber of Commerce to have a strong degree of commitment to the plant and would reject any information that might cast it in a negative light. Both of these groups, either directly or indirectly, depend on the plant for their economic livelihood. This may be true because they have contracts to provide goods or services to the plant, the plant provides jobs for area residents and support for the local tax base, or the plant is perceived as a necessary source of energy for their operations. Clearly, these groups are more concerned about the potential decay of local social institutions, brought on by economic decline, than they are about health risks from nuclear power.

The source of commitment is not as obvious for the opposition groups, although the discussions do provide some clues. For these groups, the source appears to be in deeply-seated attitudes toward technology and society. By and large, members of these groups do not have a direct tie to TMI. Just as the groups formed in opposition to a nuclear power plant in Gross and Rayner's (1985) mythical New England community, the opposition groups in the TMI area perceive an inequitable distribution of risks (borne by themselves) and benefits (accruing to powerful others as owners of the utility). They view themselves as vulnerable to technology and the whims of government, inferred from expressions of "feeling trapped," hopelessness, and the belief that the security of their homes (including the financial security of their equity), has been lost, as well as their desire to shut down the nuclear industry and their lack of faith in all those perceived to have any control over TMI (i.e., plant management; the NRC; and federal, state, and local governments).

One might argue, however, that as residents and property owners, even members of opposition groups have a certain amount of commitment to the area. This is certainly true, although the commitment is to the area and existing social networks—not to the plant *per se*. Explaining why PANE and Newberry Township Steering Committee chose to remain separate from TMI Alert, a group comprised mainly of persons residing outside the immediate vicinity of the plant, may help. The former two groups were more concerned with attending to their own "backyard problems," while TMI Alert attacked nuclear power in general.

Conclusions

Despite the uncertainty regarding the source of commitment, strong evidence of selective perception shaping pro- and anti-restart group perceptions of risk is found. For anti-restart groups, government studies were denounced because they failed to conform with a fixed notion of radiation damages; anecdotes and hearsay were judged more credible than scientific fact when they supported the group view, and substantial efforts were made to find information that would discredit the nuclear power industry. These groups were determined to find evidence to support their construction of perceived risk. At the same time, pro-restart groups perceive the accident at TMI-2 as an anomaly through which an already safe industry has become even safer. They, like the anti-restart groups, mistrust the NRC, but for quite different reasons. For them, the NRC is perceived as an arbitrary agency capable of wreaking havoc on an established symbiotic relationship between power plants and their neighbors.

The TMI restart case illustrates well the differences in how risk-benefit relationships were treated by the two factions of the population. For all practical purposes, anti-restart groups felt that a future accident at TMI-1 is a virtual certainty, while pro-restart groups felt that a future accident is extremely unlikely. This is similar to the cognitive processes displayed by individuals buying hazard insurance who tend to reduce low probability events to zero and high probability ones to certainty. Consequently, groups favoring restart conceptualized the issue primarily in economic terms, choosing to ignore potential health risks. Anti-restart groups did exactly the opposite by focusing on health risks and largely ignoring economic impacts.

This dichotomy demonstrates that the groups' perceptions start from fundamentally different positions and follow different paths of thinking. In such a case, reconciliation of views on a common metric is difficult indeed, if not impossible. Like the debate in scientific risk assessment over the "apples and oranges problem" in comparing risks, the public also frames risk comparisons in divergent terms (i.e., economic *vs.* health risks).

Because of the relatively uncontrolled environment in which the data were gathered, causal linkages between the different starting points and different perceived impacts cannot be established. Yet, in light of cognitive dissonance theory, the implications are provocative.

While these two sets of groups represent the extremes on the continuum of public perceptions concerning restarting TMI, they certainly do not represent the vast majority of the population in the local area. In the tradition of interest group participation in conflict resolution in the United States, however, these groups may represent the range of concerns that must be met in attaining a socially-viable decision. In a sense, these groups have set the boundaries of the debate by identifying the issues needing resolution. They also define the basic requirements for establishing a mutually-agreeable measure of acceptable risk.

Clearly, an optimal decision cannot be made without substantial attention not only to the processes that generate divergent views, but also to the mechanisms that could mitigate adverse impacts to particular population subgroups. The potential mechanisms for TMI-1 restart, as noted in Table 7, may well represent a range of feasible options to consider for the management of perceived risk.

The risk management mechanisms used for other technological hazards should also be considered. At Love Canal, New York, for example, local opinion was not unanimous on the appropriate course of action, but leaders of the several interest groups were aware of the dangers of factions and splinter groups. In order to build consensus, these groups concentrated heavily on developing mitigation measures expected to be most acceptable to the general populace which were then presented to decisionmakers for action. Interestingly, protection of their families' health and their major investments (equity in their homes) were the issues most consistently voiced, both of which were met through the evacuation of residents in the immediate vicinity of the toxic waste dump and a buy out of the evacuees' homes. Developing a mitigation scheme that was able to reconcile the elements often found at opposite extremes in interest group belief patterns—health protection and economic concerns—contributed greatly to the success in resolving a major source of conflict at Love Canal.

More recently, in Times Beach, Missouri, where the threat from potentially dangerous levels of dioxin have been observed in and around homes, local interest groups adopted a strategy similar to that observed at Love Canal. Although opinion was divided as to the proper actions, local groups exerted pressure on decisionmakers to implement an evacuation and a buy out of homes in the area by the government.

Negotiation and mitigation, then, are both product and process. The process by which mitigation measures are selected and authorized for implementation constitutes a significant variable in the impact analysis scheme. Others have suggested, for example, that in order to build the commitment necessary to ensure the success of mitigative measures, they should be developed in response to local initiatives. Put simply, the *who* and *how* of mitigation decisionmaking will affect the consequences of mitigation implementation and, thereby, the chances for agreeing on an acceptable risk level.

The importance of the experiences at Love Canal and Times Beach and the observations we have made based on the focus groups discussions at TMI are threefold. One, interest groups are a critical unit of analysis for understanding how beliefs and behaviors form in response to the presence of technological hazards, which is not the case for natural hazards. Two, the divergence of positions between groups, even though they may have shared the same physical experience, is understandable if not always predictable. Three, the resolution of policy debates where risks are a major theme needs to account for the legitimacy of these divergent positions by allowing participation of the various interest groups in the decision process. Such participation helps ensure that the decision strategy will be responsive to local concerns, thereby increasing the likelihood of acceptance of the ultimate decision and producing an acceptable level of risk.

The results of the focus-group discussions provide a better feel for the reasons people are concerned about restart or no-restart. Furthermore, they help establish support for the viability of the conceptual framework. The discussion also identified a number of impacts about which people are concerned. The following chapter examines a broad base of social science literature in order to help interpret what has been observed in the focus-group discussions and to develop more precise understanding of the causes of impacts.

Chapter 4

Examining The Issues: Perspectives From Social Science Research

Structuring The Review

Generalization

This literature review provides a basis for understanding and assessing the potential impacts of the restart of TMI-1 on the residents in, and social structures of, surrounding communities. It is developed from a review of social science theory and empirical work that is judged to be relevant to the restart alternatives. In that sense, it reflects the authors' biases; others may feel certain bodies of literature omitted or ignored here are also pertinent. On the other hand, findings from a diverse array of literature, which at times is overlapping, has been included.

The ability to generalize from previous research is predicated on the assumption that human response to threat is a basic social process. Research to date tends to endorse this assumption. This is not to say response is homogeneous; studies indicate that response varies, to some extent, in accordance with the characteristics of the threatening event. Relevant dimensions may include political salience of the event, frequency of threat, duration of threat, the areal extent, the predictability of risks and consequences, the level and length of available warning, the type of expected loss, and the degree to which preparations can be made for mitigating the threat (Burton *et al.* 1978; Sorensen and White 1980; Mileti 1980).

As a potentially threatening event, TMI-1 restart may differ from other hazardous events in two important respects: (1) public knowledge of nuclear-related events is relatively low, and (2) the political salience of nuclear activities is relatively high. This situation may alter response patterns noted in the literature. Given this limitation, additional research is needed to determine whether generalizations from the existing knowledge base are applicable to the TMI-1 situation.

Restart is a hazardous event because it creates a situation in which another nuclear power plant accident is possible. In responding to restart, individuals must consider potential risks and threats from an accident. This is akin to a situation in which people residing on the San Andreas fault must deal with the risk of another major earthquake, whether that earthquake ever occurs in their lifetimes.

To gain a better understanding of the limits for comparing human response to hazard, Table 9 contrasts six different events in terms of eight dimensions of hazard. Events examined include:

1. a TMI-2-type accident at a nuclear power facility;
2. an earthquake of Richter magnitude 7.0 or greater;
3. a major urban flood;
4. a Love Canal-type leak of a waste disposal site;
5. a community decision on fluoridation of water; and
6. a chemical spill from a transportation accident

Several conclusions can be drawn from reviewing the results of the comparison. First, a TMI-2-type accident is not perfectly analogous with any of the other five hazardous events. To some extent, however, every event is unique. Second, a TMI-2-type accident shares many similarities to other events on one or several dimensions of hazard. In this sense it is not totally unique. Overall, the most reasonable conclusion, based on an integration of these observations, is that the general manner in which people respond to restart will be determined by situation-specific factors, but these factors are hardly novel, given the range of human experience with hazard. The following review of the literature examines many of these factors and seeks to explain their occurrence.

Structure of Review

To structure the presentation we will examine the literature based on a nine-cell matrix. On one dimension of the matrix, three general system levels are identified (e.g., Mileti *et al.* 1975):

Table 9   Dimensions of hazardous events

Hazard dimensions	TMI-2-type accident	Earthquake R ≥ 7.0	Major flood	Love-Canal-type waste leakage	Fluoridation of water supply	Chemical spill (transportation)
Frequency of event	Rare with very low probability. Little experience	Rare with low probability	Fairly frequent	Rare event to date, probability unknown	Frequent	Rare with increasing frequency
Duration of threatening conditions	Hours to one week with ongoing threat	Minutes with aftershocks for weeks	Hours to days	Ongoing	Ongoing	Hours to days
Areal extent of threat	Fixed with 10- to 50-mile radius	Variable	Variable but not confined to floodplains	Fixed, likely a small area	Very pervasive	Variable, >5-mile radius
Predictability of events	Highly uncertain	Determinant in space but not in time	Mostly predictable	Unknown	Not applicable	Highly uncertain
Predictability of impacts	Variable and controversial	Moderately predictable	Highly predictable	Variable	Known but controversial	Variable and unknown
Level of warning for specific event	No visual warning 15- to ?-min audio warning	Probably none	Usually good	Unknown	Not applicable	None
Nature of losses	Primarily to health; very uncertain	Primarily to constructed features	Primarily to constructed features and humans	Primarily to health	No known losses	Primarily to health
Ability to prepare for losses	Low	Some preparation can be made	Well developed	Not known	Not applicable	Low

1. individuals within the context of the family;
2. families as communication and decisionmaking systems; and
3. the community and its component organizational structure.

In general, the community and the encompassing region are best viewed as the *gross context* of social behavior (Gump 1968). A more focused understanding of relevant variables is provided by research on families and organizations as micro-contexts of social activity. Community-level phenomena are conceptualized primarily as the aggregate consequences of family and organizational activities that are focused on a specific locale (Indik and Berrien 1968; Hunter 1974). While the current review is on *social* responses to various stimuli, consideration must be given to the individual and the effects of individual-level stress on social groupings (i.e., families, organizations, etc.)

On the second dimension of the matrix, research is classified into three areas:

1. general theories from the social and behavioral sciences;
2. studies of how people perceive and respond to risk and hazards; and
3. investigations of the impacts of hazardous events on people.

To some extent, the theories reviewed have guided the studies reported in the latter two areas, and empirical results have helped to refine theory. The overlap helps unite the literature in a cohesive fashion.

The Literature

Individual Systems Level

1. THEORETICAL PERSPECTIVES

The manner in which impacts are manifested on an individual level will be shaped largely by human cognitive processes and the way in which people perceive their environment and the event(s) which disrupts environmental norms. In this sense, the impact process can be viewed within a body of theory that characterizes the human processes of perception, decisionmaking, and adjustment or coping.

a. Perception

While perception was once a relatively restricted concept referring to an organism's awareness of the world, its use has shifted to a psycho-social level and typically involves a sociocultural dimension as well. As Allport (1955:368) notes, the use of the term

> ... *perception* in social disciplines has ... shifted from mere object aware-ness, physical world relations ... to a cognitive and perhaps even phe-nomenological *modus operandi* for collective activities ... and for concepts of self and society.

Given this broad conceptualization, it is not inappropriate to speak of risk perception for all social levels from the individual to the community to the entire society. It is, of course, necessary to recognize the complex interdependency of individuals, groups, and societal perceptions and the effects of interaction between those levels (Miller 1964).

For most hazards, characteristics of the agent can be objectively and relatively accurately described. However, the reality of a hazard often has little to do with how it is perceived at various social levels (VanArsdol *et al* 1964) or how it is adapted to (Mileti 1980). The per-ception of hazard is further complicated for the perceiver when the objective nature of the threat is in dispute or uncertain (Grosser *et al.* 1964), as is the case with nuclear power in general (Holdren 1982). For example, some residents of areas subject to risks of natural hazards view physical events with a different perspective from that of the expert or scientist (Kates, 1962; Mitchell 1974; White 1964). For instance, resi-dents of a floodplain may attach different meanings to the concept of the "100-year flood" than does the hydrologist (Burton and Kates 1964). Likewise, farmers may view drought in different terms than does the climatologist (Dupree and Roder 1974). In general, the behavior of people who misinterpret scientific information often differs from those with the more acute understanding.

The control a person feels that he or she has over a situation might affect perception of risk (Wortman 1976). According to Holdren (1982), individuals are more likely to tolerate a hazard if they feel they can control the situation. Sims and Baumann (1972) use the *locus of control* concept when explaining how to cope with threatening situations. Some individuals are inclined to believe in the efficacy of personal action in dealing with risky situations (internal locus of control); others, particularly those from fundamentalist religions, tend to feel that the situation is in God's hands, and, hence, little can be done in response (external locus of control) (Sims and Baumann 1972). The notion of control has implications for social adjustments made to hazardous situations, a subject considered below. When an individual's sense of control is threatened, negative psychological and emotional states can follow (Carver 1966, Baum and Davidson 1985). On the basis of experimental data, Milburn (1977) argues that *control* of a situation and not the *size of a threat* is the key in coping with threatening situations. Perceptions are related to other factors such as sex, ethnicity, age, and socioeconomic status as well, but the exact relationships are not well understood. Furthermore, perceptions are dynamic in that they change over time, but the cause of shifts is not well understood.

In a different manner, perceptions relate to how persons subjectively evaluate probabilities of rare events. Studies have shown that, while people are generally poor probabilistic thinkers (Tversky and Kahneman 1974), they are good at estimating the frequency of some risks (Hewitt and Burton 1971).

b. Decisionmaking

Second, and in a related fashion, impacts can be viewed in the context of the way people make decisions during times of risk and uncertainty. In the face of hazardous events, individuals and groups must choose among a theoretically immense number of alternative paths of behavior. Although the choice is often to do nothing, in most situations alternative courses of actions are feasible. The process by which such choices are made appears to be similar, despite a wide variety of decisional contexts. A simple model suggests that the individual or group (1) appraise the likelihood of hazardous events, (2) examine a range of alternative behaviors or adjustments, (3) evaluate the consequences of each perceived action, and (4) choose one or more actions (Slovic *et al.* 1974).

Field study shows that this general process is modified by several factors. First, people are not highly competent estimators of the likelihood and consequences of extreme events. Second, people rarely are aware of a wide range of alternative adjustments. Third, information-processing bias limits the ability to compare alternatives. Finally, people demonstrate a wide and diverse range of goals to be satisfied by the decision outcomes (Sorensen and White 1980).

In addition, evidence exists that information on alternatives is not simultaneously processed, but that alternative actions are considered in a sequential, ordered process (Kunreuther 1974; White *et al.* 1972). For example, the occupant of a floodplain in the United States does not carefully weigh the probabilities and consequences of disaster against premium costs in arriving at a decision to purchase flood insurance but tends to base a choice on whether a flood has been experienced and whether a neighbor has purchased insurance (Kunreuther 1978).

c. Stress

Another way of describing the manifestation of impacts in theoretical terms is as a stress-response phenomenon (Lazarus 1966; Selye 1956; McGrath 1970; and Manderschied 1981). In this regard, Lazarus (1966) has dealt with the notion of threat and resultant stress. Stress is the result of the transaction of an individual and a situation, and threat is conceptualized as the intervening factor between the experience of stress and the coping response (Lazarus 1966:25). The individual is most likely to perceive a situation as threatening when it appears salient to his or her future goals. However, if only some goals are threatened and not others, tensions can emerge.

Other dimensions of threat include the level of awareness of threat (Lazarus 1966:80). Awareness of threat may be a function in the restart case of the amount of media attention likely with the resumption of generation (Molotch 1979; McCombs and Shaw 1972), as well as national coverage of other nuclear power relevant issues (Marshall 1982).

The major means by which the proposed action will cause negative mental health impacts is through the stress-response phenomenon. This rests on the assumption that exposure to a risk or experiencing a disaster is similar in nature to going through a stressful life event (Logue *et al.* 1981). The model of life events and mental health suggests three stages of the phenomenon. First, a person is exposed to an initial stressor event. The nature and magnitude of this event and the way in which it is perceived as harmful are important determinants of impacts (Lazarus 1966). The second stage involves exposure to a series of events which may mediate response to the stressors; such events can help reduce stress or, conversely, raise somatic stress levels (Perry and Lindell 1978; Perry 1983). Finally, the increased stress levels may result in both physical and mental impairments. Such impairments are diverse in type and severity (Baum *et al.* 1980). One major problem in predicting mental health effects is a weak knowledge of the social and environmental determinants of perceived stress levels and the mechanisms by which stress results in debilitating illness (Sorensen *et al.* 1983; Perry 1983).

Stressors

Baum *et al.* (1980) define *stress* as a "complex set of emotional, mental, behavioral, and biological responses to the threat of being harmed or loss of something dear." Something must, however, produce that threat. Stressors or stress events cover a broad range of incidents which may elevate stress levels. Such stressors occur constantly yet do not cause stress-related impairments to mental health.

One way of examining stress phenomena differentiates between acute and chronic stressors (Baum and Davidson 1985). Acute stressors are short-lived phenomena, usually producing a sudden elevation of stress levels that endure for the length of time the stressor is present. On the other hand, chronic stressors are events that are either constantly present over long time frames or repeat themselves over longer time periods. In a similar fashion, Lazarus and Cohen (1977) identify cataclysmic and background stressors. The former are defined as strong, sudden, unique, and rare events or groups of events. The latter are defined as ordinary, persistent, or repetitive events.

Frederick (1980) has begun to investigate in more depth the characteristics of cataclysmic stressors that may affect stress levels. He classifies stressors as to whether they are natural or man-made, are preventable or nonpreventable, have short or long recovery periods, have been prepared for or not, have resulted in widespread evacuation and displacement or not, and have resulted in irrevocable or recoverable damages.

Perry (1983) discusses factors relevant to the manifestation of mental health impairment from natural disasters. He suggests, based on Barton (1970), and later confirmed by Bolin (1985), that duration of impact defined by long repetitive events or steady manifestation of a condition is a key factor in determining impacts. He also suggests that scope of impact defined by geographical coverage of the disaster agent is the second key characteristic of the stressor event. Perry also identifies disaster-specific effects as determinants of impacts. These include the extent to which friends and kin are killed or injured by the disaster and the level of personal property loss experienced.

As yet, we do not have a firm notion of the way such factors determine stress levels or stress-induced debilitating effects. In part, this is due to lack of field and experimental research on risk and disaster-induced stress. Additionally, it is attributable to the factors that mediate stress.

Mediators of Stress

A variety of factors related to the individual, the social setting, and the situational context of the threat will mediate stress or heighten it. Individual factors which seem to play major roles in shaping stress response include previous susceptibility to stress (Selye 1956) or psychological instability (Perry 1983), coping ability (Sorensen *et al.* 1983), coping resources (Lazarus 1966) or coping skills (Perry 1983), perceptions of the hazard and risk (Slovic *et al.* 1979; Sorensen *et al* 1983), individual grief reactions (Perry 1983), perceptions of control (Seligman 1975), and concern with other issues and problems (Sorensen *et al* 1983).

Factors related to social setting that influence stress include social support networks (Bolin 1982; Drabek and Key 1984; Perry 1983), community and group ties (Sorensen *et al.* 1983; Perry and Greene 1982), and crisis intervention (Hartsough 1982; Tierney and Blaisden 1979).

Situational factors that play a role include experience with witnessing death (Perry 1983), experience with evacuation (Frederick 1981), media influences and coverage (Sorensen *et al.* 1983), and post-disaster relief (Bolin 1982, Bolin and Bolton forthcoming).

Stress Effects

Distinctions are usually drawn between psychological reactions to stress and physiological responses (Baum *et al.* 1980). Furthermore, it is often desirable to view effects as direct effects, which are immediate responses to the stressor, and second-order effects, which are longer-term manifestations of stress impacts.

Direct psychological responses are numerous. First reactions often involve a feeling of shock or increased anxiety. Some stress victims may develop apathy and depressive mental states. Others may become irritable and resentful. Oftentimes a feeling of being trapped or of helplessness will accompany the stress.

Direct physiological responses are often associated with increased levels of adrenalin and other catecholamines. This increases heart rates and blood pressure and accelerates respiration, perspiration, and other physiological functions. Stress can also cause a numbing reaction whereby people experience a stunned or dazed feeling and are unable to respond in a normal fashion. Physical symptoms of these responses include muscular tension, memory lapse, headache, insomnia, tiredness, sweating, dizziness, and general weakness.

Second-order impacts are defined as reactions to or consequences of the first-order psychological and physiological impacts, and are divided into coping reactions and behavioral and physical manifestations of stress. *Coping* is usually defined as behavior taken to reduce or eliminate the danger posed by the stressor, and it might involve conscious and purposeful actions to remove the stressor, to get away from it, or to eliminate the stressor's effects. It also may include actions that are not directed toward the stressor, such as excessive alcoholic drinking or chronic drug use. In addition, coping may be solely cognitive; that is, people might make mental adaptations to deal with the stressor. Such adaptations are frequently referred to as *defense mechanisms*. Extensive documentation indicates that social support structures such as kinship and friendship ties play an extremely important role in the coping process and may be one of the major ways in which stress is mediated.

Behavioral and physical manifestations of stress are longer-term reactions to the first-order symptoms, which are often caused by chronic experiences with stress or from repeated episodes of acute stress. The most severe problems are probably produced by repeated catecholamine releases. Such releases exert a toll on various bodily functions which, in turn, can lead to cardiovascular problems or coronary heart disease. Other physical problems have also been associated with stress, including hypertension, arthritis, ulcers, and arteriosclerosis. In addition, coping responses may also produce negative consequences. Increased drinking leading to alcoholism can result. Excessive drinking can lead to a variety of problems both physical and social. Drug use can also lead to interpersonal difficulties, causing the loss of friends, divorce, and job-related problems. Furthermore, longer-term psychological manifestations of stress may occur. These are often not diagnosable as stress impacts, nor are they debilitating. Such problems may include general irritability, antisocial behavior, feelings of worthlessness, impatience, harshness, decreases in analytical abilities, and general contrariness. Such problems, when severe, can lead to clinical diagnosable mental illness.

Threat appraisal is affected by the ambiguity of environmental cues and the imminence of harm. Coping problems and stress increase when the threat is uncertain and the impact agent does not materialize (Lazarus 1966). Uncertainty as to risk is repeatedly identified in the literature as a problematic and stress-producing phenomenon in hazard assessment (Fiddle 1979; Turner *et al* 1979; Tversky and Kahnenman 1974; Danzig *et al.* 1958; Withey, 1962). Uncertainty, in turn, has been found to be associated with stress and the physiological consequences of stress such as psychosomatic illnesses (Miller 1964).

Personal stress occurs in situations where the threat stimuli is constant, whether due to predispositions of the individual to view it as such or from the characteristics of the environment (Lazarus 1966). States of chronic threat are stressful on individuals and may erupt into crises easily (Lang and Lang, 1964). Such effects are compounded if the anticipated effects of the hazard are not perceived as manageable by the target population. In such cases, Lang and Lang (1964:71) suggest that *demoralization* is an outcome.

2. RESPONSE TO RISK AND THREAT

The two bodies of literature most useful in projecting potential impacts study the way people perceive risk and hazard, consequent social adaptations, and human response to warnings of disaster. Earliest work in hazard studies emphasizing social adjustments came primarily from geographers (White 1945; Burton and Kates 1964; Kates 1962; Hewitt and Burton 1971) and psychologists (Wolfenstein 1957; Lazarus 1966). Sociologists (Fritz and Mathewson 1957; Barton 1970; Mack and Baker 1961; Dynes 1979; Quarantelli 1978) and anthropologists (Schneider 1957; Anderson 1968; Wallace 1956) provided additional insights by focusing on social and cultural adjustments to hazards.

a. Hazard Research

Because the primary emphasis of this literature is on cognition of hazard, additional concepts that appear important include threat (Lazarus 1966; Wallace 1956; Grosser *et al* 1964), stress as a reaction to threat (Miller 1964), coping strategies (Withey 1964), locus of control (Sims and Baumann 1972; Wortman 1976), risk assessment (Kilpatrick 1947; Kates 1978; Vlek and Stallen 1980) and social adjustments to the threats of environmental extremes (Turner *et al* 1979; Kroder 1970; Mileti 1980; Sorensen and White 1980).

To consider the role hazard awareness has in the cognitive process, the literature commonly identifies the characteristics of the environmental threat as elements affecting perceptions. Relevant dimensions include the perceiver's distance from the hazard (Manderthaner *et al.* 1978), as well as notions held about the "speed of onset, scope, intensity, duration, frequency temporal spacing, causal mechanisms, and predictability" (Burton *et al.* 1978; Barton 1970; Dynes 1970).

In addition, individuals' previous experience with and knowledge of the threat can affect their perceptions. Those perceptions then determine their reactions (Kilpatrick 1947). For natural hazards, the literature indicates a tendency for individuals to underestimate the hazard of a situation (White *et al.* 1958; Burton *et al.* 1965; Mileti 1980). In situations where persons have previous experience with a hazard, their perceptions have been found to vary as to the nature of future threat. In cases of flooding, White (1945) suggests that persons assume that worst-case events will not repeat themselves, although Kates (1962) has reported an opposite tendency. Burton *et al* (1965) found that persons living in coastal areas subject to hurricanes tended to view the storms as repetitive. Bolin (1982) found continued psychological stress in tornado victims with the onset of tornado season the year after impact, the season representing a potential increase in threatening weather. Friedsam (1961) and Drabek and Key (1984) have found that tornado victims continue to suffer heightened fear of storms.

Kates (1962:140) has suggested that people are "prisoners of experience" and tend to perceive hazards based on past experience. Likewise, Janis (1951) indicates that "near misses" are important in affecting perceptions of risk. In situations where persons do not have direct experience with physical impacts of a hazard such as in earthquakes, a tendency to minimize the expected damage or to interpret the situation as nonhazardous is found (Jackson 1981). This is suggested to be a psychological strategy to reduce the dissonance involved in placing oneself at risk. Thus, denial of risk by individuals has been found as one coping strategy in hazardous circumstances (Jackson 1981; Wolfenstein 1957), if the individual in question has little previous experience or knowledge.

According to Mileti (1980), the accuracy of risk perception improves with access to scientific information (see also Kunreuther 1978). Personal values and previous experience may predispose people to be selective in the information they choose as evidence of their judgments and actions (Hutton and Mileti 1979).

Considerable work on how people perceive risk and hazard under a *bounded rationality* model of human behavior has been undertaken by Slovic and colleagues (Slovic *et al.* 1974; Fischhoff *et al.* 1981). Their work has demonstrated that uncertainties, misperception of risk, crisis orientations, intuitions, and inability to integrate multiple information all conspire to limit the role of economic rationality in response to hazard.

Other researchers have focused on studying the adjustments people employ to mitigate risk and potential losses. Possible actions have been categorized to include preventing effects, modifying potential impacts, relocating potential victims from the risk area, or accepting the potential impact losses either individually or by distributing them across the larger social groups (Burton *et al.* 1978; Sorensen and White 1980; Mileti 1980; Mileti *et al.* 1981).

How people perceive the risks and benefits of restart is the central factor causing impacts to occur. This generalization is based on repetitive findings that human behavior in threatening situations is highly influenced by the perception of risk and the judged benefits of coping actions. Kates (1962) found in his early study of floodplain residents that inaction in the face of flood losses was guided by a denial or elimination of risk and uncertainty. Numerous studies on response to disaster warning note that threats must be perceived as real and likely before a response is made (Mileti 1975; Perry *et al.* 1981; Anderson 1968). Gruntfest (1977) showed that inaction in response to a flash flood and warning was primarily due to a lack of appreciation for the gravity of the situation. Key factors in explaining why people buy flood insurance are an awareness of a risk (Kunreuther 1978) and a perceived threat (Baumann and Sims 1978).

Mileti (1980) suggests that perceived risk is the central factor in affecting social behavior under risky conditions. Perceived risk is linked to the way individuals and organizations form "images of damages" which affect behavior (Mileti *et al.* 1981). Several characteristics of risk seem important in shaping human cognitions. Included are ability to estimate risk (Hewitt and Burton, 1971); the causes of the risk (Burton *et al.* 1978); experience with risk (Sorensen and White 1980); risk denial (Kates 1962; Kunreuther 1978), and exposure to risk information (Hutton *et al.* 1981).

Risk is traditionally defined as a set of consequences of risky events coupled with the probability those events will occur (Whyte and Burton 1980). A more behavioral or cognitive definition may be more germane to this line of inquiry. Recently, Slovic and others have shown that risk has several psychological dimensions including voluntariness, immediacy, understandability, controlability, newness, chronicness, dreadfulness and severity (Slovic *et al.* 1979), which can be categorized as two types of risks—unknown and dread (Slovic *et al.* 1982). While these authors have not attempted to explain how differences in the manner in which risks are perceived affect individuals' behavior, their work demonstrates individual and group variability in risk perceptions.

In most previous studies of human response to risk, behavior is treated as the dependent variable. In this case, the ability to cope is a factor which influences risk perception and, hence, impacts. Psychological studies suggest that coping is an important factor is reducing the danger people feel about threatening events (Lazarus 1966). Research has distinguished between coping by a change in behavior and that which involves a change in individuals' "internal environments" (Baum *et al.* 1980).

Coping, in this sense, is similar to the concept of *adjustment* and *adaptive behavior* used in the disaster and hazard literature. *Adjustments* are actions people or groups take to reduce their losses from a potential disaster. *Adaptive behaviors* are actions taken during a disaster to decrease the likelihood of injury, damage, or harm. Some evidence exists that the adoption of adjustment may increase people's perception of threat or, in other cases, create a sense of security (Mileti *et al.* 1981). For example, people who have safely coped with or adjusted to previous disasters are more cognizant of the threats (Perry *et al.* 1981; Burton et al. 1978). Conversely, coping activities (such as purchasing earthquake insurance) may create the illusion of being safe from earthquake damage (Hutton *et al.* 1981). Successful coping, even with an event of little significance, may create a feeling of overconfidence when dealing with more sizable situations (Baker 1977; Leik *et al.* 1981).

The degree to which people are sensitive to a risk will influence their coping behavior and the manner in which they perceive risk. Sensitivity is represented by people's awareness, experience, and preoccupation with a threatening situation. Previous studies have shown that awareness is an essential requirement for responding to a risk. For example, Kunreuther (1978) showed that, in order for people to purchase hazard insurance, they had to be aware they lived in a hazardous location. Experience also sensitizes threats. Previous experience with natural disaster is a major factor in shaping images of risk and loss (Mileti 1980; Burton *et al.* 1978). The level of sensitization is largely determined by the nature of the experiences. People who have experienced hurricanes without a traumatic outcome become complacent toward future events (Windham *et al.* 1977). Experience is also a powerful factor in explaining adjustment or coping actions (Waterstone 1978). Preoccupation with threat, in a similar sense, influences behavior. For example, while airplane flight insurance is a relatively poor investment based on actuarial estimates, preoccupation with air accidents distorts peoples' perceptions of the risks and leads to purchases (Eisner and Strotz 1961). At the extreme, habitual experience with risk leads to a social redefinition of what is unusual and what is often called a *disaster culture* (Quarantelli and Dynes, 1977).

b. Warning Research

Directly related to this body of research are disaster warning response studies, an area that has received perhaps the most systematic treatment of any area of disaster research (Mileti 1974, 1975; Mileti *et al.* 1975). In disaster research, the receipt of warning of impending disaster is followed by attempts to confirm the information (Danzig *et al.* 1958) and that, if the warning is received from the mass media, attempts will be made to confirm it some other way (Drabek 1969; Drabek and Stephenson 1971). Warnings that are consistent across several sources are more likely to be believed (Clifford 1956; Fritz 1957; Withey 1962) as are personally communicated warnings (Drabek and Boggs 1968).

Disaster warning belief is determined by a complex set of factors including warning sources, warning message content, the number of messages received, interpretation of environmental evidence of impending impacts, observations of the actions of others, whether the family is together or separated at the time of warning receipt, previous disaster experience, proximity to the projected impact area as well as demographic characteristics of the recipients, including socioeconomic status (SES), race, age, sex, and residence location (Anderson 1969; Mileti 1974; Mileti *et al.* 1975).

Warning belief, in turn, is associated with some type of social response, frequently evacuation (Drabek and Boggs 1968; Perry *et al.* 1981). Related to the warning literature, research on evacuation has been voluminous; therefore, only a few of the most pertinent findings are reviewed. Generally, research has found that those nearest the predicted target area are the most likely to evacuate (Danzig *et al.* 1958; Perry *et al.* 1981). Friedsam (1962) and Moore *et al.* (1963) have shown that the elderly are less likely to evacuate than others. Other research indicates that persons with a higher SES are less likely to evacuate (Moore *et al.* 1963; Young 1954), although education level has been reported as unrelated to evacuation behavior (Lachman *et al.* 1961). Perry *et al.* conclude that general predictors of evacuation behavior include perceived personal risk, belief in the reality of the warning, the presence of an individual adaptive plan, content of the message, past experience, warning source, warning frequency, personal contact, and age.

3. IMPACTS OF DISASTER

Considerable attention is given in disaster research to the existence and persistence of psychological and emotional consequences of disasters on victims (Wilson 1962). Whether disaster impacts cause persistent psychological and emotional disturbances among victims is debatable (Perry and Lindell 1978; Quarantelli 1979). One position maintains that disasters have relatively enduring negative psychosocial effects on victims (Menninger 1952; Moore 1958; Moore and Friedsam 1959; Moore *et al.* 1963; Lifton and Olson 1976). The other position is that psychological reactions occurring after a disaster tend to be relatively rare and of a short-term nature (Bates *et al.* 1963; Erickson *et al.* 1976; Fritz 1961; Sterling *et al.* 1977; Quarantelli 1979). Some have argued that often disaster victims emerge from their disaster experiences stronger and more "resilient" than before (Fritz, 1961; Quarantelli and Dynes 1977; Taylor 1976; Quarantelli 1979).

Researchers with clinical orientation have produced a considerable body of evidence documenting various psycho-social and physiological stress effects of natural and man-made disaster. Starting with one of the first clinical statements on the individual impacts of disasters (Tyhurst 1951), numerous researchers have since identified various types of stress-related psychological sequelae to disaster events (Blaufarb and Levine 1972; Church 1974; Gleser *et al.* 1981; Hocking 1965, 1970; Lifton and Olson 1976; Logue 1980; Melick 1978; Newman 1978; Penick *et al.* 1976; Rangell 1976; Tichner and Kapp 1976; *Tichner et al.* 1976). Janis (1951) has argued that the greater the sense of victimization a person feels following a stress event, the greater the likelihood that emotional disturbances will result. After reviewing these studies and others, Chamberlin (1980:238) proposed that, while many qualifications were required and much was unknown, the literature pointed to one conclusion: "Research provides evidence of long-term deterioration in health patterns and development of specific syndromes after such disasters."

In contrast to what he has labeled an"individual trauma perspective," Quarantelli (1979) argues that this evidence is weak and subject to alternative interpretations. In contrast to the Buffalo Creek, West Virginia data set are other field studies, for example, Hurricane Agnes (Melick 1978; Cohen and Poulshock 1977), flooding in Rapid City, South Dakota (Hall and Landreth 1974), and tornadoes in Xenia, Ohio (Taylor 1976), Omaha, Nebraska (Bell 1978), Wichita Falls, Texas (Bolin 1982), and Topeka, Kansas (Drabek and Key, 1984). While varying designs and measurement instruments were used in these studies, the tone and substance of the conclusions stand in sharp contrast to those offered by Erikson, Lifton, Titchener, and others.

Although some lingering consequences are reported that might be labeled as "negative," such as increased fear of future storms, the image structure is one of adaptation and positive change. Victims are not impaired acutely, if at all. Some appear to evidence signs of personal growth. Most indicators reflect no discernible change or impact which might be attributed to the disaster studies. Heightened fears of storms among some are offset by definitions of adaptive response emphasizing damage mitigation among others. Thus, the type and magnitude of psycho-social impacts that occur following disaster areas remain subject to scientific debate.

Looking at the differential distribution of psycho-social impacts of disasters, however, evidence is found that certain categories of individuals and families are less susceptible to stress-induced emotional disturbances than others. Those with higher incomes, higher levels of education, higher religiosity scores, as well as older persons, have been found to exhibit fewer disaster-related psycho-social impacts (Huerta and Horton 1978; Bolin and Klenow 1981; Bolin 1982; Drabek and Key, 1984).

Other individual factors do not appear to be significant in explaining the manifestation of impacts. Drabek and Key (1984) indicate that expectations about the future (e.g., Cantril's Ladder of Life Measure, 1963), attitudes of alienation and despair (e.g., Srole 1956), and self-perceptions of physical health (e.g., several items from the Midtown Manhattan Study, Srole *et al.* 1962) yielded no systematic differences. While patterned within hypothesized configurations (e.g., SES differences), victim-nonvictim comparisons did not indicate any long-term negative impacts, when both pre- and post-event data were juxtaposed.

While single events result in questionable impact, extended exposure to stressors has been associated with persistent, negative psycho-
social impacts, both on families and individuals (Bolin 1982; Gleser *et
al.* 1981). In the disaster literature, extended exposure to stress refers
to postimpact stressors, including the effects of evacuation, emergency
and temporary shelter on victims (Gleser *et al.* 1981) residential and
neighborhood disruption (Bolin 1976), disaster-induced unemployment
(Bolin and Bolton, 1983), and related persistent disruptions in social
activities (Drabek and Key, 1984; Trainer and Bolin 1976).

The other major element in extended exposure to stress for disaster
victims is that which originates in the threat of reoccurrence of another
disaster. Disentangling the psycho-social effects of disaster impacts from
the effects of the threat of reoccurrence is difficult. Kinston and Rosser
(1974) suggest that fear of reoccurrence can trigger deeper emotional
reactions than those experienced as a result of the original event. Howard (1980) studied the relationship between aftershocks and fear of
further damage in the San Fernando, California, earthquake area with
the extensive use of child counseling centers and telephone inquiries.
This suggests that children may be particularly adversely affected and
that parents are thereby affected secondarily.

Ample evidence suggests that families in the contemporary United
States are frequently enmeshed in relatively active networks of kin (Adams 1964, 1968; Aldous 1967; Aiken and Goldberg 1969; Babchuck
1971; Berardo 1967; Bossard and Boll 1946; Bott 1971; Lee 1977, 1980;
Litwak 1960a; Litwak 1960b; Litwak and Szeleny 1969; Miller and Reisman 1961; Petersen 1969; Sussman 1953, 1954; Sussman and Burchinal
1962; Rossers and Harris 1965; Wellman 1973). Kinship ties, as discussed
later, can affect families' definitions of a given situation, their responses
to hazards, resource availability in times of need, and their stress-man-
aging capacities.

Another major element in the social networks of families is their
linkages with bureaucratic organizations. While Weber (1947) described
the increasing bureaucratization of industrial societies as a "process of
rationalization," clearly a degree of antagonism exists between the patterns of familial organizations and of bureaucratic organizations (Parsons 1959). The emotional, personal base of families is often at odds
with the impersonal and ostensibly rational base of most bureaucracies.
Families' organizational linkages frequently impute a subordinate relationship for the families (Litwak *et al.* 1974:2), a fact that does little
to relieve the aforementioned antagonism. When families are forced to

establish additional contacts with bureaucracies, as in the case of hazards and disasters, they typically perceive the organizations to be impersonal, as well as inefficient and inept (Bolin 1982). In this regard, Taylor and his colleagues (1970) found that family experiences within the therapeutic community set a tone of negativism toward bureaucratically-organized relief agencies.

Family System Level

1. THEORETICAL PERSPECTIVES

For the purposes of projected data gathering on the social impacts of restart, a brief review of basic family structure and dynamics is presented. Herein, the family is viewed as a system of interaction (Burgess 1926), as well as an information processing and communications unit (Galvin and Brommel 1982).

a. Family Structure

While society and culture affect a person's perceptions, the immediate family has a greater effect (Galvin and Brommel 1982). Perceptions and "definitions of the situation" (Meltzer *et al.* 1975) derive from communication processes particularly as they occur in family contexts. Communication may be seen as a process of creating and sharing meanings and understandings about surrounding social events and actors (Wilmont 1975). Communication processes in families are important determinants of family cohesion and adaptability (Bochner 1976; Olson *et al.* 1979). The way families adapt to stress and to major changes in their life circumstances is affected by their communication capabilities, interactive processes, and available resources, as well as the nature of their linkages with extra-family groups and organizations (LaRossa 1977; Littlejohn 1978; Mitchell 1969; Parsons 1943, 1949; Watzlawick *et al.* 1967).

b. Families and Stress

The way families define and respond to stress situations was first considered by Burgess (1926), who studied family techniques for coping with crises such as divorce and unemployment. Subsequent research also focused on the way families dealt with the chronic stress of unemployment as a consequence of the Great Depression of the 1930s (Angell 1936; Cavan and Ranck 1938; Morgan 1939; Komarovsky 1940; Koos 1946; Elder 1974). Factors identified related to family coping with economic crisis include the level of marital adjustment prior to the stress event, the extensiveness of a kin-based support network, the suddeness of onset of the stressors and the nature of support available in the community.

One of the classic formulations of families under stress was developed by Hill (1949) and is still influential. Briefly stated, Hill's A, B, C, -X model suggests the stress event (A) interacts with the family's stress-meeting resources (B) and with the family's definition of the situation (C) to produce the family crisis (-X). According to Hill (1949; Hill and Hansen 1962; Hansen and Hill 1964), the family experiencing stress-induced crisis goes through a period of disorganization followed by a recovery phase and a restabilization of interaction and activity patterns.

The idea that stress on families depends on stress-meeting resources (financial resources, levels of marital stability, position in the life cycle, social support networks, etc.) and on the definition of the situation derives from complex communication processes that are constantly ongoing in families (Bochner 1976); the nature of the definition arrived at, itself a subjective state, determines the coping actions a family will take to deal with the perceived crisis (Hill 1949). Failure to arrive at a consensual definition of the situation can exacerbate marital conflict and disrupt family relationships due to a lack of agreement as to what course of action should be taken with regard to the external stressor (LaRossa 1977; Olson et al. 1979). Successful coping with previous crises appears to increase families' abilities to cope with current crises (Hill, 1949).

While early sociological research has tended to treat the family as an isolated system (Bakke 1949; Hill 1958; Burr 1973) as it copes with stressors, this view has been superceded with one giving more attention to the external relationships that families establish or activate to deal with stress (Hansen and Johnson 1979; Lin et al. 1979; McCubbin 1979; McCubbin and Olson 1980; McCubbin et al. 1980). These support networks include kinship groups (Cantor 1979; Hill 1970; Martin and Martin, 1978), neighborhoods (Litwak and Szelenyi 1969; Cantor 1979), and mutual aid groups (Katz 1970; Aschenbrenner 1975; Kropotkin 1914). Similarly, kin ties are important in stress reduction for victims (Wilson 1962; Vosburg 1971). Conversely, larger families, due perhaps to the likelihood of having young children present, appear more vulnerable to stress-related symptoms (Blaufarb and Levine 1972; Bolin 1982; Bolin and Bolton forthcoming). Several researchers have documented separation anxieties in children as a result of their experiences in disasters including earthquakes (Blaufarb and Levine 1972), floods (Titchner *et al.* 1976; Erikson 1976), and tornadoes (Bolin 1982).

c. Family Mobility

Several studies have investigated the social and cognitive aspects of population mobility, typically focusing on two aspects of family mobility: Why people move away from their locations, and why they move to certain new locations. Current thinking suggests that the combination and meshing of these two factors leads to a change in family location. A review of mobility literature suggests nine factors that explain family mobility (Michelson 1977):

1. financial considerations, including family income levels and change;
2. stage in the life cycle, including marital status, age, and family structure;
3. neighborhood characteristics, including ties, feelings of similarities to neighbors, and status considerations;
4. interpersonal relations, including contacts and participation in social activities;
5. organizational participation, including the number and type of organizations in which people participate;
6. commuting requirements, including distance and travel time;
7. commercial activity, including access to restaurants and shopping;
8. recreational activity, including type, level, and access; and
9. housekeeping activity, including type and time involved in various activities.

As a whole, these factors explain most of the reasons families move, and they have been verified by numerous investigations (Rossi 1955; Ducan and Morgan 1975; Speare *et al.* 1972). In normal situations, factors concerning environmental hazard and risk have not been identified as significant elements of migration decisions.

An alternate theory has been advanced by Wolpert (1964; 1965; 1966), who emphasizes the cognitive dimensions of migration decisions. His model is based on a satisfier theory of human decision in which a person or group will tolerate certain residential conditions until a threshold is reached. In his stress-threshold mobility model, Wolpert assumes that people attach various "utilities" to the benefits and costs or satisfactions and dissatisfactions of a place. If stresses cause a distinct imbalance between positive and negative utilities, then people are stimulated to find locations with more positive utilities and migration follows if resources permit.

2. Response to Risk and Threat

Little applied work has been done on the manner in which groups such as families respond to risk and threat from hazardous events. Many of the findings discussed for individuals appear to be applicable to the family level, but lack empirical validation. Research to date reveals the following observation.

A central contextual factor affecting the process of risk assessment is family and kinship ties. Lucas (1966; 1969) examined variation in perception of "ambiguous stimuli" in a coal mining community that was subject to continuous threat (mine collapse). His research found that expert knowledge of the hazard did not affect the perception of hazard (1966:234), but primary role (family) relationships did. Persons tended to view the risk as real if they felt kin were at risk. This finding is supported by an examination of stress produced by the Mt. St. Helens volcano (Leik *et al.* 1982). Results indicated that a major stressor, such as the presence of a volcano, created a commonality of self-appraised stress levels in members of the same family, which is in marked contrast to variable stress levels in family members usually found in everyday situations. Furthermore, the study found that the perceptions and definitions of risk were fairly consistent across family roles. The saliency of risk elements, however, varied among roles. Husbands appeared to be more sensitive to the likelihood of a hazardous event, while wives were more sensitive to the threat of damages. Children gave the two risk factors similar weights.

When confronted by threat from a warning of impending disaster, the family appears to be primary as the social context of decisionmaking for evacuation (Clifford 1956), as an evacuation unit (Bates *et al.* 1963; Drabek 1969) as well as in choosing a location to evacuate to (Drabek and Boggs 1968; Drabek 1969; Perry *et al.* 1981).

Evacuees often exhibit anxieties over the home they left behind (Bates *et al.* 1963), and these anxieties are compounded if the family did not evacuate as a complete "unit." Having the family intact prior to evacuating and then evacuating as a unit is a prime concern of those in imminent disaster situations (Drabek 1969). Evacuation and subsequent emergency shelter arrangements can be stressful on family members, particularly if the evacuation is protracted (Instituut Voor Sociaal Onderzoek 1955; Milnc 1977). Families typically seek to return to the impact area and to their homes as quickly as possible (Dacy and Kunreuther 1969), often before the situation is safe (Bates *et al.* 1963).

Few empirical investigations have been made of the role disaster or risk plays in residential location and mobility decisions. Following disasters, however, most people return to their original locations in hazardous areas (Burton *et al.* 1978). Reasons for this behavior include the lack of resources to move elsewhere, ties to location, and cognitive biases in thinking about risk. This latter factor suggests people fall prey to the "gamblers' fallacy"—if it happened once, another occurrence in the near future is not probable. The extent to which and the reasons why people move away from hazard following disaster have not been seriously researched.

The role hazard or risk disclosures play in shaping residential home purchases has been investigated in earthquake-prone areas (Palm 1981; 1982). The results of these studies indicate that the mandatory disclosure of earthquake risk to prospective home buyers at the time of closure was irrelevant and insignificant in purchase decisions when compared to other attributes which have traditionally explained why people buy certain types of housing. Earthquake risk disclosures at a time when people have committed themselves to a decision are not persuasive in changing that decision.

In a context more analogous to TMI restart, the impact of an earthquake prediction on residential and industrial/commercial mobility has been examined. A study of families' plans to move from an earthquake-prone area due to hazard threat shows that threat perception and proximity to high-risk areas are not strong indicators of intentions to move. Instead, traditional factors such as ties to community and stage of life cycle have greater explanatory powers (Kiecolt and Nigg 1982).

Slightly different conclusions were derived in another study of response to earthquake prediction (Mileti *et al.* 1981). While the study concluded that predicting the number of families who would move in response to information about increased risk was impossible, propensity to move was explainable by five factors. Relocation was positively related to level of resources, previously-adopted protective actions, and levels of perceived damage. Mobility was negatively influenced by the purchase of hazard insurance and commitment to existing locations. These findings provide some support for the theoretical perspective of the stress-threshold mobility model.

3. IMPACTS OF DISASTER

The effects of disaster on families has received much broader and more intense attention than have other social system levels. Disaster research generally shows that families recover more slowly from the effects of disasters than do communities (Haas *et al.* 1977; Bolin 1982). In general, disaster impacts vary across populations, resulting in differential rates of recovery. Recent research indicates that elderly disaster victims are less likely to experience long-term emotional disruptions from disasters than others (Cohen and Poulshock 1977; Bell 1978; Bolin and Klenow 1983; Huerta and Horton 1978; Kilijanek and Drabek 1979), although they appear to encounter difficulties in the areas of housing and economic recovery (Drabek and Key, 1984; Bolin 1982). Younger families affected by disasters experience reduced levels of marital happiness (Drabek and Key, 1984). This is expected as younger families, particularly those with young children, frequently are undergoing stress (LeMasters 1974); a disaster presents them with additional stresses that are often beyond their capacities to handle, resulting in marital deterioration.

Research centering on long-term family recovery has developed a theoretical model that incorporates a set of explanatory factors within a longitudinal framework (Bolin 1982). Important variables explaining family recovery include a family's predisaster socioeconomic characteristics, disruption levels, past stress exposure, vulnerability (as measured by a family's stress-meeting capacity), and aid-seeking behaviors. This research suggests that recovery has four dimensions: economic, housing, quality of life, and emotional, the former two functioning as preconditions for the latter two in longitudinal sequence. Central among findings is that social class factors affect not only economic and housing recovery but emotional components of recovery as well. Furthermore, certain family types (e.g., families at early stages of the life cycle, larger families, rural families) are more vulnerable to disaster-induced stress at the outset, and, hence, will have more trouble recovering.

Drabek and Key (1984) found that no major differences occurred in internal functioning across such dimensions as patterns of family decisionmaking, role differentiation, or conflict after disaster. Kin linkages were tightened, however, among victim families. Most affected were their definitions of kin as future help sources, if future problems occur. This work also showed that primary group linkages were altered, although the pattern was varied. Bonds of the victim family to friends were intensified, but those with neighbors were weakened. Slight deterioration was evidenced in social and civic group participation, except for one category—churches.

For disaster victims, emotional recovery from the event is apparently the most difficult to accomplish, particularly for large families, younger families, and those in lower SES categories (Bolin and Trainer 1978; Bolin 1982; Bolin and Bolton forthcoming). Extrapolating from previous studies, it can be generalized that elderly and higher SES families may "recover" from restart-induced stress the most easily, while those of lower SES, large families, and young families will have the most trouble overcoming such stress.

If only one individual in a family experiences emotional trauma from a disaster event, that trauma can nevertheless affect other family members either through "contagion effect" or through adjustments that must be made in family roles and interaction patterns to accommodate the upset emotional state of that family member (e.g., Bolin 1982; Gleser *et al.* 1981; Laing 1972; Lindy and Grace 1985). In particular, research has shown that children often experience negative emotional impacts from disasters (Perry *et al.* 1956; Perry and Perry 1959; Erikson 1976; Gleser *et al.* 1981; Newman 1978; Solomon 1985). Children can either create anxieties in their parents or incorporate and amplify their parents' disaster-induced anxieties (Erikson 1976; Gleser *et al.* 1981; Bolin 1982). Holmes and Rahe (1967) report that residual stress from crisis situations can be reinforced by unrelated life stresses. Families at early stages of their life cycle typically experience developmental stresses and, hence, may be more vulnerable to additional external stresses (LeMasters 1974; Bolin 1982). Stress can also be reinforced by reminders or visual cues of the disaster (Church 1974).

Community Systems Level

1. THEORY

a. Community Structure

Evidence from community research is important in understanding the significance of the locale on the well-being of its citizens in addition to providing insights into the dynamics of community-level social behavior. The behavior of groups and families cannot be aggregated and referred to as community behavior because of the synergistic nature of collective social behavior. As the previous section has indicated, the way families define situations, act, and respond to demands on them, depends in some measure on the way families (and community organizations) affect each other in an interactive sense (Schelling 1978).

The community and its component organizations constitute an important frame of reference for individuals and families (Fried 1966). Communities constitute symbolic objects of orientation (Hunter 1974, 1975) and form the basis of persons' cognitive maps (Suttles 1972). These mental maps render the local area familiar, safe, and accessible for residents. Communities also provide symbols of identification for residents, symbols that constitute an element of personal identity (Hunter 1974). Cognitive identity with the locale increases with length of residency, and participation in local organizations increases further the cognitive significance of the community as a frame of reference (Hunter 1975; Bell and Newby 1971).

In crisis situations in communities, groups and organizations frequently emerge to deal with the crisis (Quarantelli 1970; Walsh 1981). While most emergent groups necessarily disappear with the subsidence of the crisis, some persist and become part of the changed postcrisis community structure. In crisis situations with prolonged impacts, emergent organizations have the chance to formalize and institutionalize their existence (Gillespie et al. 1974; Levine 1982). By meeting community needs, such organizations may help to reduce stress at the community level; through their persistence the social order of the community is transformed permanently (Gillespie et al. 1974; Haas and Drabek 1970).

Participation in community organizations and the incumbent cognitive effects are associated with locality-relevant issues (Warren 1972). Salient issues are likely to promote participation in action-oriented organizations and are also likely to be associated with conflict at the level of the community (Litwak et al. 1974). Gamson (1966) suggested that political conflict in the community is a sign of community vitality. Coleman (1957) argued that the degree of citizen involvement in local organizations and issues is positively related to the frequency of community conflict. The issues in dispute, to generate community involvement and conflict, must touch central parts of the lives of citizens, must have differential impacts, and must be an event on which action can be taken (Coleman 1957). Even if such conditions do lead to conflict, the resultant social impacts are not necessarily negative ones.

b. Community Well-Being Research

The analysis of well-being within various geographical areas has taken two different approaches. The first has dealt with subjective or perceived facets of well-being. Research has primarily concentrated on individuals' satisfaction with various aspects of their lives (Campbell *et al.* 1976; Andrews and Inglehart 1979). Three dimensions of subjective well-being have commonly been tapped (Waserman and Chua 1980), including:

1. life variables such as personal happiness and satisfaction with one's life;
2. specific life domain variables such as satisfaction with housing and health; and
3. global life space variables such as satisfaction with community or attributes of a place.

Research shows, however, that a high level of intercorrelation exists between measures at these three levels (Wasserman and Chua 1980; Andrews and Withey 1976).

A second approach to measuring well-being has used objective indicators (Liu, 1975; Smith 1973). Typically, a wide range of variables are used and reduced into clusters using multivariate techniques. For example, Golant and McCutcheon (1980) condense 92 variables into 11:

1. growth and change (e.g., population change);
2. congestion and crowding (e.g., population density);
3. safety (e.g., crime rates);
4. family welfare (e.g., divorce incidence);
5. economic status (e.g., income);
6. education and professional status (e.g., level of education);
7. availability of services (e.g., indices of various professional and commercial functions);
8. physical health (e.g., death rates);

9. housing stock status (e.g., vacancy rates);
10. economic health (e.g., unemployment rates); and
11. mental health (e.g., suicide rates).

A chief criticism of this approach is that by producing an index based on these factors, one still fails to know what they mean in terms of well-being; any interpretation is ultimately subjective.

In light of these problems, several researchers have attempted to compare objective and subjective measures. In general, they have found no overall relationships between the two approaches to rating geographic areas (Schneider 1975). Furthermore, specific variables attempting to measure the objective dimensions of well-being are not highly correlated with subjective measures of that same dimension (Wasserman and Chua 1980), which has led to considerable skepticism about the utility of objective measures as a means of capturing the human dimension of well-being. Subjective measures, on the other hand, have been attacked on the basis that people tend not to make honest evaluations of their lives when questioned. Research is beginning to dispel this criticism (Atkinson 1982). From this literature, examining the effects of the accident and restart using an objective is difficult. Ultimately, well-being involves the perceptions and attitudes of local people.

2. RESPONSE TO RISKS AND THREAT

a. Response to Hazard

When the unit of analysis shifts to the level of community, much of the available literature is directed toward the adjustments that communities make regarding perceived hazards (Dynes and Wenger, 1971; Mileti 1980; Hutton and Mileti 1979). Response to hazard at the community level is typically made problematic by the propensity to deny risk (White and Haas 1975; Mileti 1980; Mileti *et al.* 1981). For some hazards, this is reinforced by the tendency of the media to underplay potential hazards (Turner 1979), although the media can also create community-level anxiety if they promote rumors (Prasad 1935; Danzig *et al.* 1958; Turner 1979). In situations where the credibility of official information is questioned, rumor could be a likely outcome.

Other studies show that communities who have repeated experiences with a disaster agent are better able to maintain an organized response capability to deal with future impacts (Fritz 1961). However, if the community prepares for an anticipated disaster based on past experience, dysfunctional consequences can follow if the new disaster is different from their earlier experiences (Parr 1969). Prior experience may also add familiarity to the event, reduce sensitivity to the event, and reduce the adequacy of the social response to it (McLuckie 1970). One interesting variant of this aspect of the research is that some communities have disaster subcultures incorporated into their environments as a consequence of repeated exposure to risk and threat (Moore 1958; Anderson 1968; and Hannigan and Keuneman 1978). Substantial variability in this tendency may be considered as an intervening variable in the community's response to threat.

Some evidence leads us to believe that communities may vary in their abilities to define and/or tolerate risks. This is based on observations of community variability in the definition of flood risks (Kates 1962), adoption of erosion control strategies (Mitchell 1974), adoption of earthquake building codes (Nilson 1981), implementation of floodplain regulations (Hutton and Mileti, 1979), or acceptance of hazardous technologies (Kasperson 1980). Such variability suggests that regional differences in risk perception and saliency of hazard lead to different community decisions about environmental hazards.

In general, disasters result in human responses which have "therapeutic" impacts on the social functioning of communities (Fritz 1961). Collective social responses to disaster tend to promote four major positive impacts according to Quarantelli and Dynes (1976). First, they resolve and reduce personal and social conflicts. Second, they prevent disorganizing behavior. Third, they reduce antisocial behavior due to losses caused by disaster. Fourth, they motivate people to constructive tasks. As a result, a relative lack of social conflict appears to follow disasters.

Yet, in some circumstances, conflicts do arise and are significant. Table 10 identifies the major conditions that have been identified as promoting social harmony or conflicts following disaster. The table also estimates the presence of factors which may cause conflict to emerge over the potential TMI-1 restart decision. The evidence tends to support the idea that conditions are more conducive to conflict than to harmony, although this does not mean conflict is certain to occur. Furthermore, conflict, *per se*, is not inherently good or bad. Conflict can lead to a more socially desirable decision on restart or a breakdown in social unity and dysfunctioning. The end outcome is not predictable.

Table 10   Conflict and harmony concerning hazardous events

General factors[*]	TMI-specific factors
Factors which promote harmony	
External threat	Threat comes from source near the community
Understandable/identifiable threat	Radiation is not readily understandable or identifiable
Consensus on problem solution	Community is divided
Recognition of impacts and problems	Impacts and problems are complex
Focus on present	Concerns are over long-term effects
Leveling of social distinction	Social distinctions are not prominent
Strengthening of community identification	Identification is not apparent
Factors which promote conflict	
Lack of warning	Warning for accident was poor, existing capabilities questioned
Lack of emergency response capacity	Capability has not been well demonstrated
Allocation of resources	Questions exist over resources for clean-up
Interjurisdictional disputes	Insider-outsider conflicts exist
Social inequities	Are not highly apparent except for cost of power issue
Emergence of groups	Have formed over TMI issue

[*]After Quarantelli and Dynes, 1976.

b. Conflict over Fluoridation

Another analogous situation is the issue of fluoridation of community water supplies. Since 1950, fluoridation of domestic water supplies has been one of the most prominent technological issues with perceived health risks that is faced at the community level. It is characterized by an underlying scientific debate over the carcinogenic nature of the fluoride, a debate which still continues in the scientific literature (Kinlen and Doll 1981). Several theories have emerged from rather extensive social science research on public opposition to fluoridation, and these theories may shed some light on the issue of conflict over TMI-1 restart.

Mazur (1975) identifies some basic theories as to why people oppose both fluoride and nuclear power and categorizes these as danger, ignorance, alienation, beliefs about larger issues, and social influence. The *danger theory* suggests that conflicting information over the health risks of fluoridation lead to public doubts about its safety. Such doubt and adherence to beliefs endorsed by a few scientists concerning adverse health affects lead to social and political conflict. The *ignorance theory* suggests that people have not been adequately informed about fluoridation benefits or have been misinformed about risks and, therefore, express opposition. The *alienation theory* concludes that opposition to fluoridation is a reflection of a social movement against a centralized larger social order. According to this idea, opponents are alienated against technology, government, and science. As individuals, they are characterized as being deprived, powerless, and outside the mainstream of society. The *beliefs about larger issues theory* suggests opposition to fluoridation is a means by which people react against the loss of individual freedom and socialist political ideologies. Finally, the *social influence theory* holds that opposition is a result of the personal influence held by opinion leaders over others in society. Opposition is generated by information passed through social networks led by certain charismatic people.

Alternatively, another theory of opposition to fluoridation has been offered, which suggests that conflict occurs because of basic weaknesses in the decisionmaking structure of local governments (Crain *et al.* 1969). The defeat of fluoridation comes about because of normal social processes; conflict, when aroused, encourages opposition to the issue because of public doubts and emotions. When brought to the public forum, the rejection of fluoridation becomes much more likely because of public conflict.

Walsh (1981) documents the existence of seven anti-TMI organizations that constitute an organizational infrastructure that appears to play a central role in sustaining a disaster subculture in area communities. At least one single interest pro-restart group has also formed. A disaster subculture provides families with definitions of the situation, definitions that alert them to the hazardousness of a locale (Barton 1970; Dynes 1970; Bolin 1982). Disaster subcultures reflect a general social and cultural adaptation to persistent or recurring disasters. Such a subculture also constitutes an institutionalization of previous disaster experience, that, in turn, affects social responses to future disasters in a number of ways.

Emergent norm theory (Turner and Killian 1972) has been used to describe and explain social processes as they occur when persons are confronted with situations where previous norms are not applicable (Hufnagle and Perry 1982). In this view, a crisis creates an unstructured situation that can be responded to only when new norms emerge to guide social behavior (Drabek 1968). In crisis situations, nontraditional modes of behavior typically are developed to cope with perceived environmental changes.

The restart issue is likely to sustain the protest organizations which emerged after the TMI-2 accident. In light of the complex set of issues surrounding restart (health, property values, employment, the cost of electricity, TMI-2 cleanup, etc.) and on the basis of analogies from disaster literature and the fluoridation issue, rancorous conflict could result at the community level as a result of restart (e.g., Gamson 1966).

3. IMPACTS OF DISASTER

a. Economic Impacts

Several recent studies (Friesema *et al.* 1979; Wright *et al.* 1979; Wright and Rossi 1981) indicate that natural disasters have few detectable long-term effects as measured by aggregate socioeconomic indicators such as employment rates, business starts, or population growth. The lack of long-term impact has been attributed to the integration of local communities and economics into the larger society, thereby allowing communities to externalize and distribute their losses (Friesema *et al.* 1979). If natural disasters have few detectable long-term community impacts, restart by itself would probably not have any negative economic or demographic impacts at the aggregate level of community or region.

Within the limits of the units studied and the dependent variables selected, this conclusion stands. Critics, however, have not been willing to see the matter put to rest in view of some of the interpretations and policy recommendations offered by the study teams (Drabek 1981; White 1981). Therefore, while limited exploration of macro-system impacts has occurred, the overall issue is far from resolved despite the propensity by some to generalize this conclusion to all forms of disaster, in all locations. To date, however, no comparable data set has been published indicating discernible long-term effects—either negative or positive—on such macro systems.

b. Impacts to Social Cohesion

Social cohesion is the ability of groups and organizations to establish and maintain bonds, interactions, and solidarity. To address the question of social cohesion, two experiences with hazardous waste incidents are reviewed: Appendix C summarizes the nature of the experiences at Love Canal, New York, and Wilsonville, Illinois, based on four characteristics of these incidents. These characteristics are (1) type and timing of public involvement, (2) major public concerns, (3) the role of information, and (4) mitigation and closure. Each of these factors helps explain impacts on social cohesion. The appendix also displays the analogous impacts of TMI-1 restart based on the hazardous waste experience.

Type and Timing of Public Involvement

In reviewing this information, we see a process in which the social visibility or public awareness of an event is followed by"alarmed perception" with rapid dissemination of information, after which "chronic adaptation" (saturation and disinterest) occurs. This type of reaction is more likely in short-term acute pollution crisis situations; long-lasting exposure is often tolerated or disregarded because of feelings of inevitability, impotence, or uninvolvement (Battisti 1978). For example, people buying houses in Love Canal may have known that the neighboring park and school grounds were given to the city by Hooker Chemical Company after its use as a waste disposal site without becoming concerned until physical evidence of chemical release, such as strong irritating odors or standing pools in yards, became quite common in the area. This visible physical evidence generated concerns about further potential effects such as physiological damage. In the case of Wilsonville, the absence of a solid buffer zone between the town and the hazardous waste landfill facility, and the truck access roads running through the town, were identified as real dissatisfactions with town residents and officials (Bolch *et al.* 1978). These dissatisfactions probably provided the spur to the increased citizen involvement when it was proposed that polychlorinated biphenyls (PCBs) from outside the state be disposed of at the Wilsonville facility. In the TMI-1 restart situation, the high visibility of the TMI-2 accident (particularly because cleanup after the

accident will be ongoing long after the proposed restart of TMI-1) will
spill over as an issue on restart.

Major Concerns

In all three of these cases, health and safety concerns are very
important, largely because neither chemical pollution nor radiation damage can be easily detected by the human senses, their effects may have
a long latency period, and often they cannot be measured or even con-
clusively attributed to these sources. These problems exacerbate the
uncertainty of the overall situation.

Economic concerns exist in each situation but are more diverse than
similar. However, the fact that economic factors play a major role in
each situation is in itself analogous.

Institutional issues play a pivotal role in the resolution of problems
in each of the categories under discussion. Who is in charge, who is
responsible, and how decisions are made, interpreted, and implemented
are key elements in the entire scenario.

Role of Information

The role of information in analyzing these three situations can be
divided into subissues of access, credibility, and feedback mechanisms.
Immediate easy access to reliable information is an ideal never attained;
not getting the requested information has led to law suits for information
at Wilsonville and Love Canal.

Equally as important as access is the credibility of the information
and/or information source. The Environmental Protection Agency
(EPA) severely damaged its credibility in the Love Canal case when it
issued a health study that came under heavy scientific criticism, and a
second, independent study fared no better (Seligman 1981). At Wilsonville, citizens did not believe SCA, Inc. (the facility owner), or the
state agency (which granted operating permits on a determination that
land for the disposal site was sufficiently impervious to safely contain
toxic wastes) and persuaded the court to close the site (*Environment
Reporter* 1978). This subissue is further underscored in the case of Three
Mile Island by Goldsteen and Schoor's (1982) TMI-area survey, which
concluded that a lack of confidence in government and utility officials
with respect to nuclear power exists; this conclusion is particularly not-
able because the most respected sources of information in many disaster

situations have traditionally been government officials. This conclusion is strengthened by a finding that while Harold Denton of the NRC was perceived by laypersons to be the single source of reliable information during the TMI- 2 emergency period, laypersons currently do not feel that any one is fulfilling this role (Social Impact Research 1982).

The related issue of communication or feedback mechanisms at both Love Canal and Wilsonville have been characterized as "too little, too late." In both cases, the citizens have resorted to the court system in order to be heard.

Mitigative Strategies

The two hazardous waste cases discussed herein were chosen partially because they were allowed to progress past most mitigation opportunities before any serious attempts were made to address the issues at hand. At Love Canal, state and federal aid for some evacuation and purchase of the most severely affected homes were granted only after a great public outcry and the bungling of health studies for the affected area. "Superfund" aid is still pending release of the latest federal environmental data study (New York Department of Environmental Conservation 1982). Civil suits for more than $2 billion (Wolf 1980) have been filed by citizens.

The Wilsonville situation has reached an impasse. Court-ordered exhumation of all wastes buried there has not been done and is a multimillion dollar task. While citizens won their case to close the facility, it remains visible at the perimeter of town. Access roads not passing through town and a sizeable buffer zone have been suggested as two of the few improvements SCA, Inc., could have made on their original plan. In all cases, more information on health issues, final cleanup, emergency plans, and monitoring appear to be minimum requirements.

Implications

Fear, anger, and frustration over the government's handling of the situation were prevalent at Love Canal and will probably cause impacts over TMI-1 restart as well. Creation of the Love Canal Homeowners Association (Holden 1980) as an instrument for political expression by the impacted population is analogous to the creation of seven antinuclear organizations around TMI (Walsh 1981). However, although the chronic threat of Love Canal and Wilsonville may be similar to the chronic threat that TMI constitutes for some, the social consequences of these three events may be divergent. In the case of Love Canal, much of the area has been evacuated and the local community, in a sense, has been effectively destroyed (Holden 1980). Likewise, preliminary evidence indicates that the chronic stress of that situation has taken a significant toll on family stability and cohesion, including a 40 percent divorce/separation rate for the first wave of evacuees (Holden 1980:1243). While opposition to Hooker Chemical and the EPA's treatment of local residents may have been initial sources of cohesion for the impacted population, that cohesion seems to have been short-lived.

These types of problems have not been observed at Wilsonville, where the sense of community has been preserved. These differences imply that if the proposed restart of TMI-1 does cause severe stress, which leads to a breakdown in community cohesion and stability, then impacts similar to those at Love Canal could occur. Evidence suggests, however, that the physical loss of community as represented by the total displacement at Love Canal caused the breakdown in cohesion. Other factors, such as local culture, beliefs, and economic status, may also be factors in the loss of cohesion. This is supported by the findings of Erikson (1976) about Buffalo Creek. The lack of physical destruction in Wilsonville, as well as from the accident at TMI-2, suggests that a major loss of cohesion will not occur in the vicinity of TMI due to restart unless physical displacement due to physical loss or other causes develops and becomes widespread.

Hypotheses

Based on the results of the focus-group discussions and the literature review, the following hypotheses are offered with regard to the causes of impacts of restart.

Coping Ability

As a person's ability to cope with potential accidents at TMI-1 after restart decreases, the likelihood of that person contributing to impacts increases. A good example is the perceived ability of an individual to evacuate successfully from a threatening situation. In holding that belief, a person is less likely to perceive a high level of risk than a person who feels unable to cope and is, therefore, less likely to create impacts.

Disaster literature has shown that those who have evacuated un-
necessarily in the past are less likely to evacuate in a similar future
situation (Bates *et al.* 1963). The question is to what extent evacuees
from the TMI-2 accident considered their actions as necessary and functional in terms of personal safety and health. Flynn's data (1979:37)
indicate that an average of 61 percent of those surveyed were concerned
about radioactive emissions during the accident. Overall, 91 percent of
evacuees thought the TMI-2 situation threatening, 83 percent felt information on the situation was confusing, and 61 percent left to protect
their children (Flynn 1979:18).

Level of Sensitivity

As a person's sensitivity to a potential accident increases, the level
of perceived risk also increases. The material issue for TMI-1 restart,
of course, is to what extent the TMI-2 accident is perceived as a "near
miss" by area residents and thus to what extent can residents be expected
to become "hypersensitive" to the signs of reoccurrence (Mack and
Baker 1961). Evidence indicates that restart will probably produce stress
analogous to any other chronic threat situation, at least for individuals
predisposed to define the situation as risky. For example, individuals
who had a bad or traumatic experience in the TMI-2 accident will probably be more prone to impacts than those who did not have negative
experiences with the accident.

Concerns over Other Issues

As the salience of the TMI-1 restart issue increases, the likelihood
of impacts increases. For example, an individual who places restart low
on his or her "agenda" of important topics is less likely to perceive it
as a threatening event. Those who see restart as a significant issue will
be more likely to perceive higher risks from restart. In the TMI accident,
for example, one of the main reasons cited for not evacuating was that
they were "unable to leave their jobs" and a smaller number had "things
to do at home" (Flynn 1979). This suggests that employment and other
work tasks, when viewed as important concerns, may not allow any
room for fear or concern over restart.

Attitudes toward TMI Management

As the credibility of those persons managing TMI increases, the
likelihood of impacts decreases. If individuals trust the people who are

in positions of preventing and managing accidents and risk, they will be less sensitive to an accident. Conversely, distrust of risk managers including Met Ed, NRC, and state and local governments will cause greater sensitivity to future problems.

In illustration, one of the distinctive characteristics of the TMI-2 accident, when compared to many natural disasters, was the confusion and uncertainty over the precise nature of the accident, what kind of dangers it posed, and what warnings should be issued (Marshall 1979b). The confusion among officials served to threaten official credibility (Schorr and Goldsteen 1980). This, in turn, could create high levels of distrust and subsequent stress regarding official pronouncements about the safety of restart, particularly in the context of a disaster subculture that reinforces distrust of official sources of information (Walsh 1981).

Attitudes toward Nuclear Power

As people's concerns about nuclear power increase, the likelihood of impacts increases. Those who oppose nuclear power (and restart) probably will be more sensitive to a future accident and more likely to perceive greater risks. Those supporting nuclear power will be less likely to perceive restart as a threatening event.

The role of attitudes has already been demonstrated by the emergence of the protest organizations in the area after the TMI-2 accident. These organizations constitute an existing social complex that has assumed the task of preventing restart of TMI-1. As Walsh noted (1981:17), the "multiplicity and severity of individual and collective grievances . . . created a large pool of people available for protest mobilizations." As general surveys of the local populations have indicated, they are predominately middle class (Flynn 1979), residentially stable (Goldhaber et al.1981), and homeowners (Shearer 1980; Gamble and Downing 1981), and many are engaging in political protest for the first time (Walsh 1981). Given a population with reasonable availability of resources and a salient issue (restart), renewed and expanded protest at the community level should be anticipated. These protest groups (as well as those favoring restart) may become important sources of information that can affect the intensities of attitudes and concerns, thereby affecting the values of other "independent" variables.

Information/Knowledge

The more information a person receives that conveys images of danger and threat, the more likely impacts will occur. Levels of sensitivity and coping ability will be affected by this type of information. An additional important dimension of information is the consistency of that information. Because information conveys a more clear and consistent pattern, the likelihood of impacts decreases. Conflicting information increases sensitivity, decreases coping ability, and causes the perception of higher levels of risk. As Houts and his colleagues (1980b) point out, the constant media attention to the TMI-2 accident created much sensitivity to any potential problem at the TMI facilities. This is reinforced by findings that almost one-half of the public were dissatisfied by information during the accident and felt confused about what information to believe (Flynn 1979).

The media has an important agenda-setting function (McCombs and Shaw 1972) by focusing community attention on specific issues. Discussions and disagreements among experts over the effects, for example, of ionizing radiation (Marshall 1979a), the risks of low-level radiation (Marx 1979; Marshall 1981), and the so-called brittle reactor hazard (Marshall 1982) may all affect definitions of the situation and feelings of safety among community members. This must also be considered in light of the reported lack of trust in officials and the fact that 1980 evidence indicated a majority of community residents were in opposition to the restart of TMI-1 (Schorr and Goldsteen 1980; see also Houts *et al.* 1980a). The importance of the community and its constituent organizations on perception of hazard is addressed in more detail in the section on hazards.

Demographics

People most vulnerable to the restart and, hence, those that will perceive greatest risks are pregnant women, adults with small children, women in general, and people furthest removed from the mainstream of social organization and the existing power structure. Education and income levels by themselves probably will not explain variations in perceived risk, although they may interact with other factors in the model.

These hypotheses are supported in general by risk and hazard research and studies of the accident and related work. Evidence is found that women, particularly mothers, were inclined to view the accident as a threatening situation (Flynn 1979) and to distrust official handling of the event (Schorr and Goldsteen 1981). The fact that women were more likely to define the situation as dangerous also suggests that conjugal conflicts could increase in families in which disagreement exists with regard to the danger involved in restart. However, the presence of children in families appears to mitigate disagreement tendencies in families as Flynn's (1979) data shown for the TMI-2 accident.

On the other hand, given TMI-2 evacuation experience, families with children could feel directly threatened by restart activities (Bromet 1980). This is supported by another study, dealing with how children react to the threat of nuclear plant accidents (Schwebel and Schwebel 1981), which found that females were more likely to expect an accident to happen. Schwebel and Schwebel report (1981:268–69) that most of the children in their study reported feelings of resignation and powerlessness regarding nuclear power. This, according to the authors, implies an increased likelihood of emotional problems for adolescents undergoing already stressful life transitions (Schwebel and Schwebel 1981).

Another factor related to demographics is geographic proximity to the plant site. A recent study (Manderthaner *et al.* 1978) examined the effect of geographic distance on risk perception. In terms of perceived threat of a nuclear facility, the group living 0.9 miles from the reactor perceived the situation as riskier than comparison groups living 0.3 miles and 6 miles from the plant. According to the authors, this fact indicates that frequent exposure with threatening objects reduces the perceived hazard, which suggests that those nearest TMI would experience the least stress at restart because of their constant exposure to the facility. This does not appear to have been the case in TMI-2 accident, as impacts appeared greatest in the 0- to 5-mile radius (Flynn 1979; Houts *et al.* 1980b).

Family and Group Structure

The ability to cope and the way threats are perceived will vary with the strength of kinship ties, support from peers, and organizational participation. Those most prone to impacts will have weak family solidarity and interaction on which to base support, have weak bonds with friends and community, and be disassociated with community organization.

While neighborhoods, kin, and community can aid families in dealing with stress, they can also determine to what extent a family defines a situation as a stressful event. In both general hazards research and the specific case of the TMI-2 accident, clear evidence shows the role of kin in housing evacuees from the area (Flynn 1979; Houts *et al.* 1980a, 1980b). Houts *et al.* (1980a) indicate that 69 percent of the evacuees went to the homes of relatives. The same authors also suggest that many evacuees did so because of pressures and requests from their kin, who viewed the accident as dangerous. Those same kin (and friendship groups) will affect the way area families respond to future events at the TMI facilities. The evidence from TMI-2 research (Houts *et al.* 1980a) indicates that external support networks contributed to influencing family definitions of the situation. The presence of a number of antinuclear and anti-TMI restart groups in surrounding communities (Walsh 1981) also may have an effect on family definitions of the proposed restart.

Another significant feature of the evacuation behavior that warrants attention in assessing the social impacts of TMI-1 restart was the incidence of families who had only some members evacuate after the TMI-2 accident. In addition, disagreements over evacuation were evidenced in 18 percent of the households surveyed by Flynn (1979:31). Failure to evacuate as a family unit and the inability to arrive at consensus regarding the propriety of evacuation could indicate several things. The lack of consensus regarding these decisions suggests that restart could engender conflict within families regarding how threatening restart will be. Heightened levels of family conflict over restart could be stressful, although this can only be confirmed with further research.

Adjustments to and the impacts of TMI-1 restart ultimately will be affected by definitions of the situation arrived at by individuals, families, and communities. As discussed, the presence of what may be called a disaster subculture has provided a sociocultural frame of reference which may be expected to influence risk perceptions. In the case of natural hazards, the cultural frame of reference tends to normalize threat by placing it in a familiar cultural context (e.g., Wallace 1956; Schneider 1957; Lachman and Bonk 1960; Anderson 1968). For technological hazards the uncertainty of effects mitigates against such a normalization process, particularly where a "near impact" event has precipitated changes in perceptions of risk for individuals, families (e.g., Flynn 1979; Houts *et al.* 1980a, 1980b; Bromet 1980), and organizations (Walsh 1981).

Conclusions

This chapter sought to ground the proposed model of impacts within social science theory and research and to develop hypotheses about why impacts will or will not occur. In doing so, it has integrated general social science knowledge with findings specific to disasters in general and the TMI accident in specific. The processes at work in the focus group discussion (Chapter Three) are understandable given our general knowledge of human response to disaster and risk. In this case, however, the accident at TMI-2 was a significant mediator of the process described in the model. In light of this, the next chapter takes a more in-depth look at the relationship between accident and restart.

Chapter 5

The Accident and Restart

Analysis of the Conceptual Model

Introduction

When people are confronted by a release of radiation from a nuclear power plant failure, an approaching funnel of a tornado, the ground motion of an earthquake, the headlights of an out-of-control automobile, or a variety of other situations, they are faced with possible physical harm or death. Frequently, this results in a disruption to their normal patterns of behavior, irrespective of whether they are personally injured or harmed. Both disruption and harm are thought to have longer-term impacts, although the nature of those impacts are widely debated. The accident at TMI presents a unique opportunity to study the impacts of an impending disaster in which no identifiable physical harm was inflicted. Thus, we can focus on the impacts created solely by the disruption to normal activities and the unusual levels of intense fear and uncertainty created by the situation.

The inventory of previous literature on the social effects of experiencing disaster or preparing for it discussed in the previous chapter provides a good base of knowledge on which to formulate a conceptual model of the factors, which may explain why impacts would be experienced in a nuclear power accident in which no damage actually occurred. Of course, in any disaster where damages occur, those experiencing damages probably would be impacted by the natures and magnitudes of those damages and their personal experiences with the hazard event.

The issue of whether research results can be transferred among hazards in general and from natural to technological hazards in specific, has received increasing attention in the literature. Some argue it is erroneous (Baum *et al.* 1983; Walker et al. 1982), others argue that, with some care, they can be compared (Perry 1982). In this chapter, the empirical results which will provide added insight to this debate are discussed.

In the first section, we examine the appropriateness of the conceptual model as an integrative guide to examining the restart issue. Next, we highlight some of the impacts of the accident as reported by various studies and revealed by available data sources. In the final section, the existing conditions in the vicinity of TMI are examined in an effort to understand the extent of possible impact.

To help evaluate the hypothesized causes of impacts portrayed in the Figure 3 conceptual model, the data collected by an independent research organization for the NRC approximately six months after the accident was analyzed (Flynn 1979). These data were gathered by a random digit dialing sampling procedure. One thousand, five hundred and four (1,504) households were selected from within 89 miles of the power station at TMI. This data base is unique in that it is the only source of information of the TMI accident impacts that is representative of the surrounding population.

Variables were chosen from the data set to approximate or represent constructs defined in the flowgraph (Figure 3). Where hypothetical constructs or latent variables are posited, the logic of factor analysis is employed to test the validity of the expected relationships and to estimate the relative weights and reliabilities (Kerlinger 1973) of the indicators comprised by the constructs. These data are presented in Table 11. While the variables are not ideal measures of the constructs in the model, they are judged to be adequate to test the presence or absence of the hypothesized relationships. Better measures are needed to explain greater levels of variance than can be achieved with the ones being utilized.

Statistical Procedure

The hypothesized causal model includes nine latent variables and three measured variables. The expected direction of the relationships among these variables (i.e., paths) are represented by Figure 3. No measure of coping was included due to a lack of an appropriate variable.

TABLE 11 DESCRIPTIONS OF VARIABLES

Variables Definition (Construct/Indicators)	Range	Factor Size
DISTANCE (Household Distance from TMI)		
Distance	0 < 1 mile - 89 = 89 miles	1.0
SES (High Socio-economic Status)		
Income (Family Income)	1 < $5,000 - 7 > $30,000	
Occupation (Occupational Prestige)	1 = Professional - 17 = Unemployed	-.49
Married (Single/Married)	1 = Single - 2 = Married	.67
Own Home (Ownership of Home)	1 = Own - 2 = Rent	-.57
FLS (Early Family Life Stage)		
Hhsize (N of household residents)	1 = 1 - 8 = 8	.71
Kids (Children < 6)	0 = No - 1 = Yes	.79
Age (Respondent's Age)	18 = 18 - 97 = 97	-.76
NUKEATT (Attitudes About Nuclear Power)		
Nucom (Compare Nuclear)	1 = Advantages > - 5 = Disadvantages >	.76
Nucdist (Preferred Distance)	0 < 1 Mile from home - 996 = 996 Miles	.76
TMIATT (Negative Attitudes Toward TMI Management)		
Meteda (Met. Ed. Info.)	1 = Extremely Useful - 4 = Useless	.68
CompTmi (Compare TMI)	1 = Advantages > - 5 = Disadv. >	.78
Emitb (Pre-TMI fear of emissions)	1 = Not concerned - 3 = Very Concerned	.57
SENSITIV (Sensitivity to Nuclear Risks)		
Threata (Perceived Threat)	1 = Not serious - 4 = Very serious	.89
Upset (Upset at impact)	1 = Not Upset - 4 = Extremely Upset	.85
Emita (Concern at Impact)	1 = Very Concerned - 3 = Not Concerned	-.87
CONCERN (Concern About TMI vs. Other Issues)		
Disarea1 (Disadvantage of area #1)	1 = TMI - 2 = Other	1.0
Disarea2 (Disadvantage of area #2)	1 = TMI - 2 = Other	1.0
FEAR (Fear of Emissions Today)		
Emitt (Concern over emissions now)	1 = Not Concerned - 3 = Very Concerned	1.0
DISTRESS (Few Psychophysiologic Symptoms of Distress)		
Irrit (Irritability today)	1 = No - 2 = Yes	.64
Stom (Stomach trouble today)	1 = No - 2 = Yes	.65
Head (Headaches today)	1 = No - 2 = Yes	.69
Sleep (Insomnia today)	1 = No - 2 = Yes	.62
Shake (Felt shakey today)	1 = No - 2 = Yes	.63
FAMILY (Disruption of Family Life)		
Activa (Disruption during incident)	1 = none - 4 = high disruption	.80
Activt (Disruption Today)	1 = none - 4 = substantial	.80
COMMUNITY (Perceived Negative Impact on the Community)		
Rateare (Rate area as a place to live)	1 = excellent - 4 = poor	.63
Areaecon (Rate expected economic impact)	1 = help - 3 = hurt	.63
Move (Anyone in household consider moving)	1 = yes - 2 = no	-.73

TMI-REV.26

An ordinary least squares (OLS) regression approach utilizing techniques developed by Alwin and Hauser (1975) whereby coefficients are derived from computations of reduced-form, semireduced-form, and structural equations was employed. OLS has been proved unbiased and consistent under many conditions provided certain assumptions are met (Netter and Waserman 1974). These assumptions are that the relations among the variables are linear, additive, and causal; that the disturbance terms are uncorrelated with the variables that precede them in the model, and that they are uncorrelated among themselves. While Kerlinger (1973) also suggests that variables should be measured on an interval scale, several researchers have demonstrated exceptions to this rule using ordinal and indicator variables (e.g., Kim 1975; Netter and Wasserman 1974; Boyle 1967). Kerlinger also notes that the causal flow must be assymmetric (i.e., recursive); the model presented is a recursive model meeting the assumption documented by Kerlinger (1973).

The results of the statistical analysis are presented in Appendix A (Tables A-1; A-2). Examination of the correlation matrix reveals that the directions of the relationships among the constructs are consistent with those discussed earlier. The reduced model with nonsignificant paths removed along with the path coefficients is illustrated in Figure 4.

Discussion of the Results

Much of the literature on the social and psychological impacts of disaster has focused on what impacts have occurred and at what levels (Perry and Lindell 1978; Gleser et al. 1981). In fact, a major disagreement between researchers is whether or not disasters have noticeable adverse impacts and, if they do, how persistent they are (Quarantelli 1979; Chamberlin 1980; Tichner and Kapp 1976). Our research, however, assumes that impacts exist, even if they cannot be precisely measured, and then endeavors to explain why they do or do not occur. In doing so, an attempt is made to determine whether the causes of impacts in natural disasters also help predict the impacts of a technological hazard such as the accident at TMI.

The results of the path analysis suggest that sensitivity toward risk, as measured by accident-specific experiences, is a key factor in explaining why impacts occurred. Sensitivity was the strongest cause of postaccident fears ($\beta = 0.50$) of nuclear power. In other words, people who had a negative experience with the accident (e.g., were upset and threatened) were likely to remain fearful of an accident. Sensitivity also had a strong effect on the concerns people have about TMI in relating to other problems in the area ($\beta = -0.40$). To use a common analogy, a bad experience with a threat seems to alter the way people subsequently distribute their supply of "worry beads." Sensitivity also had strong direct effects on individual distress ($\beta = 0.25$) and family disruption ($\beta = 0.47$) which are unmediated by existing fears or concerns.

Preaccident attitudes and perceptions, in contrast, have weaker

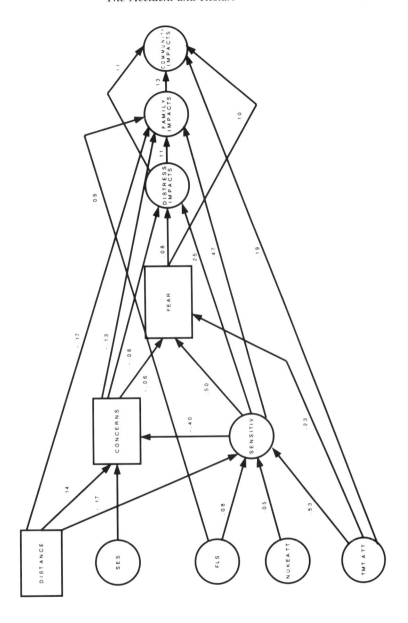

Figure 4. Reduced Causal Model.

relationships with impact measures. For example, general attitudes towards nuclear power are weakly related to sensitivity ($\beta = 0.05$), but not to impacts or to perceived fear. Specific attitudes toward TMI, developed in part because of the accident, have a stronger relationship with the constructs of sensitivity ($\beta = 0.53$) and fear ($\beta = 0.23$) and with perceptions of aggregate community level impacts ($\beta = 0.19$), but not with distress or family disruption. These findings suggest that general feelings about nuclear power do not cause impacts but more specific accident-determined perceptions are significant causes. These findings are in contrast with the nonempirically derived hypotheses of researchers who suggest impacts from experiencing a nuclear power plant accident are due to the innate fear of radiation, and predisposed attitudes toward nuclear energy (Johnson and Ziegler 1983).

A second major finding is that family life stage (FLS) plays an important role in the model. Families in an early life-cycle stage appear to be more likely to be sensitive to the accident ($\beta = 0.08$) and to have experienced family disruption ($\beta = 0.09$). This is consistent with findings concerning the family level impacts of natural disasters (Drabek and Key 1984, Bolin 1982). Families in an early family life stage seem to be more vulnerable to crises despite the cause.

Third, distance plays an interesting role in the model. While sensitivity, concerns and family disruption increase as distance decreases, distance has no direct effect on fear or other types of impacts. This suggests that distance plays a much more minor role in determining impacts than it does in determining accident-specific responses such as evacuation (Cutter and Barnes 1982).

Finally, the model provides reasonable explanation of disruption ($r^2 = 0.44$) but not individual distress or community change ($r^2 = 0.12$ and 0.15). Several possible explanations for these results warrant consideration. First, consider distress. One possible reason for the low explanation of distress is that the stress-measure of the NRC survey may not be accurate or that it lacks validity hence biasing the results. In retrospect, a validated stress-measure would have reduced the possibility that measurement error resulted in poor explanation.

Another explanation is that individual characteristics not measured by the survey cause and mediate distress. For example, individual distress levels may be determined primarily by other situational factors that are far more dominant than the accident-specific or other nuclear power determinants included in the model. Our analysis suggests that while the complex of factors, which includes sensitivity, concerns, and fear, may significantly explain some portion of the distress that people experienced, other factors must be explored to explain further the way other distress occurred. This observation tends to dispute the notion that stress is a stimuli-specific response but, instead, may endorse the notion that stress is a social condition, prevalent throughout a population. Thus, stress symptoms may be falsely attributed to a disaster because, simply, it happened, and then stress levels were measured.

Second, consider family disruption. The relatively high explanatory powers of family-level impacts suggest that a situation like TMI results in the most prominent impacts at the family level. Increased family disruption may be, in part, a manifestation of the effects of individual coping with the situation. The construct of sensitivity, however, has the largest direct effect on family disruption. Being upset and fearful at the time of the accident has a strong influence on the breakdown of family cohesion.

Third, questions and answers arise regarding the explanation of community impacts. While the perception of community change builds upon fear, TMI attitudes, distress, and family disruption, it is obvious that nonaccident, nonnuclear factors also play an important role in determining perceptions about community level impacts. Thus, community change may be affected in a small way by the presence of the plant and in a slightly larger fashion by the accident. The analyses suggest, however, that nonaccident related forces that traditionally affect change will be the predominant cause of impacts. In the absence of physical destruction such as that observed at Buffalo Creek (Erikson 1976), community change will probably not result from the accident experience.

This section examines why impacts, both objective and perceived, occurred following the accident at TMI. The analysis confirms the appropriateness of the theoretical model as a guide to estimating impacts from restart. While the model cannot be used in a statistical way to predict impacts, it is valuable for understanding why they could or would not occur.

In addition, several findings warrant attention. The major finding is that impacts on people seem to be caused by individual and group experience with the accident much more than prevailing preaccident population characteristics. From this we conclude that pre-emergency actions to educate people about nuclear power will not substantially reduce impacts. Conversely, pre-emergency fear arousal concerning radiation risks will also not lead to greater impacts.

The major way in which impact levels will be affected is by the situational warning and emergency response effort. A good warning and efficient handling of the accident will tend to minimize impacts. A poor warning and ineffective emergency response will elevate impacts. This underscores the importance of good emergency planning for technological hazards in general and nuclear power in specific.

Second, families at an early stage of their life cycle seem more susceptible to impacts than those at other stages. This suggests that special attention should be placed on mitigating impacts to this social group if an accident occurs.

Finally, consistent with the findings in the natural hazard literature, we find that the correlates of disruption include perceived threat, FLS, concern over other problems, and sensitivity to the hazard. Furthermore, these relationships held in the absence of any direct physical damages, suggesting that research findings in studies of natural disasters can, with care, be used to help understand response to technological risks and to help dispell the notion that all technological hazards are unique.

Impacts of the TMI-2 Accident

Introduction

This section highlights some of the impacts of the accident as reported by various studies and revealed by various data sources. It is not a comprehensive summary of impacts; rather, it reports accident impacts in the context of the model examined previously. The first part of the discussion reviews changes in factors that the model suggests may contribute to the manifestation of impacts. The second part of the discussion focuses on the impacts observed in various social units.

The TMI-2 accident had a definite and measurable impact on the social and psychological well-being of people and social groups in the TMI vicinity (Sills *et al.* 1982). Studies which examined the impacts suggest that the levels have decayed, to a greater or lesser extent, over time. However, whether the impact of the accident has completely disappeared is unclear. No doubt the accident is the singular, significant event which will intervene for determining restart impacts. Accordingly, assessing the possible influence of accident-related impacts on potential restart impacts is important.

The *Workshop on Psychological Stress Associated with the Proposed*

Restart of Three Mile Island, Unit 1 (Walker *et al.* 1982) suggested that the impacts from the accident set an upper bound for restart impacts. While this was treated as an assumption in the workshop, it is viewed here as an empirical question: Does the accident set an upper bound for restart-related impacts, and under what conditions will impacts exceed or fall short of that level? When viewed as an empirical question, reviewing the nature and level of impacts associated with the accident, reviewing conditions as they existed following the accident, reviewing the implications of these conditions for identifying impacts, and suggesting situations that will lead to acceptance or rejection of the upper bound hypothesis are possible.

Data used in this section have been drawn from several sources including surveys conducted for the NRC (Flynn 1979; Flynn and Chalmers 1980) and GPU (Field Research 1980; 1981) and unobtrusive measures (Webb *et al.* 1966).

The chief criteria for utilizing previously collected survey data were the use of a random probability sampling frame for the selection of respondents to ensure that the results are representative of the population of the study area and the use of relatively unbiased questions. Data not meeting these criteria were excluded from use. This is not to say that the data which were acceptable do not have other problems or that they perfectly meet the needs of this analysis. Caveats in interpreting the data are pointed out in the text.

Impacts

1. PSYCHOLOGICAL/BEHAVIORAL FACTORS

a. Perceived Risk

Prior to the accident, few people in the vicinity of TMI felt threatened by the presence of a nuclear power plant (Flynn and Chalmers 1980). While no comparable time series data exist, perception of a threat probably jumped markedly as the news of an accident filtered to the public and details were made known. In retrospect, the TMI accident was labeled as a very serious threat by almost one-half of the public living within 15 miles of the plant (see Appendix A, Table A-3a). Conversely, it posed no threat to a small percentage of those in the same area (11 to 14 percent). Levels of perceived threat dropped markedly beyond the 15-mile radius. Data on perceived fear for personal safety permit an examination of another dimension of "perceived risk." Over 50 percent of the respondents in the 25-mile radius indicated some degree of fright (Appendix A, Table A-3b). Almost an equal number, however, indicated no fright at all. This suggests that perceived risk may be determined by factors other than personal safety. This is partially borne out by data presented in Appendix A, Table A-3c, which reveals the way people view the outcome of the accident. Roughly two-thirds had confidence that they emerged from the ordeal satisfactorily, although the remainder expressed strong doubts about their safety. Confidence in survival increased with distance, although the data indicate that those remote from the TMI site still felt threatened by the situation.

Another way of looking at perceived risk is through beliefs about exposure (Appendix A, Table A-3d). Despite many statements made to the public about no health risks, 14 percent of the people surveyed within 5 miles of the site felt they received a dangerous dose of radiation from the accident. Even more significant, however, was that 25 percent were unsure. Such uncertainty is another component of perceived risk. Again, perception of risk and uncertainty decrease in the 5- to 25-mile radius and for the statewide control population.

In sum, roughly one-half of the population within 15 miles of the plant felt seriously threatened by the accident, while only a few (about 12 percent) claimed not to be threatened at all. At the other extreme, only a small number viewed the accident as dangerous to their health, although sizeable doubts over radiation effects exist.

b. Coping Ability

Successful coping or the perceived ability to do so helps to reduce certain impacts, although the coping behavior may lead to other impacts. Ability to cope can, in part, be explained by feelings of control and helplessness. A high level of helpless feelings occurred during the accident (Appendix A, Table A-4a). Levels of helplessness do not significantly decrease with distance or in the statewide control group; thus, coping with an accident may be universally difficult.

Another way of analyzing coping is to evaluate emergency response efforts. Despite the many criticisms of such efforts, less than 40 percent of the respondents were not satisfied that everything possible was being done in response to the problem (Appendix A, Table A-4b). Favorable evaluations may be related to feelings of helplessness in that the inability to control the situation may promote the belief that others will take care of it.

The chief behavioral coping mechanism during the accident was evacuation. Appendix A, Table A-5 summarizes the best available estimates of the portion of the population who chose this course of action. A peak of approximately 60 percent of the population residing in a 5-mile radius evacuated. The numbers leaving arithmetically declined to the 25-mile radius and gradually dropped to less than 1 percent at 40 miles. Evacuation extent also differed according to direction from the plant. Reviewing the behavior of households, the data indicate that the large majority of households behaved as single units. Split decisions occurred in a maximum of 18.7 percent of the households within the 5-mile radius. This result is consistent with general evacuation trends for other warning situations (Perry 1981).

While perceived danger (risk) and uncertainty seemed to be the chief factors influencing evacuation decisions, reasons for staying were more diverse. The lack of specific orders, fatalistic attitudes, and inability to leave a job were central factors; other reasons included perceptions of no danger, fear of looting, and a need to stay home. Lack of transportation and sheltering were not influential.

c. Information and Uncertainty

TMI has often been labeled as an "information disaster" (Sills *et al.* 1982). Information problems likely contributed to the uncertainty and were certainly a major factor in creating impacts. Attitudinal data help to confirm this, with about one-half the respondents in the NRC survey expressing dissatisfaction with the information-dissemination process. This is also reflected in evaluations of specific sources and channels (Appendix A, Table A-6). NRC and the Pennsylvania Governor's Office were the most useful sources, and electronic local media the most useful channels. Local government and Met Ed were the least useful sources.

While no empirical research data are available on the perceived adequacy and interpretability of information disseminated during the accident, two recent books (Stephans 1981; Gray and Rosen 1982) have examined the transcripts of meetings, news reports, and telephone conversations between plant and NRC officials recorded during the accident. The authors all conclude that erroneous and conflicting information was being released by all parties involved in covering the accident. Such confusion could only exacerbate, rather than alleviate, people's perceptions of the risks due to the accident.

2. IMPACTS OF THE ACCIDENT

a. Disruption to Family and Society

The accident environment was certainly not a normal one for households near TMI. Functioning in all arenas of society changed from the routine to that of coping with the newly-discovered threat. The extent of these changes in households is documented in Appendix A, Table A-7. Only 21 percent of the respondents in the 5-mile radius indicated no disruption to normal activities, while 36 percent were highly disrupted. As expected, disruption decreased with distance. Evacuation was one of the major disruptions; however the major disruptions reported were not grave, but they were inconvenient and upsetting.

Another facet of disruption can be measured by the societal costs of the emergency. To households, these were mainly in the form of evacuation and other emergency responses and lost wages and income. Table 12 summarizes estimates of the direct costs of the emergency. The cost of evacuation to households (the average equals $247 to $342) represented a significant expense to many. The costs of not evacuating were small by comparison. Cost, however, did not appear to prevent anyone from leaving.

Lost income from decline in sales and from wages foregone are more difficult to calculate. The data in Table 12 show a total economic loss from the accident of nearly $100 million, although these estimates are subject to interpretation.

b. Changes in Societal Trends: Unobtrusive Measures of Community-Wide Stress

TMI created fears, disrupted activities, and left people confused and upset. Such impacts do not normally result in drastic societal changes, because people, groups, and communities are adept at returning to normalcy after an emergency in which no physical losses occurred (Quarantelli and Dynes 1977). If this were not the case, however, detectable changes in communities surrounding TMI should be measurable during and following the accident. Mileti *et al.* (1982) reconstructed data sets for six unobtrusive indicators of increased stress levels in the vicinity

Table 12   Economic impacts of the accident

a.   Estimated direct cost to households

Group	Average cost in dollars		
	Evacuating households	Nonevacuating households	Average
0-5 miles	247	42	177
5-10 miles	259	57	156
10-15 miles	342	34	136
Total (0-15 miles)	296	41	146

Source: Flynn and Chalmers, 1980.

b.   Estimated direct losses to economic sectors

Sector	Accounting area	Production sales losses ($)	Wage losses ($)	Average per employee ($)
Manufacturing	20-mile radius	7.7 million	1.5 million	75
Nonmanufacturing	6-county area	74 million	5.5 million	276
Tourism	Southcentral Pennsylvania	Combined: 5 million		?
Agriculture	20-mile radius	Minimal	Close to 0	?

Source: Pennsylvania's Governor's Office of Policy and Planning, no date.

insert table 12

(Table 13). The results suggest that short-term impacts likely accompanied the accident. Long-term effects were not discovered. Such results hardly lay to rest the question of whether significant societal impacts occurred or continue to occur. Such questions of causality are difficult to assess, using this type of measure. Both the limited time frame and scope of the indicators leave the problem only partially addressed.

c. Changes in Societal Trends: Professional Practices

PANE, in its contention, states:

Table 13   Summary of changes in unobtrusive measures
of stress following TMI-2 accident

Measure	Was there a change?	Where? 0-5	Where? 5-10	Where? Control	What happened?	Interpretation
Consumption of alcohol	Yes	Yes	Yes	No	Increases in consumption for several days after accident	Consumption increases likely due to stress and more leisure time
Cardiovascular death	Yes	Yes	Yes	No	Slight increases for several months after accident	Cannot be linked to accident or stress
Crime	No	No	No	No	No change	
Psychiatric admissions	No	No	No	No	No change	
Suicide	No	No	No	No	No change	Samples too small to make inferences
Traffic accidents	Yes	No	Yes	No	Slight increase after accident for a week	Could indicate stress in population and increased highway use for evacuation

From: Mileti et al., 1982.

The perception, created by the accident, that the communities near Three Mile Island are undesirable locations for business and industry or for the establishment of law and medical practices or homes compounds the damage to the viability of the communities. Community vitality depends on the ability to attract and keep persons such as teachers, doctors, lawyers, and businesses critical to economic and social health. (PANE vs. U.S. Nuclear Regulatory Commission, 1982)

To test one aspect of this statement, the locational changes of professional practices in the area were documented over a five-year period surrounding the accident. Data were collected from the 1977 to 1981 telephone books for three communities in the area: Middletown (less than 5 miles), Hummelstown (5- to 10-mile radius), and Mechanicsburg (15-mile radius). Three professional practices were included: physicians (all types), attorneys, and dentists.

This effort is limited in several ways and, therefore, no causality can be attributed to the changes observed. First, it looks at only select communities instead of the entire area. Second, dates of change are only approximate due to the year-long time interval. Third, the lag effects are due to the use of telephone books as a data source. Fourth, the small size of the populations under examination make inference difficult. Given these caveats, Figure 5 illustrates the results of the data collection efforts.

These results do not offer any firm conclusions about the impact of the accident on community well-being. The trend for attorneys (Fig. 5a) is similar for all three locations, showing fluctuation with a downturn between 1980 and 1981. The trend for physicians is quite different: Middletown and Hummelstown show sharp decreases, while Mechanicsburg shows an increase. The downturns, however, reflect trends beginning prior to the accident. In contrast, the change in dentists over time shows slight increases in both Middletown and Hummelstown, and a fluctuation pattern in Mechanicsburg.

In order to gain a more detailed picture of the changes, Table 14 distinguishes among professionals relocating in the metropolitan area versus those who are no longer practicing in the vicinity. Of the physicians and attorneys leaving Middletown and Hummelstown, roughly one-half relocated. This is not the case for the more distant Mechanicsburg. The opposite is true concerning dentists, although the lack of change in Middletown and Hummelstown makes comparison difficult.

Many speculative reasons for these patterns of change could be offered, however, without detailed investigative work, they are mean-

Figure 5.   Practicing Professionals in Communities Surrounding TMI.

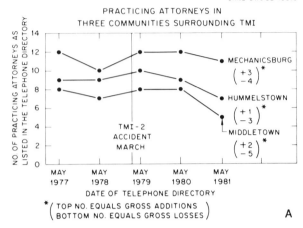

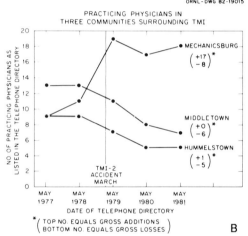

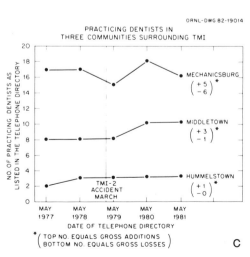

Table 14   Reasons for relocation of professionals

	Middletown	Hummelstown	Mechanicsburg
Physicians			
Relocated within area	3 (50%)	3 (60%)	3 (37.5%)
No longer listed (moved, retired, deceased, etc.)	3 (50%)	2 (40%)	5 (62.5%)
Totals	6	5	8
Attorneys			
Relocated within area	3 (60%)	2 (66.6%)	1 (20%)
No longer listed (moved, retired, deceased, etc.)	2 (40%)	1 (33.3%)	4 (80%)
Totals	5	3	5
Dentists			
Relocated within area	0	0	5 (83.3%)
No longer listed (moved, retired, deceased, etc.	1 (100%)	0	1 (16.6%)
Totals	1	0	6

ingless. Based solely on the numbers observed, the two communities within 10 miles are experiencing an attrition of professionals in two fields. Whether this is due to the accident is unknown. Moreover, the degree to which these trends will continue if restart occurs or does not occur is an empirical question that only can be partially answered over time.

d. Real Estate and Financial Impacts of the TMI-2 Accident

One specific dimension of well-being that has received considerable attention is the impact of TMI–1 restart on real estate prices. Because a home and property represent a major means of accumulating savings and investment, the value of real estate plays a major factor in both psychological and economic well-being. To gain a better understanding of the real estate and financial markets in the TMI area, an objective study of real estate prices (Gamble and Downing 1981) and subjective appraisals of individuals involved in that market are reviewed herein.

Despite several weaknesses in the Gamble and Downing study, including the failure to treat distance as a continuous variable (Peterson 1982), the study effectively made the case for negligible impacts on housing values beyond approximately 5 miles from TMI. By using time series data on housing transactions in the area, a sharp but temporary decline is seen in sales immediately following the accident. Whether deleterious impacts remain in the immediate vicinity of the plant (approximately 1 to 2 miles) is subject to debate.

As part of the community profiling, an effort was undertaken to resolve this question, to supplement the findings of the Gamble and Downing study on the impact of the accident at TMI-2, and to assess the perceived effect of the TMI-1 restart on property values in the surrounding area. Local realtors, lending institutions, contractors, and tax assessors were contacted. The following is a summary of the preliminary results of those interviews.

Several groups were contacted by telephone April 26—30, 1982, and asked about the effect of the TMI accident on their businesses, as well as the effect of a possible restart of TMI-1. The chief assessors in each of the four counties within a 10-mile radius of TMI—Dauphin, Lancaster, York, and Cumberland—were called. Nine individuals and firms were called. All realtors in Middletown and four within a 5-mile radius were contacted. The two appraisers who did most of the work for the class-action property valuation suits were also contacted. Ten banks were contacted, including the four banks located within a 5-mile radius of TMI. Six savings and loan associations were called, including the one within the 5-mile radius. Two Middletown contractors were called. One of the contractors is also a real estate agent, and his responses are also listed in that category.

With regard to the effects of the TMI accident on property values and lending institutions, none of the persons contacted believe the accident in 1979 had a major adverse impact on property values in the area, and proximity to the site has not affected appraisals or mortgage policies. Some believe that some properties very close to and generally downwind from the plant have appreciated in value less rapidly than might otherwise be the case. However, these people also commented that the few families who moved out have been replaced, generally, by those more comfortable with nuclear technology. These persons may have come as part of the TMI cleanup force. All consider the area to be comparable to the rest of Pennsylvania and the United States, with high interest rates and a generally slow economy the determining factors in home sales and construction. Although a few lending institutions reported that some deposits were withdrawn or accounts moved during the week of the accident (March 28, 1979), this was only a temporary phenomenon.

With regard to the effects of restarting TMI-1, several of the persons contacted foresee small negative effects on property values in the immediate area of the plant when TMI-1 is restarted. The two persons who have conducted most of the recent property reappraisals say that they cannot predict what effect restart would have. The majority of those contacted believe that neither an effect on nor a benefit to the area would occur, primarily because of stabilized electric rates. A number of persons added that if technical problems occurred with restart, there could be an adverse impact, and two commented that if another accident comparable to the TMI-2 accident occurred, it would be a "disaster."

With regard to the concerns expressed by the persons interviewed, several persons expressed the opinion that generating electricity from nuclear reactors is reasonable and necessary, however, they also showed concern about (1) the ability of the utility to manage efficiently, (2) the credibility of the NRC, (3) the recent news stories about operators cheating on examinations, (4) the effectiveness of the cleanup proposals for TMI-2, (5) the location of the TMI plant in relation to population centers, and (6) the ultimate disposal of the radioactive wastes. One person suggested the creation of a local oversight group to add credibility to the utility and NRC activities, as well as providing an independent source for information and education.

Several persons commented that the *indecision* about whether TMI-1 will be restarted and all the attendant publicity have more of an effect on persons living in the area than either restarting or a firm decision not to restart would have. The general feeling seemed to be that residents wanted to "get back to normal and out of the limelight." One person commented that there would be a grumbling for several days, but then other issues would take TMI's place in people's thoughts.

TABLE 15   STRESS AT THREE MILE ISLAND (TMI) AND CONTROL SITES

Stress Measure	Site			
	TMI[a]	No Plant	No Accident Nuclear Plants	Coal Plant
Distress Symptom Index	26.0	14.5	16.2	16.6
Standard Deviation	(21.0)	(11.5)	(13.5)	(11.8)
Becks Depression Inventory	6.0	3.6	3.5	3.5
Standard Deviation	(6.5)	(3.3)	(4.2)	(4.2)
Catecholamines				
Epinephrine, ng/mL	12.3	8.9	7.5	6.2
Norepinephrine, ng/mL	25.7	21.0	13.7	15.7

[a]Seventeen months after accident.

Source: Baum et.al., 1983.

e. Stress Effects of the Accident

Few studies have investigated the linkages among being exposed to a threat, stress, and stress effects. This is not only due to methodological difficulties in sorting out the causal effect of various stressors when stress levels are fairly small, but also can be attributed to the lack of any compelling theoretical reasons for such investigation. Studies that have been conducted deal mainly with response to ongoing threat after a disaster has occurred. Based on the cumulative record of stress research, no sound reason is found to expect that the stress effects of threat are significant unless an accident or disaster has occurred.

Empirical evidence for this conclusion is provided by Baum *et al.* 1983. In one of a series of studies of the stress effects of the accident at the TMI Nuclear Power Plant in 1979, the researcher compared populations at TMI (17 months after the accident) with a site operating a nuclear power plant, with a site operating a coal-fired power plant, and with a site having no power plants. Backgrounds and demographic characteristics of each group were comparable. Major stress measures used in the study are presented in Table 15 along with mean scores at each site. The results show that the TMI population is under greater stress than the other populations. No significant difference was found between the site exposed to risk from a nuclear power plant and the two control groups. While this does not mean that the threat in the no-accident site does not play a role in determining stress, it suggests that the threat does not elevate stress above normally found levels.

Another study by Baum investigated stress associated with the venting of radioactive gases from the damaged reactor at TMI (Baum *et al.* 1982). The results of this study suggested that the accident at TMI has led to some elevated chronic stress among the population around TMI. The venting of radioactive materials led to elevated acute stress before the release. The venting and post-venting measurements revealed a lowering of the anticipatory pre-venting stress. In all cases stress levels were subclinical.

f. Mobility Impacts of the TMI-2 Accident

Findings from a study of mobility within a year after the TMI-2 accident parallel the earthquake investigations (Goldhaber *et al.* 1981). This study concluded that mobility rates remained fairly stable after the accident and that the people who moved away from the area possessed characteristics of people who are likely to move. The findings suggest that TMI was cited as the main reason that some people moved within the 5- mile radius (7 percent), from the 5-mile radius into the 6- to 20- mile band (19 percent), and outside 20 miles (19 percent). The analysis strongly concludes, however, that these people were highly mobile types. If we return to the stress-threshold model, it can be postulated that the people who indicated TMI as the reason for moving may have viewed their locations at the time of the accident as having high negative place utility, and the accident became the stressful event that prompted the migration decision.

The same situation could occur after restart. The magnitude of the impact, if this theory is valid, will be shaped by the way highly mobile people perceive the risks from restart.

Examination of Existing Conditions

Introduction

In preceding sections of this chapter, the utility of the conceptual model used to explain how and why impacts may occur due to the restart of TMI-1 was examined and the impacts that arose due to the accident as intervening events which will influence potential restart impacts were explored. In this section, the extent of possible impact is addressed by examining existing conditions in the TMI vicinity. Furthermore, the way conditions have changed since the accident are examined where possible, although this is somewhat constrained by the lack of meaningful data. By examining conditions from both a static and dynamic reference, added insight is gained into the process that is postulated to explain the manifestation of impacts from restart.

Prevailing Conditions

Conditions are discussed, in turn, according to the framework of the conceptual model as dictated by data availability. Key components include attitudes toward TMI management, attitudes toward nuclear power, information credibility, knowledge, sensitivity to a future accident, coping ability, concerns over other issues, perceived risks from restart, and attitudes toward restart.

1. ATTITUDES TOWARD MANAGEMENT

Generally, people in the vicinity of TMI have negative attitudes toward Met Ed. Using judged reliability and believability of information toward Met Ed as an attitudinal measure, more than 50 percent of the population have doubts about TMI management (Appendix A, Table A-8). Fewer than 10 percent felt that Met Ed is very reliable or believable. Attitudes are more favorable statewide, but they are still skewed toward distrust.

2. ATTITUDES TOWARD NUCLEAR POWER

Support of, and opposition to, increased use of nuclear power in the United States is roughly split equally, although slightly more have a favorable attitude (Appendix A, Table A-9a). This is true for both the TMI vicinity and the larger statewide sample. Similar questions in national opinion polls typically showed a similar split following the TMI accident. In this respect, the TMI population does not differ from others in their general attitude toward nuclear power.

More specific measures of attitudes help confirm this split and demonstrate the strength of nuclear support and opposition. About 30 percent of the population have strong convictions against nuclear power, and about 15 percent are moderately opposed (Appendix A, Table A-9b). At least 50 percent of the population have strong pronuclear attitudes. Furthermore, the strength of antinuclear sentiments appears to decrease with distance from TMI, although the shift is minor (48 percent).

3. INFORMATION/KNOWLEDGE

People vary widely in their evaluations of differing sources of information on TMI (Appendix A, Table A-10). Using data on judged reliability and believability, people appear not to distinguish between these criteria, as rank order does not greatly differ for comparable categories. The results also indicate that scientists have greatest credibility, while the utility, media editorials, interest groups, and local government have the lowest. In both cases, the NRC demonstrates credibility as a nuclear expert.

In general, although residents of the TMI area are more knowledgeable about nuclear power than people from the entire state (Appendix A, Table A-11), their knowledge is not perfect. Using three different measures of knowledge, the percent responding correctly ranged from 33 to 86 percent, indicating significant variance in knowledge levels.

4. SENSITIVITY TO NUCLEAR POWER RISKS

Slightly more than one-third of the population is troubled by the possibility of another accident (Appendix A, Table A-12). A somewhat erroneous belief that the plant may "blow up" does not frighten many (3 percent). Fear of radiation leaks and exposure is far greater for the statewide sample than for TMI-vicinity residents. This is also true of the belief that TMI causes fear and anxiety for those living near the plant. These results suggest that people in the TMI vicinity are sensitive to a repeat of an accident, but they tend to deny the risks of radiation, a catastrophic accident, or the fear of living in the presence of the plant.

5. COPING ABILITY

The events of TMI caused people to think about their ability to deal with the risks of the accident, subsequent alarms, and possible future problems. While one-half the population in the TMI vicinity are aware of improvements in emergency planning, 63 percent feel helpless about the current situation (Appendix A, Table A-13). Lack of coping ability is confirmed by 54 percent of the TMI respondents indicating that TMI has not been allowed to restart because of evacuation problems and inabilities. Finally, only 38 percent felt that Met Ed has demonstrated competence at nuclear power plant operations since the accident. These results indicate that a majority of the population has doubts about being able to cope with nuclear power accidents and related risks.

6. CONCERN OVER OTHER ISSUES

While people living near TMI are concerned about other issues such as inflation and unemployment, TMI is their greatest concern (Appendix A, Table A-14). This is particularly true for those living near the plant. TMI is not a significant concern statewide where people are more concerned with many other issues, chiefly economic ones. Over time, TMI concerns appear to be dissipating. Nevertheless, TMI concerns are not being suppressed by other social problems.

7. PERCEIVED RISK

TMI-1 restart is viewed as a risky event by about one-half the population in the vicinity. Within 5 miles, 49 percent believe that they might receive a dangerous dose of radiation from TMI (Appendix A, Table A-15a). Exactly 50 percent within 25 miles feel that regardless of differing opinions, restarting either unit is unsafe. This is supported by the fact that 52 percent believe that studies do not support the safety of TMI-1 (Appendix A, Table A-15b). Perceived risk is a dominant issue of concern associated with restart, which is reflected by the similar portion of the population who oppose restart (Appendix A, Table A-16).

The results of voting in nonbinding referendums in Dauphin, Cumberland, and Lebanon counties provide a different result. On May 18, 1982, the following question appeared on primary election ballots in the three counties: Do you favor the restart of TMI Unit 1 which was not involved in the accident of March 28, 1979? In Dauphin County, the county in which the plant is located, 71 percent of those voting voted against restart. In Cumberland County, across the Susquehanna River from Dauphin County, 64 percent voted against restart. In Lebanon County, directly east of Dauphin County, 57 percent voted against restart. Such voting results should be regarded cautiously, due to the nonrandom nature of voter turnouts. Given that only 26 percent of the

Figure 6.   Percent of Sample "Very Concerned" about Radioactive Emissions from TMI.

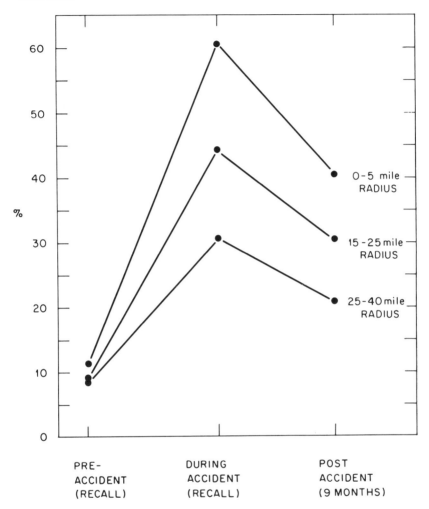

Source: Flynn 1979.

Table 16   Summary of TMI population characteristics
in light of model components

Attitudes toward TMI management	Metropolitan Edison officials are not trusted by a majority of population in local area
Perception/attitude toward nuclear power	Pro/anti split about 50/50
Information	Perceptions of reliability of various sources are highly variable
Knowledge	Local population more knowledgable than state as a whole (but variable)
Group ties	No data
Demographic/individual characteristics	No data
Sensitivity toward risk	30-50% of population are sensitive to another accident taking place
Coping ability	Majority have doubts about coping ability
Concerns over other issues	TMI is one of the top three greatest concerns in the local area
Perception of risks/benefits from restart	About 40-50% of the population feel threatened by restart; a smaller number oppose restart

registered voters actually voted and that political activism of the restart opposition was high, these results probably are not representative of the entire population.

Additional survey data, however, suggest that Unit 2 cleanup is an important mediating factor in formulating attitudes concerning restart. A greater portion of the population supports restart of TMI-2 after cleanup than supports restart of TMI-1 during cleanup of Unit 2 (Appendix A, Table A-16).

Summary and Conclusions

Table 16 summarizes characteristics of the TMI population discussed in this chapter. Based on this assessment, approximately 30 to 50 percent of the population within a 25-mile radius are vulnerable to restart impacts. This numerical range is based on the portion of the population that was consistently measured on each of the various factors presented in a direction of possible vulnerability. Indeed, roughly 30 percent state that they feel threatened by restart or related risks, which is not to say that this proportion of the population would be significantly affected by restart, but, rather, that they have a potential for being impacted. The exact nature of the impacts and number affected will depend on the circumstances surrounding restart and the manner in which information about it is disseminated to the public.

Given the evidence at hand, does the accident set an upper bound for restart-related impacts? The data presented in this section suggests that restart *per se* will not cause a greater level of impacts. An accident of any magnitude, however, has the potential of creating impacts as great as or even greater than the TMI-2 event.

Some supporting evidence for this conclusion is provided by Figure 6. The curves show that sensitivity toward radioactive emissions from TMI were fairly low before the accident, peaked during the accident, and dissipated following the accident. While we do not know how low they will fall, sensitivities were higher after the accident than before. The figure also shows a distinct pattern in the three distance-determined groups reported, and the effects were smaller as distance increased. Thus, according to this measure, communities as a whole are more worried or stressed about TMI following the accident than before. Whether greater or lesser impacts occur as a result of restart cannot be predicted with great precision.

Chapter 6

Forecasting the Impacts

The focus-group discussions, the literature review, and the investigation of the TMI accident all help provide a picture of what impacts might occur from restart. In this chapter, these diverse analyses are brought together to give a coherent picture of the range and likelihood of impacts. In addition, the community profiling activities (Chapter One) are recast to examine the way impacts might be distributed among the functional social groups in the TMI vicinity.

As discussed earlier, the projection or prediction of future effects of technological change is not exact and subject to the limits of science in general. The approach to the projections made in this chapter attempt to capture those limits and are not meant to be deterministic in nature. They reflect the uncertainties in what can occur and reasoned opinions based on the multiple modes of analysis used in the study. As such, they provide the most probable categories of impacts within specified social contexts.

The first part of the chapter summarizes the potential ranges of impacts at different social levels and discusses the likelihood of impacts under alternative circumstances. The second part discusses the social and spatial distribution of impacts in the TMI vicinity.

Potential Impacts of Restart

The previous chapters have identified the range of potential impacts to individuals, families, and communities. They have also provided a detailed account of the factors which may lead to the manifestation of impacts or make conditions more favorable to impacts. Moreover, a clear picture of why impacts may differ among individuals and groups has been formulated. At this point, more speculative forecasts of what may happen in the aggregate due to restart are offered.

Based on the various factors believed to affect the incidence of impacts at all social levels, the overall prevalence probably will vary with respect to four threat scenarios as compared with a baseline no-threat situation. The first situation is characterized by the presence of a threat such as an operating nuclear power reactor. The second situation is characterized by a *threat signal* such as an accident at another power plant or a minor event or emergency. The third circumstance is a minor disaster in which an emergency takes place but no fatalities occur. The final circumstance is a major disaster in which fatalities are significant. In general, impacts are hypothesized to increase, assuming other factors are constant, as the severity of the threat and size of the disaster increased. Impacts will also be shaped to a lesser degree by the way in which information is handled, the behaviors or responses of utility and government officials, and the prevailing social climate regarding nuclear power. Impact levels are described in general terms for each threat situation in Table 17.

Individual Impacts

The major categories of individual impacts concern various stress-related effects. At one extreme, the impact could be elevated concern for the threat of the reactor; at the other, clinically diagnosable impairments could occur. In between are somatic effects and increased anxieties. Associated with these impact categories are a variety of cognitive coping strategies that may be triggered by elevated stress, as illustrated in Table 18.

Under normal operation following restart, increased concerns among some members of the population is expected, and a few might experience increased anxieties as a result. If somatic effects are observed, attributing them to restart is difficult and probably is observed at levels that are not significantly different than normal. Clinical impairments should not occur.

Under the disaster signal situation, more widespread concerns among the population is expected. Some people experience increased anxieties, and some can have somatic stress symptoms. Clinical impairment is unlikely.

In a minor disaster, effects are similar to the previous accident, although perhaps at slightly elevated levels. Concern is strong and wide-

Table 17   Impacts of Restart

Threat type	Threat only	Disaster signal	Minor disaster	Catastrophic disaster
		IMPACTS TO INDIVIDUAL		
Concerns/feelings	Some concern	High concern	Widespread and strong	Extreme trauma
Anxieties	May affect a few individuals	Some people will have anxiety	Prevalent during emergency, some longer lasting	High and of lasting duration
Somatic effects	None attributable	Some people will experience symptoms	Notably higher for some	Prevalent among many individuals
Clinical impairment	None	None	Few but difficult to attribute	Some likely

IMPACTS TO FAMILY

Family tension	Minor; possible in isolated cases	Some disruption; more widespread incidence	Widespread	Widespread; extreme
Family conflict	Unlikely	Possible conflict over appropriate action	Could occur in isolated cases	Unlikely
Family cohesion	Unlikely	Rare but possible disruption	Some disruption, short-lived	High disruption
Family break-up	None	None	Unlikely	Would occur due to fatalities, attribution difficult in other cases

IMPACTS TO COMMUNITY

Long-term population change	Unlikely	Unlikely	Unlikely	Possible decline
Change in community "well-being"	Unlikely	Possible decline in sense of well-being but not enduring	Decline in sense of well-being; long-terms effects unlikely	Possible loss of communiality, effects may persist
Economic disruption	Unlikely	Isolated cases possible overall no effect	Short-term disruption likely	Long-term disruption possible

Table 18. Cognitive coping mechanisms

Mechanism	Example
Deny risk	
Deny existence	Nuclear power is foolproof
Deny seriousness	The accident didn't hurt anyone
Structure risk	
Eliminate uncertainty	An accident "will happen"
Assign authority	The NRC will take care of it
Compare risk	
With benefits	It's needed to lower utility rates
With other risks	It's safer than coal

spread. Anxicties exist and persist after the accident. Clinical impairment can occur, but attribution is difficult to establish. In a major disaster, somatic effects are prevalent among surviving victims, with evidence of some clinical impairment.

Less understood are the cognitive coping mechanism that might be used to deal with both the threat and the uncertainty of another accident. People may deny risk by not acknowledging its existence or seriousness. People may seek to structure risk by reducing the uncertainty or ascribing the responsibility to another party. People may cope by rationalizing risk by comparisons with other risks or the benefits of the risk. Such coping mechanisms all serve to reduce the mental preoccupation with the threat. The incidence of various forms of cognitive coping are not readily estimable because of the lack of data regarding this potential type of response.

Family Impacts

Four major categories of family level impacts are increased family tensions, conflict among family members, a loss of family cohesion or the sense of belonging to the family unit, and, at the extreme, the breakup of the family unit. Family impacts are heavily intertwined with the incidence of individual impacts among family members.

Under the threat situation, increased tensions among family members might occur in isolated cases, but are not generally prevalent. More severe effects are unlikely. Under the disaster signal scenario, tensions are more prevalent and could result in conflicts in some families. A breakdown of family cohesion is rare. Family breakup is expected to occur.

Under the minor disaster, tension is more widespread and conflict could occur in some isolated cases. Cohesion is disrupted, but short-lived. Family breakups could occur, but attribution is difficult. If a catastrophic disaster took place, tension is experienced by most, which does not necessarily lead to conflicts, although high levels of disruption to family well-being can occur. Families breakup due to fatalities and, in the long run, due to stress of recovery although incidence rates are difficult to prove.

Community Impacts

Three broad categories of community impacts, changes in the well-being of a community, long-term population decreases, and economic disruption, are relevant. Under the threat condition, no evidence exists to suggest that any of these impacts could occur. Given the disaster signal, impacts are also unlikely.

A minor disaster usually creates a short-term decline in the community's sense of well-being. Isolated economic disruptions can also occur. A catastrophic disaster could result in population decline, depending on the extent of damage. Long-term effects on well-being are also expected. Economic disruption is experienced and could endure depending on the adequacy of relief efforts.

Impacts: Identification and Distribution

The profiling of functional social groups enables estimation of the vulnerability of different social groups to impacts. The results of the profiling have been summarized in tabular form for each group (Appendix B). Information collected includes main group characteristics, changes in the group after the accident, baseline or current situation, expected attitudes and impacts on a decision to restart TMI-1 or a decision not to restart TMI-1, and some possible mitigation strategies. The group characteristics and possible mitigation strategies represent the judgment of those conducting the community profiles, while the remainder of the information are the changes, impacts, and attitudes as perceived by the persons interviewed. In this respect, the data on impacts do not represent predictions of impacts but, rather, estimates of potential impacts. Table 19 briefly summarizes a less comprehensive survey of community characteristics for communities located in the 10-mile radius of TMI. More detailed community profiles can be found in Flynn *et al.* (1982) and in Social Impact Research, Inc. (1982) from which this summary was prepared.

The data collected as part of the profiling activities allow us to make some judgments about the characteristics of each group as they pertain to the conceptual framework (Figure 3). In many cases, a group can be appraised on the basis of a component of the framework with relative ease; in others, this is difficult because data are lacking or because the lack of consensus among group members or factions creates confusion. In this subsection, each group is reviewed in terms of eight factors: their attitudes toward TMI management, attitudes toward nuclear power, information and knowledge, levels of sensitivity, coping ability, concern regarding other issues, and perception of risks and benefits of restart. In view of the way each group relates to these factors, insight is gained with regard to their susceptibility to restart or nonrestart impacts based on the hypotheses generated in Chapter Four. Susceptibility is a condition that denotes a greater likelihood that impacts will occur under certain conditions which, currently, are unknown. Conversely, some groups, because of their characteristics, may be less susceptible to experiencing impacts. At times, the conclusion of the analysis may be ambiguous about susceptibility when groups show characteristics in both directions or have factions with divergent characteristics. In no case does the analysis suggest that every individual associated with a group will be characterized by the group norm. Given these limits, each group is reviewed according to factors in the framework and speculating on the group's susceptibility to impacts.

Farmers—West

These farmers, in general, have little faith in Met Ed as nuclear managers and do not trust what the utility has to say. As a group, however, they appear to be split over favoring nuclear power as an energy source. Prior to the accident, the farmers knew little about nuclear power, a condition that has since changed. Still, they see a need for more reliable information on nuclear power. This group is charac-

Table 19   Distribution of major impacts by social group

Group	Vulnerability	Perceived impacts of restart	Perceived impacts of no-restart
Farmers-West	Moderate	Increased industrialization; increased property values; lower taxes	Slower growth
Retirees-West	Moderate	Some out-migration; safety and health threatened; anxiety over accident	Higher taxes; decrease property values
Other long-time residents - West	Low	Reduced electric rates; increased development	Higher taxes; higher property values
Harrisburg suburbanites	High	Out-migration; increased political activities; decline in property values; health and safety decline	Slower growth
Other newcomers- West	Moderate	Few effects; increased concern over accidents; increased political activities	Slower growth

Transients-West	Low	Increased industrialization; increased property values	Increased political activity; slower growth
Old Middletowners-West	Moderate/split high and low	Highly variable; threats to health and safety; increased growth	Decreased economic activity
Blacks-East	High	Protest; increased concern over safety	None
Long-time residents-East	High	Property values decline; increased concern over accident; in-migration; higher taxes	Slower growth
Royalton-East	Low	Few changes; increased concern over safety	None
Farmers-East	Low	Increased development; in-migration	Slower development and industrialization
Newer residents-East	High	Health problems; concern over safety; hostility or social protest out-migration	Slower growth; tax increase

terized by close-knit structure emphasizing a family orientation and ties. Despite this fraternal nature, the group is tolerant of divergent views. The TMI–2 accident created a great deal of sensitivity to safety and health issues surrounding nuclear power even though most of the members of this group did not evacuate. Overall, the farmers appear to be split over the restart issue with some focusing on the risk of radiation damage, while others are concerned about the economic effects of power rate increases. Given these characteristics, this group is classified as being neither highly susceptible nor immune from impacts.

If TMI is restarted, the farmers see greater industrial growth which will reduce available farmland and cause property values to rise. They expect taxes would be lowered by this situation. Overall, they feel that the area will not be affected significantly by restart.

Retirees—West

Since the accident, most retirees feel that Met Ed has lost credibility, and they lack faith in the ability of Met Ed to operate the plant. Overall, the group's attitudes toward nuclear power range from indifference (the majority) to mild support. The retirees mainly rely on news media to obtain information about TMI and cannot be considered highly knowledgeable. A strong majority are well-integrated into the community through kinship and group ties.

Since the accident, many have expressed anxiety over unscheduled events at the plant or over sirens sounding. Most are, however, indifferent about needing to cope with a TMI-related incident. With the majority having fixed incomes, the retirees are highly concerned with economic consequences of the issues and inflation in general. The attitudes toward restart range from a small faction in support to indifference or support opposition. Most of those opposed to restart fear for the health and safety consequences of an accident.

Overall, we feel that the retirees are only moderately susceptible to impacts from restart. Those who are indifferent or support restart are less susceptible. All in this group are sensitive to the economic ramifications of any decision.

If the reactor is restarted, the majority feel their safety and health will be threatened. Some may leave the area when opportunities exist. Others, despite opposition to restart, will remain because they feel restart will lower taxes.

Other Long-Time Residents—West

This group is split into two factions and, for the most part, differ on most elements in the framework: the first, and larger, faction has faith in the utility and feels that the plant can be operated safely. They are supportive of nuclear power and feel that it is necessary to the economic vitality of the area. They view the media as irresponsible, and they are somewhat knowledgeable about nuclear energy. Although they are not concerned about future accidents, they support the need for better evacuation planning even though most did not evacuate during the accident. This faction is supportive of restart and is more concerned about the economy and the cost of power than about accident risks.

The minority faction, supported by the same extensive network of social ties, is more negative to nuclear power and has little confidence in the utility. A major concern is the repeat of another accident for which they have no confidence in emergency planning efforts. As with others against restart, they have deep concerns about the safety of an operating reactor.

Accordingly, the majority, as represented by the first faction, are not highly susceptible. Some, however, are characterized by certain attributes which can be associated by high susceptibility. If TMI-1 is restarted, the group feels that electric rates will drop and they will benefit from more industrial development, thereby leading to more jobs and higher property values. They did feel, however, that businesses near the plant will suffer.

Harrisburg Suburbanites

Again, variance is found within this group on some of the components of the framework and agreement on others. The group as a whole does not trust the utility, although some feel that the government can compensate for the utility's inability, while others have no faith in the government either. This first faction tends to support the notion that power from the plants is essential for regional growth. These people are concerned about the availability of accurate information and, despite their general attitudes, dislike the irritation of sirens and unusual events at the plant. Moreover, they are afraid of having to experience another evacuation. This faction tends to be greatly concerned with the economic conditions in the area and feel restart will have distinct benefits.

The second faction has negative attitudes toward nuclear power, ranging from mild to extreme opposition. They believe the media before they believe official information sources. As with the others, they are irritated by sirens and, additionally, fear a repeat of the accident. They view restart as a life-threatening event at the extreme and are generally concerned about the health impacts of TMI. Thus, a portion of this group appear highly susceptible, while the others appear neutral or slightly susceptible to impacts.

If restart occurs, some of the group will move outside the 5-mile zone. They fear a negative impact on property values near the plant, but increasing values at greater distances. All, regardless of support, saw positive effects on industrial growth and the economic prosperity of the area.

Other Newcomers—West

This group, while differing from the Harrisburg suburbanites on the basis of demographic features, has much the same constitution when viewed through the conceptual framework. Again, a range is found, differing only in that extreme antinuclear attitudes are not found. Most share the same concerns about the utility but vary much like the former group. Overall, this group ranges from moderately unsusceptible to moderately susceptible to impacts.

This group largely views favorable effects on industrial development and electrical rates. They do not feel that restart will affect property values. Some who are concerned with safety will move further away if the chance existed.

Transients—West

Little data exist with regard to this group to provide a comprehensive description in relation to the conceptual framework. Their most solvent characteristic is their indifference toward the utility, nuclear power, and restart. Most were not in the area at the time of the accident and are not worried about another one. Overall, they are highly unsusceptible to restart impacts.

If the unit is restarted, the group expects lower utility rates, increased industrial development, and more job opportunities. Rising property values, however, may cause displacement of members of this transient group.

Old Middletowners—East

Old Middletowners hold widely divergent views, ranging from strong support for nuclear power and TMI management to strong opposition toward restart because of fear of nuclear power in general and of TMI as a danger to health; some distrust TMI management and the NRC. Others, generally those more neutral, believe that cleanup of TMI-2 before restarting TMI-1 will increase the credibility of TMI management and of nuclear power. Many were initially supportive of nuclear facilities on TMI, particularly since they were affected by emissions from the coal-fired plant that was replaced by TMI. Although the level of concern for the decision is high in residents regardless of their inclinations for or against restart, patterns of family and group interactions are unlikely to change very much. Old Middletowners have a close-knit community and social organization with extensive family ties, local political and business activity, and social participation. Economics (including the cost of power, loss of borough revenue, and possible side effects on business revenue) concerns many Old Middletowners. Therefore, this group is only moderately susceptible to impacts.

If restart occurs, this group is unlikely to migrate from the area. Again, the group expects positive economic impacts on the community and increased property values.

Blacks—East

Before the TMI accident, Blacks were not concerned with nuclear power in general or with TMI facilities. Their heightened level of sensitivity is based on fears that their health and safety may be affected by radiation and that their property may be destroyed by a second nuclear accident. They also believe that the Black neighborhoods are most vulnerable in case of accident. A paucity of private transportation further heightens concerns over the community and school emergency evacuation. The health of the economy and employment opportunities are the overriding issues of interest to the Blacks, and few Blacks are employed at the TMI complex. These factors indicate that Blacks are quite susceptible to impacts.

If restart occurs, this group suspects increased civil protests against the action and greater political opposition against nuclear power.

Londonderry Township Long-Time Residents—East

The Londonderry Township long-time residents share many characteristic attitudes and impacts of the Old Middletowner's group, with the exception that even those supporting restart do not trust the TMI management and would like to see cleanup of TMI-2 before restart to demonstrate good faith and credible operations by Met Ed. This group has strong values on rights of private property ownership and sees possible increased industrial development, jobs, tax base, and property values as highly beneficial. Like Old Middletowners, they are quite interested in the decision regardless of opposing viewpoints, but they are unlikely to change social, political, and economic patterns of behavior. Overall, this group exhibits high susceptibility of impacts, although this is not true for all individuals.

If restart occurs, the group sees both positive and negative impacts. Some fear health problems will increase due to operations, however, they do not believe it is a reason to leave. Overall, they see some profitting by restart due to higher property values, as well as higher taxes.

Royalton—East

Royalton is a small, aging, somewhat closed community with few formal organizations; the local school has closed, and one grocery store is the only business. Residents were not concerned with nuclear power or TMI before the accident, and they are still not major issues in the community. Community leaders hope to encourage younger families with good incomes to settle there, but it is unlikely that economic benefits from restart will significantly affect Royalton. Given these characteristics, the Royalton group appears fairly immune from impacts.

If restart occurs, this group anticipates that negative or positive impacts will not occur.

Farmers—East

These farmers are not particularly concerned with TMI. While they lack faith in Met Ed's ability to manage TMI, they maintain faith in government authorities and nuclear power experts. They believe that a reliable power source is essential, that for the most part nuclear is a safe power source, and that increased nuclear power generation will minimize rising electric rates. Generally, the farmers exhibit a low level of sensitivity to another accident because they feel that sufficient safety measures have been instituted to prevent future accidents. Most perceive the risks of nuclear power to be minimal and the benefits to be abundant. Economics (the cost of power and increased electric power available for commercial and residential development) and a variety of farm operation and agricultural policy issues are more important to almost all of the farmers than are the TMI issues. In summary, this group does not appear to be susceptible to impacts.

If TMI is restarted, this group sees favorable economic impacts. Rising property values could, however, hurt members in the group.

Residents of Newer Developments—East

Residents of new developments are less cohesive and/or socially interactive than other groups. The majority commute to jobs, often in other communities. However, they do exhibit strong concern for environmental and community issues and successfully engage in political activity. The TMI accident divided this group into pro and con factions with considerable hostility apparent. The level of sensitivity is high, particularly for the decision outcomes, regardless of viewpoint. Patterns of group interactions may be affected, including the possibility of increased hostility, political action, and even some out-migration within the 5-mile zone. Overall, these residents are split on restart with radiation-related health risks as the major concern on one side and a variety of economic issues on the other. Given the propensity for strong reaction whatever the decision, this group is thought to be highly susceptible to impacts.

Conclusions

From the above tasks—profiling, impact identification, and the estimations of susceptibility—several issues and themes provide insight into community impacts. The profiling reveals that the population potentially impacted by restart is not homogeneous. Diversity among groups is found along each social characteristic investigated. Despite such differences, certain issues and impacts appear on the agenda for most groups regardless of their attitudes toward restart. There is a consensus that growth will increase in the future regardless what decision is made about the restart. Most feel that out-migration will be very minimal, even given the most negative circumstances. Clearly, the cleanup of TMI-2 will do much to increase public trust in and the credibility of Met Ed and help demonstrate the utility's capability to operate a nuclear power plant. Most groups agree that public education and credible sources of information will allay their fears and concerns, particularly over the health effects of radiation. Finally, there was a consensus that an improvement in emergency preparations is needed, including installing more reliable alarms and demonstrating that evacuation is feasible.

If TMI-1 is restarted, the two negative impacts most frequently cited are possible health effects and fear or anxiety over another accident. On the positive side, the major impacts were the increased availability of power, the deflationary effects on the cost of power, and accelerated industrial development.

If not restarted, the major benefit to the area mentioned include a prospering of the locations near the plant that have been adversely impacted due to the accident. On the other hand, negative effects include decreased development, higher utility rates, and population decline.

Overall, this analysis indicated that the majority of the people in the area are concerned about the decision. Most groups, while sharing similar social characteristics, are divided over the restart issue. Even though most are not politically active, the decision will be politically sensitive. Regardless of the decision, groups in the area probably will continue to appear and continue their opposition through the courts. Finally, certain groups exhibit characteristics that shape their susceptibility to impacts; some appear more likely to be affected than others.

Chapter 7

Mitigating the Impacts

Generally, impact mitigation can be defined as measures taken to alleviate impacts that are considered undesirable or to accentuate those impacts that are considered beneficial (Murdock and Leistritz 1979). The CEQ has defined mitigation to include actions which avoid, minimize, rectify, reduce or eliminate, or compensate for adverse impacts (CEQ 1979).

Mitigation may affect most of the variables within the heuristic model of individual and community change resulting from the TMI-1 restart decision. This may occur as a result of the particular mitigative measure addressing either an initial variable within the framework (i.e., attitudes toward TMI management, perceptions/attitudes toward nuclear power, information/knowledge, and demographic/individual characteristics) and analyzing its effect as it winds through the conceptual model to first-order impacts, second-order impacts, and group and community impacts; or by addressing the various impacts directly with changes in the initial variables resulting from feedback processes.

While a mitigation program can be developed from either of these perspectives, mitigation should be based on an understanding of the dynamics of individual, group, and community change that may result from the TMI-1 restart decision. Mitigation does not merely comprise a sociotechnical "fix" that works or does not work. Rather, mitigation is an intervention ancillary to the restart decision itself, which requires equivalent levels of investigation, analysis, and planning.

The *process* by which mitigation measures are selected and authorized for implementation constitutes a significant variable in the impact analysis scheme (Carnes *et al*. 1982). Mitigation can be thought of as both a product and a process, and both of these elements may affect the composite effectiveness of a particular mitigative measure or set of measures. Put simply, the "who" and the "how" of mitigation decision-making will affect the consequences of mitigation implementation. For instance, a mitigative measure might be interpreted as a bribe rather than as an attempt to offset or mitigate real or perceived adverse impacts when the mitigation proposal is initiated by facility sponsors or external decision-makers (e.g., the utility or the NRC); conversely, if the proposed mitigation is developed in response to local requests, it is more likely to be interpreted accurately, and its effects are more likely to be perceived as salutary and straightforward (Carnes *et al.* 1982). Thus, the NRC staff and subcontractors asked local groups and individuals to assess the impacts of a restart decision and to suggest potential mitigating measures.

Classification of Mitigation

It is important to distinguish mitigation functions so that one can determine why a particular mitigation measure might be offered, to whom it might be offered, and what institutional and administrative arrangements might be necessary to implement the mitigation. Mitigation can (1) ameliorate anticipated adverse impacts of a decision or action through preventive or corrective actions and/or (2) compensate for actual damage if abnormal or unanticipated events occur. Table 20 defines these types of mitigation, identifies a range of options within each type, and provides examples of mechanisms that might be used for implementing the particular mitigation measure (these options and mechanisms are offered as examples and are not necessarily relevant to the TMI-1 restart decision).

In addition to anticipatory and compensatory mitigation, establishing a monitoring program to discern unanticipated adverse impacts resulting from the decision and informing the public about the planned future mitigation activities should they be detected might be necessary. That is, unanticipated impacts may occur that require noncompensatory mitigation. Compensatory mitigation is applicable only in the case of an abnormal event (e.g., a future accident), and anticipatory mitigation is applicable for those impacts expected to occur as a result of the "normal" operation of the TMI-1 restart decision (e.g., either normal operation of the plant with restart or possible adverse regional economic impacts with no restart). Monitoring can discover unanticipated "nor-

Table 20   Mitigation classification system

Mitigation type	Brief definitions	The range of possible strategies	Example of corresponding implementation mechanisms
Anticipatory	Actions geared toward preventing, reducing, or eliminating adverse impacts before they occur	Buffers/land use management	Purchase of easements
		Monitoring/detection	Establish dosimeter program
		Emergency preparedness	Develop contingency plan
		Safety design	Establish acceptable risk level
		Public education	Distribute information brochure
		Socioeconomic impact mitigation	Develop job-training program
		Land value guarantees	Property dedication program
Compensatory	Payments for actual damages in the event of an accident or other abnormal and unplanned event	Trust funds	Excise taxes on wastes
		Insurance programs	Government-backed policies/
		Assumption of liability	Price-Anderson Act

Source: Adapted from Carnes et al., 1982.

mal" or nonextraordinary impacts and allows the development and implementation of appropriate mitigation measures.

Mitigation Effectiveness

The effectiveness of any potential mitigation measure(s) has two basic dimensions: its ability to prevent or ameliorate adverse consequences of a given action and its ability to increase the probability of public acceptance of the action. While the particular criteria for evaluating the effectiveness of potential mitigative measures are outlined in detail elsewhere (Carnes *et al.* 1982), the criteria can be clustered into the following groups: (1) prerequisites to the use of mitigation measure(s); (2) objective characteristics of the mitigation measure(s); (3) characteristics of community understanding of the mitigation measure(s); and (4) the projected consequences of implementing a particular mitigation measure(s). These criteria characterize alternative mitigation measures for comparative purposes. Figure 7 presents a simplified version of this evaluative framework, with the criteria appropriately grouped.

Given the diversity of potential impacts and their probable variable distribution among numerous social groups in the TMI area, a single mitigation measure cannot successfully ameliorate all adverse consequences of the ultimate restart decision. The existence of multiple and occasionally incompatible objectives across groups and, perhaps, even within groups, makes the design of a perfectly responsive mitigation strategy an unlikely event or outcome. What can be sought, however, is a strategy that is responsive to the major concerns of a pluralist social structure, one that does not systematically ignore the concerns of any social group. In this sense, the two effectiveness criteria (i.e., ability to ameliorate impacts and to increase probability of public acceptance of the decision) are inextricably interrelated; even if one group's concerns are not perfectly met, their inclusion in the mitigation design process should increase the probability of that group accepting the decision.

Prior Experience with Mitigation

Most experience with mitigation has concentrated on conventional impact areas (i.e., measures to lessen demands on local systems or to increase local carrying or infrastructure capacities), and much of that experience is instructive for the purposes of mitigating impacts of a TMI-1 restart decision. As indicated earlier (comparison of Love Canal, Wilsonville, and TMI-1), however, finding situations strictly comparable or analogous to the TMI-1 restart decision is difficult because of the unique circumstances of the TMI-1 restart decision, such as the prior history of the TMI-2 accident and subsequent events (e.g., venting, embrittlement, and radioactive water at TMI-2); the interposition of "dread" and "fear" associated with the plant due to the accident; and the paucity of "normal" benefits associated with the facility (e.g., rebates on utility bills for Middletown residents through local municipal distributor but no direct facility-related property taxes to local jurisdictions).

The legal responsibilities of the NRC for mitigation have been rather narrowly interpreted in the past. In addition to how the way information is handled, the potential role of key NRC personnel with the public, and the quality of emergency planning (USNRC 1982), the NRC has conditioned licensing on a variety of applicant commitments and NRC staff requirements. For example, in the case of the proposed construction of the recently aborted Greene County Nuclear Power Plant (USNRC 1979), the application was rejected, but the EIS noted that *if* a decision was made to issue a construction permit, it would be conditioned on a number of requirements such as transportation corridor maintenance, local government and school services augmentation, fair financial compensation to affected landowners, and sufficient monitoring to ensure environmental compliance. At the Tennessee Valley Authority's (TVA) Hartsville Nuclear Power Plant, a comprehensive monitoring program was conducted for several areas subject to impact by construction, including population, secondary employment, education, housing local planning assistance, water and sewer requirements, health and medical services, local government budgets, and local recruitment and training (TVA 1980). Mitigation activities were directed at education, housing, local planning assistance, and health and medical services.

Perhaps among the most relevant of NRC's experience with mitigation has been with respect to those conditions specified for the operation of both units at TMI. The original Final Environmental Impact Statement (FEIS) for operating both units (U.S. Atomic Energy Commission 1972) stipulated that continued construction and operation were conditioned on a variety of factors to protect the environment including environmental and health monitoring and development of a course of action to alleviate problems resulting from the operation of the plants (USAEC 1972: iii-iv). These requirements were continued by the NRC in its subsequent reevaluations of the TMI plants in 1976 (USNRC 1976b: iii; 1976a: iii).

As noted in these examples, the NRC has had extensive experience with monitoring and mitigation as conditions in their licensing actions. It is less clear that NRC, or any agency for that matter, has had much experience with the kinds of monitoring and mitigation that might be appropriate for the TMI-1 restart decision. That depends substantially on the kinds of impacts anticipated in the impact area.

We have earlier identified some analogous elements from hazardous waste experiences that illustrate some state government mitigation experience. The most relevant one is the Love Canal situation at Niagara Falls, New York, where a school, park, and residential neighborhood were developed atop a closed chemical waste disposal site. Love Canal was declared a federal disaster area in August 1978, and approximately $3 million was spent by the Federal Disaster Assistance Administration in the Love Canal area for citizen relocation, security, and construction of a drainage tile system to divert leachate flow from the contaminated site. However, not paid by the agency was the $12 million spent to purchase private homes, $8 million for construction of a drainage project, about $800,000 for family health surveys, and more than $100,000 in salaries/overtime pay that state officials say is directly related to the cleanup efforts (Solid Waste Management 1979). This work is still being funded by numerous state and federal agencies under coordination of the state's Love Canal task forces.

Over 200 families have been evacuated and their homes purchased. Recent health studies by the state and federal government have been published (Janerich et al. 1981; Smith 1982a, 1982b), and environmental monitoring is continuing. The homes purchased by the state are scheduled for demolition, and the site will be considered for further cleanup in the coming months under Superfund (Kovak 1982). A U.S. senator from New York estimated that cleaning up Love Canal and two other Hooker Chemical Company disposal sites in Niagara Falls could reach $280 million; pending citizen lawsuits seek up to $2 billion in damage (Wolf 1980).

The relevance to TMI-1 restart studies is not to the type of facility nor to its estimated danger to the public, but that it was perceived to be a major emergency situation without accident or known casualties that reached crisis proportions based on public fears, health concerns, and conflicting information.

Potential Mitigation Measures for TMI-1 Restart

Tables in Appendix B identify the key issues and impacts perceived by local functional groups to be associated with alternative TMI-1 restart decisions. These tables also identify mitigative measures, suggested by community key informants and profile analysts, which may be perceived to be responsive to these concerns.

These mitigating mechanisms have been combined into eight broad categories: (1) improved communications, (2) decisionmaking, (3) public education, (4) emergency preparedness, (5) relocation assistance, (6) job training, (7) land use, and (8) subsidies. With the exception of some measures under emergency preparedness, all of the suggested measures are anticipatory (see Table 20), although many of the remaining measures could be modified to be compensatory.

Furthermore, just as measures have been reduced to eight functional categories, measures could also be grouped within categories. For instance, under decisionmaking, both pro-restart and anti-restart groups perceive that changing decisionmaking processes would improve the situation and, presumably, mitigate the effects of either delayed or unresponsive decisionmaking. More detailed strategies for changes to decisionmaking processes include public participation in negotiations on a mitigation plan or local representation through a citizen advisory review board. Table 21 provides an overview of major mitigative measures perceived by local groups and the literature to be potentially useful in ameliorating perceived adverse impacts due to the TMI-1 restart decision.

The potential usefulness of any of these mitigation measures can best be judged by an ability to accomplish two objectives—ameliorate actual or perceived impacts of the restart decision and increase the chances of public acceptance of that decision. These, in turn, can be evaluated according to a variety of criteria as noted in Fig. 7 (see also Carnes *et al.* 1982). These mitigation measures and other potential measures have not, as yet, been subjected to such a scrutiny but should be during subsequent research.

It is highly unlikely that each and every adverse impact can be

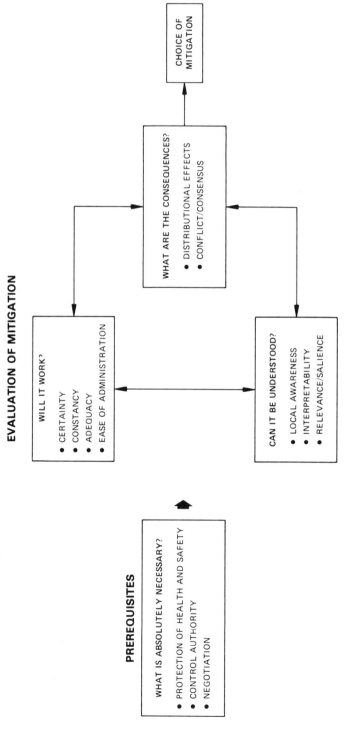

Figure 7. A Framework for Evaluating the Utility of Mitigation.

mitigated. The development of a consensus regarding projected decision impacts is not likely to occur; consensus regarding the ability of a mitigation strategy to ameliorate these impacts is perhaps even less likely to occur. Since the perception of impacts obviously varies with one's perspective, the adequacy of any mitigation measure to address a given impact will likewise vary. In short, different mitigation strategies may be more or less helpful for different groups.

Conclusions

Review of other mitigation programs offers some confirmation that the general tenor of mitigative efforts will need to take into account many of the initial variables of the model of individual and community change resulting from the TMI-1 restart decision: perception/attitude toward nuclear power, information/knowledge, attitudes toward TMI management (and government), and demographic and individual characteristics.

Mitigation strategies should be devised that consider both conventional and innovative approaches to ameliorate impacts, particularly those perceived by local residents. For example, an extension of the focus-group discussions held in this phase of the study might be used to facilitate information transfer to area residents and to provide local inputs to the decisionmaking process. Two options available include local assessment of decision impacts and potential mitigating measures (Carnes *et al.* 1982) and use of innovations in telecommunications (Linderman 1980). Either of these two approaches allow all of the initial model variables to be addressed.

The effectiveness of mitigation is determined by its ability to address specific actual or perceived adverse impacts and its propensity to increase acceptance of the decision by various interested parties or the public. Any potential mitigation measure must be evaluated on the basis of these two broad criteria. Information collected in the impact area through focus-group discussions and community and group profiling activities demonstrates that while considerable diversity exists in perceived anticipated impacts and in potential mitigation measures, some measure of concurrence or consensus is found on some items. It may be essential, for instance, to clean up TMI-2 before restarting TMI-1, or at least to be well along the way toward cleaning up TMI-2 before a positive TMI-1 restart decision will be acceptable to local residents.

Table 21   Overview of possible mitigation measures

Improved communications	Relocation assistance
On emergency preparedness Credible information source Process to provide undistorted flow of information Full monitoring program (radiological) Publication of monitoring information	For displaced TMI-1 employees (no restart) For residents (restart) Purchase property at pre-accident values
Decisionmaking	**Job training**
Change process NRC not appeal court decision Negotiation on mitigation plan Clean up Unit 2 Decommission both units New management of TMI Raise operation standards Retrofit for other fuel source	For displaced TMI-1 employees (no restart) For residents (no restart) For residents (restart)
Public education	**Land use**
Risks/benefits of nuclear power Tours of TMI facilities Nonbiased information on health effects of radiation Health education program	Preserve agricultural land Efforts to attract industry Joint planning Tax assessment based on present/best use
Emergency preparedness	**Subsidies**

Substantially revised community evacuation
  plan
  — those without personal transport
  — schools
  — institutionalized, handicapped
  — low income
Improved alert system
Provide potassium iodide
Advanced warning on venting
Stress management training
Develop local radiological health unit
	Home improvement programs
	Liberalized tax credits
	Assist elderly in tax assistance and
	  selling homes
	Energy conservation credits
	Rebate on electric utility rates
	Cash grants
	Compensation for acquired properties

Similarly, increased attention to emergency preparedness appears to be warranted by local concerns. These and other issues (see Table 21) have been identified as potential mitigation measures. The design of actual mitigation measures should be informed by local participation in the design process so that the mitigation strategy is responsive to the concerns and interests of a diverse public in the local area and, therefore, more likely to result in acceptance of the ultimate restart or no restart decision.

Chapter *8*

Implications for Environmental Management

This chapter seeks to extend the results of this case study of the TMI restart issue to the broader arena of hazard and environmental management. Some may argue that the situation at TMI, both with respect to the accident and to the circumstances surrounding restart, are unique. We feel, however, that they are antecedents to major concerns of the future. As such, they provide an indication of the type of environmental management issues that will command public attention in years to come. Concern over the environment will focus increasingly on the catastrophic risks that humans face. Although these concerns may not dominate policy agendas, they will start to erode the emphasis on more deterministic types of environmental alterations. Perhaps the most noticeable indicator of this trend is the growing scientific debate over and public concern with nuclear winter, the hypothesized cooling of the earth following a large nuclear attack. Similarly, the potential for drastic climatic change is beginning to draw attention. As for technology, the debate over recombinant DNA also raises the spectre of extreme risk.

The consequences of these extreme events are unknown and may be beyond our imaginations. Still we must live in the shadow of their threat. The extent to which these environmental extremes will shape the quality of our immediate existence and our expectations of the future is largely unknown. To some degree, this will depend on the way we individually and collectively define images of the future in the face of these risks. It will also depend on the way political and social institutions incorporate risks into their agendas. Whatever the range in the outcome of such events, our society must face the eventuality of dealing with catastrophic risks either in a direct or a vicarious manner. The restart of TMI can be viewed as a precursor of human response to surfacing environmental risks. Although we cannot generalize that response will be identical to that observed at TMI, we can hypothesize that many of the processes will be manifest in other public controversies over risky technologies.

To extend this analysis, the major conclusions from this study are summarized below, which is followed by discussions of relevant issues that logically extend from the analysis. First, the implications of research for measuring psycho-social impacts in specific and assessing socioeconomics effects of risk in general are discussed. Second, the implications for NEPA and preparing environmental impact documents are considered. Third, a rationale for and application of mitigation actions for the development of hazardous technologies is developed. Finally, the approach and findings of this research is interpreted in light of the broader fields of hazard and risk management.

Major Findings

This study used multiple methods to examine the type and nature of the impacts from restart. By employing multiple methods, we are able to discern whether impact types converge or diverge across method. This approach helps to identify the full range of possible impacts, to establish general confidence bounds concerning the likelihood of impacts, and to identify conditions under which impacts may occur.

The Range of Impacts

The literature review, the focus-group discussions, the review of analogous situations, and the community profiling helps to identify the types of impacts that may occur due to restart or are perceived by the people in the vicinity of TMI as possible consequences. Table 22 summarizes the major types of impacts revealed by the various approaches utilized to identify impacts. By comparing impacts in each category, constructing a reasonable picture of the types of anticipated impacts, as well as those derived from theory and experience with analogous situ-

Table 22 Impacts by method

Impact category	Method/Approach		
	Focus groups	Profiling	Reviews
Individual psychological impacts	Fear; anxiety; hopelessness	Distrust; fear of health effects; anxiety; worry	Concern; some anxiety
Manifestations of stress	Disease; sleep-lessness; lethargy loss of job	long-term health problems	Minor somatic effects
Group level impacts	Social stigma; loss of home; conflict; protest; neighborhood loss; harrassment; prosperity	Protest; violence hostility	Inter-group conflict; loss of family cohesion
Community impacts	Higher taxes; outmigration; property values decline; loss of well-being; economic growth; stable taxes; lower utility bills	Higher taxes; outmigration; property values decline; increased development; lower taxes; property values increase; lower utility bills	No measurable impacts

ations, is possible. Although we cannot exclude other potential impacts with complete confidence, Table 22 provides a reasonable portrayal of impacts of concern.

By comparing the empirically derived impacts identified in the focus-group discussions and the profiling with those from reviews of analogous situations, establishing some general levels of confidence in the validity of various impact types is possible. At the individual level, all three activities suggests that people will be concerned with restart and potential effects and some may develop anxieties and fears. These types of concerns emerged and are verified by both theory and experiences with related incidents.

Some minor individual stress effects may occur. The focus-group discussions indicated a broad range of effects at both clinical and subclinical levels. The profiling did not reveal much anticipation of stress effects. Intermediate to these two points, the various reviews suggest some potential somatic impacts, but at subclinical levels. Although some serious stress-related problems may occur coincident with restart, causality is difficult to infer. Thus, we can be confident that some stress effects will occur, but they will not pose serious medical problems.

At the group level, all three activities suggest increased strain and possible conflict. Focus groups indicated the most severe impacts with the reviews showing only more ambiguous forms of conflict. Restart probably will cause dissention among communities, organizations, social groups, and perhaps families. While this conflict probably will not manifest itself in widespread violence, some forms of protest are likely. Clearly, some families have been affected by the accident, and restart might possibly rekindle feelings of insecurity.

At the community level, we find the most divergent range of possible impacts. Both sets of field activities show perceptions of opposite outcomes ranging from increased prosperity to economic recession and from growth to decline. Our reviews, however, suggest that these types of impacts are unlikely to occur and would be difficult to attribute to restart if they did. In part, the differing perceptions may reflect a process by which some of the positive impacts that may result compensate for negative impacts resulting in little net difference.

Conditions for Impacts

Our research shows that restart as a technical decision *per se* will not be the cause of impacts, but rather, the events surrounding restart may be. The analysis of the impacts of the accident at TMI showed that perceived threat, fear, and mistrust were major antecedents of impacts. The same types of concerns surfaced in the focus-group dicussions. Four major possible intervening factors will shape the extent and magnitude of impacts. The first concerns the manner in which a restart decision is reached. If it is perceived to be done in a manner of secrecy, further distrust in the utility and the government agencies that help regulate the industry will probably result. As distrust grows, the probability of impacts also increases. If, on the other hand, the public is given signals that increase their confidence in the institutions managing nuclear power, the likelihood of impacts should decrease. Among those activities that may raise public confidence are demonstrations of competent corporate management, progress toward cleanup of the damaged reactor,

TMI-2, improved coordination of emergency response capabilities, and public involvement in plant affairs.

A second major factor concerns the type and level of information people receive about the restart. The extent to which restart is characterized by the news media as a symbol of other larger issues will be significant. If it becomes associated with issues such as nuclear war or arms proliferation, impacts are more likely. The degree to which experiences with the accident are relived will also be significant. Finally, the extent to which the media focuses on potential impacts may lead to self- fulfilling prophecies.

The third factor concerns operating experience after the reactor resumes operations. A series of minor problems may act as reminders of the accident or signals of the potential risks and consequences. The manner in which the utility handles such problems, if they do occur, is also significant. Cover-ups or perceived secrecy may generate further anxiety among the public. Downplaying of risks may actually elevate perceived risk among the population. Even minor problems such as false sounding of alarms may raise sensitivity to risk.

Another emergency would trigger the greatest possible level of negative impacts. The level of impacts would be likely to rise with the severity and uncertainty of the incident. While predicting the precise nature and magnitude of those impacts is still difficult, they would probably exceed those of the 1979 accident.

The final intervening factor is the extent of the effort put into mitigating potential impacts. If a mitigation scheme is developed with the assistance and approval of the public, impacts are less likely to occur. Although a mitigation program cannot satisfy all the concerns of each individual, the process of developing one should, by itself, help ameliorate negative affects.

Distribution of Impacts

Every person or group in the vicinity of TMI will not be affected by restart. The review of various surveys conducted in the vicinity allows us to identify the portion of the population, based on their characteristics and perceptions, vulnerable to impacts. In reviewing data on the various factors postulated to be associated with the occurrence of impacts, we find that consistently 30%–50% of the population within 25 miles exhibit characteristics that suggest vulnerability. This is not to say they will experience severe impacts but, rather, have the greatest potential.

The people are not evenly distributed throughout the social fabric of the area.The community profiling indicated certain social groupings of people are more susceptible to impacts. Of the 12 distinct groups identified, four are more likely to experience impacts, another four are less likely to experience impacts, and the final four are only moderately susceptible. This does not mean that all members of the groups will be affected. The prevalence of impacts may be higher in the groups most vulnerable.

The analysis of the TMI accident data also suggests the way impacts may be distributed. Families at the early stage of their life cycles were most vulnerable to the accident. This group is comprised of young married couples, often with preschool children. They are also more vulnerable to restart due to their concern over the effects of ionizing radiation. In addition, distance plays a role in determining vulnerability. Those families living closest to the reactor site are most vulnerable, and vulnerability decreases as the distance from the plant increases.

These findings must be interpreted in the context of the multiple means approach utilized by this study and within the limits of social science research. In the next section, the relationship between this research and the broader area of research methods is discussed.

Measuring Psycho-Social Impacts

The Limits of Research

The major principle underlying social science research is making causal judgments by systematically excluding competing explanations. The philosophy of science teaches that one cannot logically know what is true (Popper 1973). At best, one can know what has not yet been ruled out as false (Cook and Campbell 1979). Each successive attempt at gaining understanding is a search for a better approximation to the truth through the elimination of competing explanations for observed causal relationships. The extent to which research conclusions are valid depends on the researcher's ability to rule out factors other than the hypothesized cause as plausibly responsible for the observed change.

This process of exclusion, however, cannot be based on a single line of evidence, for, as Campbell (1969; Cook and Campbell 1979) points out, this evidence is also susceptible to threats to its validity. Rather, multiple, related lines of evidence, each one independently imperfect, are needed. Each line is susceptible to a different set of threats to its validity, while adequately controlling for weaknesses of the other lines. Taken together, these overlapping sources converge to produce a pattern of evidence that approximates the actual relationships.

To produce such patterns requires the use of not only multiple procedures, but also multiple operationalizations of measures of potential impacts. Campbell and Fiske (1959), Webb, Campbell, Schwartz, and Sechrest (1966), and Cook and Campbell (1979) have warned of the pitfalls inherent in utilizing a single method and/or indicator of a given concept. Rather than relying on a single indicator which cannot perfectly reflect on underlying process, a number of overlapping measures that have different patterns of irrelevancies are needed. When the effect has been confirmed by more than one independent measurement process, uncertainty is reduced and greater confidence can be placed in a conclusion.

For example, a more limited approach along these times was used in an assessment of the impact of Concorde supersonic transport operations at Dulles International Airport in Washington, D.C. Two independent types of measurement were used: a replicated survey of community reations (an attitudinal measure) and the telephone log at the complaint center (an unobtrusive behavioral measure) (Dintzer and Soderstrom, 1978). Within the survey, multiple measures of community satisfaction were obtained: reactions toward noise pollution; housing values; access to government leaders; etc. Theoretically, the two measures should not be influenced by the same sources of bias, but will still measure the same traits (i.e., reaction to Concorde operations).

The extent to which a similar pattern of change is evident across multiple measures and procedures affects the credibility of the conclusion that an impact has occurred. In corresponding fashion, determining the validity of any generalized understanding of an observed relationship is based on the extent to which a pattern is detected at another time, at a different place, and with different people. Obviously, one's confidence in the general proposition concerning the presumed causal relationship increases with successive tests under different conditions revealing a similar pattern of evidence.

This confidence in a general proposition allows analysts to generalize about potential impacts from one studied situation to another similar, but untested, situation. The ability to anticipate effects is directly related to the depth of understanding of causal relationships and the extent of similarities between situations. If experience with any given event is high and the conditions for response are well-known, then predictions are facilitated and more likely to be valid. Conversely, if the event is novel and the bases for human response are vague, prediction is not justified.

Although the situation presented by a restart of TMI-1 is unique, the basis for understanding human response to risky or hazardous events is more firmly established. Thus, although it may be infeasible predicting the extent of any human behavior or manifestation of psycho-social impacts is not feasible, understanding and explaining why they may or may not occur is possible.

Even in social situations that have been the focus of much empirical research, predicting human response to a future, seemingly unrecognizable, event is not a precise or exact art. Although learning from analogous events and extending general findings regarding human behavior in response to disruptive events, such as natural hazards, is possible, this type of knowledge can only be used to develop estimates of a range of impacts. To the extent that TMI-1 restart is unique, making inferences from any historical evidence is subject to error. Actual predictions are impossible to make with a high degree of confidence by borrowing solely from related incidents.

Application to TMI Restart

Recognizing the limitations of prediction in the social sciences, a research plan comprised of five major activities was developed: (1) a review of the literature on behavioral response to risky or hazardous events; (2) focus, group discussions; (3) community profiling; (4) assembling data on unobtrusive indicators; and (5) surveys of community residents. Each of the problems with prediction discussed earlier are addressed by at least one of these activities.

The literature review and focus-group discussions were employed to ensure appropriate and adequate coverage of the most socially important variables and to identify the likely causal factors that might lead to observed impacts. Community profiling was undertaken to explore changes in social organizations and interrelationships. The unobtrusive indicators and community surveys developed information on the nature and extent of the existence of the potential causal factors, and, from this, examined the range and magnitude of psycho-social changes that might occur as a result of restarting TMI-1.

Although the methods employed in this study sought to control for many of the weaknesses in social science research, Soderstrom (1981) points out a fourth class of problems that is not easily handled: the possibility that certain aspects of social interactions are inherently unpredictable. Polanyi (1966) argues that this incapability exists because the process of evolution is "emergent":

> The characteristics of what evolves cannot be predicted from the characteristics of the parts which compose it. We cannot predict the meaning of this paragraph from the words which comprise it, nor a new theory in science from the problems that inspire it . . . The whole is more than the sum of the parts, and what the whole will be cannot be predicted from the parts or their partial interactions.

If this emergent condition also applies to evolving social systems, as Michael (1978) suggests, then the future state of a community becomes very difficult to project.

Although this perspective has a good deal of truth, it may be, as Cronbach (1975) suggests, that this emergence is the result of complex interactions involving time. In this regard, the emergent state may be merely an unstudied phenomenon. Credence is lent to this position by virtue of the replicated pattern of results of studies on behavioral responses to the environmental hazards reported earlier. The examination of analogous situations was used to identify and examine similar elements in other unique hazardous events in order to determine how closely the restarting of TMI-1 might parallel these events and how useful the experiences with these events might be in understanding the potential impacts at TMI. To the extent that the conditions and interrelations surrounding TMI-1 restart are reflective of those found in previous research, predictions are based on a sound empirical foundation. Conversely, the extent to which restart is a unique event, unlike other environmental hazards, then the emergent condition of which Polanyi wrote may hinder predictions. The purpose of using multiple lines of evidence is to determine which of these alternatives is most valid.

Psycho-Social Impacts and NEPA

As noted in the introduction, our analysis grew out of a request by the NRC, subsequent to a decision of the U.S.Court of Appeals for the District of Columbia Circuit (People Against Nuclear Energy v. United States Nuclear Regulatory Commission, 1982), to assess the psychological and community well-being impacts of restarting TMI-1. The research was to be used by the NRC in its preparation of an environmental assessment, as required by the appellate court prior to the NRC's granting license to Met Ed to resume operations of the undamaged reactor. Subsequent to the completion of our research, the U.S. Supreme Court overturned the appellate court's decision and voided the order for an environmental assessment or any other NEPA documentation on the issues under contention (Metropolitan Edison Co. v. People Against Nuclear Energy, 1983).

Although the Supreme Court has addressed these particular issues as they relate to the TMI-1 restart, it has not closed the door on these issues entirely. Indeed, the court recognized that the law evolves as does our capability to understand and explain the consequences of purposive collective action. The court's fairly narrow reading of the purpose of NEPA and other germane issues may have been, as noted by Hartsough and Savitsky (1984), simply the result of a desire to establish boundaries on a potentially enormous field of litigation or to challenge the social sciences to distinguish authoritatively between fraudulent and legitimate claims. The court may have also hoped that other, nonjudicial means might be established to ameliorate or even preclude the emergence of such concerns.

The following discussion addresses the implications of our analysis for NEPA and the preparation of EISs. Specifically, the cognizability of psychological and community well-being impacts under NEPA with a critical review the Supreme Court's decision regarding TMI-1 restart is considered, the utility of focus-group discussions in NEPA and other social science assessments is evaluated, and the possibilities for conflict resolution in similar cases involving public controversies over hazardous technologies is discussed.

Cognizability of Psycho-Social Impacts

The Supreme Court's rejection of PANE's contention that psychological impacts of TMI-1 restart should be assessed under NEPA was based on a number of critical elements, including consideration of NEPA's legislative history, the length of the causal chain between a restart decision and psychological impacts, the relevance of the accident at TMI-2 to the contention, and the ability of NRC to address impacts outside of its primary charter.

The Supreme Court interpreted the NEPA in light of the original congressional debate over its passage in late 1969. At that time, the court argues, Congress was interested in protecting the physical environment—the air, water and land—to ensure the quality of the human environment:

> Congress was talking about the physical environment—the world around us so to speak . . . although NEPA states its *goals* in sweeping terms of human health and welfare, these goals are *ends* that Congress has chosen to pursue by means of protecting the physical environment. (Emphasis in original.)

Citing various statements by U.S. Senator Henry Jackson and U.S. Representative John Dingell in their remarks to their colleagues on the Conference Report that was eventually enacted, the court emphasized that Congress had no intent of charging the federal government with the responsibility of protecting the social or psychological well-being of Americans except insofar as those environmental concerns were adversely affected by a change in the physical environment. Although we acknowledge and understand the court's reliance on original congressional intent as a convention in judicial decisionmaking, we suspect that the evolution of the NEPA during the intervening 14 years, particularly as indicated by the CEQ in its various implementing regulations during that period, does not make that approach persuasive. Too many EISs and too much litigation have gone well beyond changes to the physical environment to make original congressional intent a dominant factor in reaching a decision on this issue.

The court's opinion was also based strongly on the length of the causal chain involved in the NEPA analysis. Although the court concurred that psychological impacts, *per se*, are cognizable as a health impact under NEPA, it found that the chain between the change in the environment (i.e., restart of TMI-1) and the effect (i.e., adverse psychological consequences) too remote:

> · [The NEPA requires] a reasonably close causal relationship between a change in the physical environment and the effect at issue. This requirement is like the familiar doctrine of proximate cause from tort law. . . [a] *risk* of an accident is, by definition, unrealized in the physical world. In a causal chain from renewed operation of TMI–1 to psychological health damage, the element of risk and its perception by PANE's members are necessary middle links. We believe that the element of risk lengthens the causal chain beyond the reach of NEPA." (Emphasis in original.)

Such a rationale was and probably is prudent for the vast majority of EISs prepared by federal agencies. However, increasingly we find that hazardous technologies that have associated with them the possibility of low probability/high consequence events (i.e., highly improbable catastrophes) are squarely on the public policy agenda and are proving troublesome to the public and to decision makers. As such, insisting that assessments of psychological impacts be related to improbable accident scenarios and not to the risk or perceived risk of such a scenario is a valid requirement. However, exempting such concerns from the NEPA process entirely is probably invalid. Recent analyses of the health and environmental impacts of disposing of M55 rockets filled with a chemical nerve agent have examined both normal or routine operations and accident scenarios, and psychological impacts of both scenarios have been identified on a qualitative basis (Carnes 1985). Less than a year after the TMI-1 restart decision, the City of New York sued the U.S. Department of Transportation over the shipment of radioactive materials through its jurisdiction in part on the basis of the Department of Transportation's own assessment of the impacts of highly improbable accident scenarios (City of New York v. United States Department of Transportation, 1984). Although these and other analyses do not guarantee a certain relationship between the federal action and environmental consequences, the court's decision in Met Ed v. PANE is cause for concern if it means that an environmental impact statement (EIS) need not be prepared if that certainty does not exist (Mandelker 1984). Federal courts have already found that the risk of environmental damage is sufficient to initiate the preparation of an EIS, even if the consequences are not certain. Furthermore, the CEQ's recent rulemaking on the preparation of EISs regarding worst-case analysis indicates that federal agencies are responsible to bound their analyses with a scientifically valid and defensible range of accident scenarios for projects involving low probability/high consequence events (CEQ 1986). The psychological and social well-being impacts of such events are surely a part of the required analysis in such cases.

A third critical element of the Supreme Court's decision on the TMI-1 restart case, and one which overturned the majority opinion at the circuit court level (PANE v. NRC) concerned the relevance of the accident at TMI-2. The District of Columbia Circuit Court noted that it "cannot believe that the psychological aftermath of the March 1979 accident falls outside" NEPA. The Supreme Court, on the other hand, found that:

... NEPA is not directed at past accidents and does not create a remedial scheme for past federal actions. It was enacted to require agencies to assess the future effects of future actions.

The Supreme Court's admonishment to disregard the TMI-2 accident in any consideration of future licensing for TMI-1 seems incredible. Adopting a *tabula rase* approach simply violates good science and certainly would not be tolerated in "conventional" impact assessments. For assessments of the psychological and community well-being impacts of restarting TMI-1, such an admonition is tantamount to assuming that the accident never happened. Litigation would be swift and sure if an agency were to ignore the seismic history of a region in its assessment of future seismic activity for the construction of seismically sensitive facilities; assessments of impacts on ecologically sensitive areas that did not take into consideration such sensitivity would be thrown out of court; health assessments that assumed that all members of a population were no more sensitive than a healthy 160 pound man would be deemed unprofessional by biologists and epidemeologists. In short, the Supreme Court erred seriously with respect to this part of its analysis. The citizens in the TMI vicinity experienced the accident at TMI-2 and incorporated that experience into their cognitive structures. For some of them, the accident reaffirmed their belief that nuclear power was and is safe because no casualties occurred; for others, however, the "impossible" accident occurred and seriously threatened their personal and financial security; for most of the population, the accident served as a signal value and may have enhanced their understanding of nuclear power and appropriate behavior if a future accident occurs. However, in no way should the accident at TMI-2 be divorced from considerations of the future of TMI-1.

Finally, the Supreme Court argued that consideration of psychological impacts would place an undue burden on the NRC and that such concerns were outside the charter of the NRC. Although the Court is certainly correct that NRC's primary duty is to protect public health from the adverse consequences from exposure to radiation, it seems inappropriate for the court to conclude that impacts outside the scope of an agency's charter should be ignored during the NEPA process. Such guidance, applied for other issues and settings, indicates that the NRC could ignore adverse impacts on aquatic species from the thermal effects of cooling waters, that the Department of Energy could ignore the possible health effects of its hazardous wastes, that the Department of

Interior could ignore the socioeconomic impacts of boom towns caused by coal development on federal lands in the Northern Great Plain. The court may be correct in assuming that existing resources at the NRC were and are insufficient to address psychological impacts, but that is not a persuasive reason why the NRC should not be required to address the issue when it arises, particularly for the NRC and other agencies confronting hazardous technologies characterized by the possibility of low probability/high consequence accidents. The implications of this argument are that Congress and the Office of Management and Budget (OMB) may well have to reconsider existing statutory and budgetary commitments and amend them where necessary. In fact, former Administrator William Ruckelshaus initiated an Administration-wide effort to consolidate risk assessment activities prior to his recent departure from the EPA; such an initiative may well lead to such reconsideration. In short, however, the court erred in its conclusion that since psychology was outside the expertise of the NRC, it was not responsible for assessing the psychological impacts of restart.

The extant analysis does, we believe, identify the kinds of psychological and community well-being impacts that could occur with restart. These impacts derive from a reasonably exhaustive consideration of the literature on natural and technological hazards and disasters, sustained discussions with many affected publics in the region, and an ethnographic characterization or profile of the region. While our heuristic model of TMI-1 restart impacts is not unique, it both incorporates the relevant empirical evidence and offers a plausible structure for the consideration of psychological and community well-being impacts of restart or no restart. Our work may not satisfy the requirements for tort litigation (i.e., proximate cause), but it satisfies the NEPA's requirements to assess the impacts as well as is reasonably possible, had the Supreme Court decided to require such an assessment.

This Supreme Court decision and this research also demonstrates a need to evaluate the environmental impacts, including psychological and community well-being impacts, of alternative futures associated with federal actions involving low probability/high consequence facilities (or other highly uncertain sociotechnical decisions such as nuclear war, the carbon dioxide problem, or recombinant DNA); that is, what are the expected environmental impacts associated with normal operations, a minor accident, and a catastrophic accident involving a risky facility or operation. Such an analysis, including the probabilities associated with each scenario, would be responsive to CEQ's recent proposed rule and would provide decision makers with sufficient understanding of the implications of alternative decisions to make their decisions cognizant of average or maximum net expected losses or gains resulting from their decisions. This approach necessarily entails greater costs than currently incurred, of course, but many of these costs are already being incurred in Safety Analysis Reports (SARs) and similar documents (e.g., probabilistic risk assessments). Other incremental costs would be incurred, however, in terms of integrating all of these probability and consequence analyses far more than has been the norm. More important, such an approach may well demonstrate to the public that government agencies are sensitive to the risks of technological facilities, thereby ameliorating some anticipatory psychological impacts, as well as enhancing the institutional credibility of government and industry.

Scoping via Focus Groups

This research may also point to some possible improvement in the NEPA analysis in terms of some of the methods employed. Specifically, using focus-group discussions may have use in other NEPA analyses and, more important, point toward an alternative philosophical approach to impact analysis. First, and as we have noted elsewhere (Soderstrom *et al.* 1984), such an approach allows both the analyst and the decision-maker to bound the problem from a public policy perspective. Opposing interest groups can and will identify what they think are the relevant issues at conflict, thereby focusing the attention of the analyst and the decision-maker on socially relevant concerns. While this does not obviate the need for an objective, outside analysis (i.e., in case the interest groups have not identified all potential environmental impacts of interest, it is important to provide sufficient expertise to do so), it does respond to CEQ regulations to "scope" the issue correctly so that decision-makers are confronted with substantial information about real issues rather than "laundry lists" or boilerplate material on the insignificant issues.

Second using focus-group discussions points to a more participative approach in environmental impact assessment in which additional opportunity is provided to validate the assessment. Although the current regulations regarding the preparation of EISs stipulate the preparation of a draft EIS (DEIS) for public comment prior to the preparation of a FEIS, incorporating focus groups for the identification of potential impacts *and* mitigation prior to preparation of the DEIS allows an earlier validation, resulting, hopefully, in fewer cases of egregiously bad analysis and/or litigation. As noted by Friesema and Culhane (1976), *local* experts and *local* people are the ones who can interpret the impacts of a given project in the context of a *local* environment. To be sure, nonlocal experts and decisionmakers must also participate in the analysis; but without the benefit, early on, of local perspectives, some of the analysis probably will be erroneous. CEQ's guidance on scoping in 1978 is in the right direction, but in all too many cases public scoping meetings (i.e., open to the entire public) can result in an adversarial environment not conducive to increasing anyone's *understanding* of relevant issues.

Conflict Resolution

This research has also, we feel, pointed toward some avenues for conflict resolution that may be useful in other cases of controversial public policy. We have emphasized the importance of alternative sources of risk perception, the plurality of authority (leading, perhaps, to a vacuum of authority and responsibility), and the general dilemmas of multijurisdictional decisionmaking on issues affecting public health and the environment. While the TMI-1 restart issue is not totally analogous to other decision situations, it does point to the need for shared systems of authority when the actions taken by one political jurisdiction inevitably affect other, subordinate jurisdictions. Shared authority is undoubtedly more complex and difficult to administer than preemptive authority, but in some cases it may be essential to the promulgation of *any* decision that will be obeyed and respected. This may well be the case with nuclear power, in spite of the preemptive authority granted the federal government by the Atomic Energy Act, as this technology becomes increasingly regulated by nonfederal authorities (e.g., the State of California's successful suit to control nuclear power plant development on the basis of inadequate radioactive waste disposal policy and capacity; the shared powers approach of the Nuclear Waste Policy Act of 1982; state responsibility for low-level nuclear wastes).

The original and continuing intent of the EIS provisions of NEPA is to facilitate decisionmaking by acknowledging the intended and unintended consequences of federal actions. The meaning of the NEPA has evolved continuously since its passage. Various groups have intervened in the NEPA process throughout its relatively brief history, forcing federal agencies and the courts to reconsider the breadth and scope of the NEPA. The scientific community has simultaneously been called upon to document society's understanding of complex phenomena and controversial issues. The range of cognizable issues has grown apace, and scientists have developed new and more precise tools and methods for measuring environmental impacts. The NEPA and EIS could become important resources for use in resolving conflicts, as well as aiding decisionmaking by federal authorities. We believe that our efforts to understand the psycho-social impacts of TMI-1 restart usefully builds upon the law and could enhance its utility to society and decisionmaking.

Impact Mitigation

The traditional role of mitigation has been to prevent or ameliorate adverse consequences of a given action (CEQ 1978), and conventional impact areas have been addressed by suggesting measures to lessen demands on local systems or to increase local carrying or infrastructure capacities. In spite of this fairly straightforward characterization of mitigation, it does not comprise a sociotechnical "fix" that works or does not work. Mitigation may be thought of as both a product and a process, and the effectiveness of the mitigation process (the "who" and "how" of mitigation decisionmaking) (Carnes *et al.* 1982; Copenhaver *et al.* 1984) may be as or more important than the effectiveness of the mitigation product. Mitigation functions have evolved from purely anticipatory actions to prevent or correct adverse impacts (e.g., due to normal operating conditions) to include compensation for actual damages when abnormal or unanticipated events occur (e.g., a future accident). In addition, a monitoring program may also be necessary to discern unanticipated "normal" or nonextraordinary impacts that may require noncompensatory mitigation. Past experience indicates that many adverse impacts will be underestimated, will not be quantifiable, or will not become apparent until normal operations are underway (National Research Council 1984).

Effects of Psycho-Social Impacts on Mitigation Strategies

TMI has made profound changes in the way people perceive many things—nuclear power, NEPA, risky technologies, emergency planning—and in the way they react to such circumstances. Mitigation practices are also not immune to the changes brought about by TMI. This is partially a function of the unique circumstances of the TMI-1 restart decision, such as the prior history of the TMI-2 accident and subsequent events (e.g., venting, embrittlement, radioactive water at TMI-2); the interposition of dread and fear associated with the plant due to the accident; and the paucity of normal benefits associated with the facility (e.g., utility bill rebates, facility property taxes to local governments). The lack of opportunity for anticipatory mitigation combined with the difficulties of determining the type and extent of compensatory mitigation requires close attention to the developing case history regarding psychological stress impacts on populations surrounding an accident site.

While the decision of the Supreme Court in the TMI case has limited the role of psychological assessment under the NEPA to psychological impacts associated with physical environmental changes, psychological factors will likely continue to be litigated in the future (Hartsough and Savitsky 1984). These indications of public interest in psychological issues suggest that mitigation strategies take into consideration these types of concerns. In fact, we and others have suggested that in order to build the commitment necessary to plan and implement a successful mitigation strategy, the mitigation measures chosen should be developed in response to local public initiatives (Carnes *et al.* 1983; Fischhoff *et al.* 1980). Including the public in the decisionmaking process either through direct participation or keener attention to overtly expressed public concerns will affect the consequences of mitigation implementation and chances for agreeing on an acceptable level of risk. Failure to consider carefully public response, regardless of the legal position, can result in significant impacts on normal operation. In the extreme case, a legally permitted facility might be closed as was the case in Wilsonville, Illinois, where a hazardous waste landfill was closed without proof of significant health or environmental damage when the citizens became very concerned over a proposal to bring in PCBs from cleanup of sites outside the state (Bolch *et al.* 1978).

Many of the types of impacts considered in this study on TMI, particularly those involving social change or individual emotional states, are extremely difficult to quantify and to determine accurately their causality and temporality. Some of these impacts may be irreversible and may or may not be subject to mitigation. However, governments, in all countries of the developed world are being used to reduce or shift the risk borne by individuals. The current social order has evolved from a reliance by citizens on government for the solution of certain economic, social, and cultural problems to include pressures on government to mitigate almost every risk any individual might be asked to bear (Aharoni 1981). The evolution in EISs to address socioeconomic effects, aesthetic impacts, and broader public participation roles corroborates this point. The key to whether these factors as well as psychological factors can be addressed and considered for mitigation is the extent to which they can be reliably measured and quantified. The previous chapters indicate the extent to which we believe psychological factors can be considered at the present time.

Mitigation strategies can then be devised to address specific or perceived adverse impacts and/or to increase acceptance of the proposed action by various interested parties or the public. Chapter Four has summarized some potential mitigation measures, as identified in the focus-group discussions and in community profiling, which might be applied to specific concerns identified by the various segments of the public. These measures—including improved communication, public education, emergency preparedness, changes in decisionmaking, relocation assistance, job training, land use, and subsidies—attempt to address the range of concerns that must be met in reaching a socially viable position between the pro- and anti-restart interest groups and the vast majority of the population of the area that belong to neither group. An optimal mitigation strategy may be a combination of measures that seeks to address the basic concerns of all groups and also provides relief to particularly impacted population subgroups. If the mitigation strategy can also encompass the elements often found at opposite extremes in interest group belief—health protection and economic concerns, its success is more certain (Soderstrom *et al.* 1984). The participative approach to mitigation should ensure that those concerns most broadly shared by the public will receive first consideration in resolution of impacts.

Social Design in Technology Development

Finally, our research may point to the need to develop technologies that take into account the socio-institutional as well as technical and economic dimensions of society and societal needs. Recent work by Weinberg *et al.* (1984) and others to develop a system to design an "inherently safe reactor" (i.e., one that shuts down on the basis of laws of physics and chemistry and without requiring the intervention of man or machine) is a good beginning, perhaps, but it does not recognize that technologies are bundles of social, psychological, cultural, and political characteristics as well as technical, economic and engineering characteristics. If the production of methylisocyanate (or nuclear power, for that matter) requires a technology that precludes population settlements nearby, then such a technology needs to be developed. Although the advent of human factors engineering for nuclear power plants subsequent to the accident at TMI-2 may be a step in the right direction, it does not incorporate the human characteristics of the off-site population that a truly integrated technology design process would entail. Early incorporation of social, cultural, and political dimensions in technology design may be, ultimately the most effective mitigation strategy.

Implications for Hazard Management

The experience with the accident at TMI and the controversy surrounding restart have provided many important lessons for hazard management. A number of these lessons concern plant operations, accident prevention, and emergency response, and they are discussed in depth elsewhere (Perrow 1984; Fisher 1981; Nelkin 1981; Sills *et al.* 1982; Kemeny 1979; Copenhaver *et al* 1985). This section summarizes the implications of the restart issue for managing risky technologies.

Public Involvement in Hazard Management

The experience with restart is a prime example of the pitfall of managing in a veil of secrecy. Although the procedure to restart was itself handled in an open fashion, the legacy of elitism and secrecy that has dominated nuclear power development still prevailed in the public's mind. This was not a view simply of those attempting to prevent the restart. Opponents and proponents of restart shared at least one belief in common: many felt distrust in both public and private institutions charged with developing, operating and regulating nuclear technologies. A major source of this distrust has been the industries' isolationist attitude toward the public. Another is the feeling that the government is incapable of making decisions over nuclear power. While people may disagree over the outcomes of those decisions, all are frustrated with the lack of strong leadership in decisionmakers and the absence of a mechanism for reaching a defensible decision. As a result, people continue to believe that they are being excluded from participation in management even though this belief may be promoted by standard bureaucratic practices and not be deliberate action, deceit, or conspiracy.

Other large scale technologies with hazard potentials have also had a clandestine management history. Dams and reservoirs have been constructed through pork-barrel politics with little public involvement. These projects have, however, generated public controversy on grounds other than risk and potential catastrophe. Cost, displacement of people, and environmental loss are the frequent reasons for opposition. A major dam failure during the early development of hydroelectric power could have charted a different course for that technology as a result of public perceptions of the management of the technology. However, a major difference is seen in the signal value of the TMI accident in relation to public perceptions of nuclear power.

Similar processes can be observed at other sites where nuclear power is being debated. Power stations at Diablo Canyon (California), Indian Point (New York), Shoreham (New York), and Limerick (Pennsylvania), all face opposition. One common element in the opposition is the lack of trust people have in the managing organizations. Opponents distrust the ability to operate the technology safely. Supporters' distrust arises because of the inability of the utilities to overcome opposition and begin power generation.

Similar issues are likely to arise in the chemical industry as a result of the accident at the Union Carbide Corporation plant in Bhopal, India. Traditionally, the chemical industry has operated without much public or government scrutiny. Like TMI, the Bhopal accident has caused public awareness of the secretiveness within the industry, and the chemical industry will probably face an agonizing period of opening its hazard management programs to the public. Even instant involvement will not, however, result in automatic public acceptance.

Public Acceptance of Technology

In the book *Normal Accidents*, Perrow (1984) argues that the groups surrounding TMI reject nuclear power because they employ a "social rationality" in their thinking about technology. Unlike the risk analytic thinker or Herbert Simon's (1956) "bounded rationalist," Perrow argues that the fear of a catastrophe and the perception of a tightly coupled and complex system frames the public's view. By accepting the validity of this type of rationality, Perrow then argues that nuclear power is socially unacceptable because it cannot be made safer and low-cost alternatives are available.

This argument is sound if one accepts the premise that individuals and social groups have homogenous notions regarding a complex technology. While this may be true for basic cognitive processes, our research suggests that it is certainly not true for the beliefs that are outcomes of those processes. Unlike Perrow's public, we found the people surrounding TMI had very divergent views of nuclear power technology and its impacts on society. For a significant number, nuclear power is, in Perrow's terms, a simple (as opposed to complex) and loose (as opposed to a tight) system that can operate safely from both organizational and engineering viewpoints. This view was reinforced by the accident, which, according to this group, was controlled so as to result in no negative consequences. This is not to deny that another group residing near TMI shares some views of the accident with Perrow. They certainly feel a threat from nuclear power operations and distrust the ability of organizations to manage the technology. Perrow's analytic schema only partially accounts for these elements of public perception because chronic long-term effects also cause concerns, and not just the potential catastrophic accident. Moreover, the schema totally fails to explain the divergent perceptions found in the TMI situation which raises doubts as to its ability to explain interfaces between humans and technology.

Communication and Education

A major issue in hazard and risk management is the extent to which public education and communications are important in shaping human perceptions of risk and response to disaster. Our research on the restart issue confirms that communications play a major role in influencing public support and opposition to nuclear power. The communication process serves to reinforce beliefs and views within existing social groups. Communications do not appear to change perceptions of the risks or benefits of nuclear power. In this light, public education does not appear to have a promising future as a means of altering public support for and opposition to the technology.

In another sense, the accident and restart controversy started and has furthered the educational process about responding to an emergency. In general, the local population is far more knowledgeable about the accident hazards of nuclear power and appropriate emergency response actions than the public at large. This suggests that while education will not help nor hinder the development of risky technology, it can play a role in helping people to understand what can be done to respond to a potential emergency. For example, convincing some people that another accident will not occur if TMI is restarted is nearly impossible. However, educating the public that that accident will not resemble a hydrogen bomb and that sirens signal a potential accident at the plant is possible.

For example, following the accident, a program was started to educate and train citizens to monitor radiation during Krypton venting (Gricar and Baratta 1983). The major goal of the program was to rebuild public confidence in information about the risks of cleanup. There was no proof that the program did so and some evidence that it failed to change peoples beliefs (Key 1983). This is consistent with the results of our research, which suggests that involvement—not education—may affect beliefs.

Conclusions

This research provides further insight into the effects of hazard and perceived risk on individual well-being and on social change. The overwhelming evidence suggests that the restart issue will have no or at least no detectable effect on the communities and people in the vicinity of TMI. Several qualifications to this conclusion are warranted. First, it applies only to social groupings in the aggregate. Throughout the course of the research, individuals and groups were at least qualitatively affected by the proposed restart and the events surrounding restart. In our field work, we observed that a small number of people were distressed by the situation, but whether the restart issue was the cause of their condition was never clear. People were affected because they believed the decision would impact on the quality of their lives. Without restart, other issues probably would have demanded their attention. As such, restart was and will continue to be like other problems facing communities in general.

Second, unraveling the restart issue from the accident is difficult. The research suggests that many people fail to distinguish the two situations, or, at least, linked the accident with restart. The failure to make clear progress toward cleanup of TMI-2 confounds the problem. A comparison of analogies raised during the focus-group meetings underscores the point. To one individual, the two reactors were twins; the accident at TMI-2 was a precusor of what would happen at TMI-1. To another they were siblings; one does not kill a relative for the acts of another family member. Differentiating the restart from the accident, while feasible from a technical and administrative view, is difficult from a behavioral perspective.

Finally, demonstrating the effect of this issue on the development of society and infrastructure in the vicinity of TMI is difficult. Our analysis did not reveal any major indications that either the accident or restart would change life significantly for people of the area. Our conclusions suggest the area will continue to change with respect to the forces that normally affect social and economic change. The extent to which these normal forces enabled the original siting of the reactors at TMI as well as other developments in the region, in juxtaposition to the dramatic accident and subsequent events, will influence the impacts of restart is difficult to sort out. Those forces possibly served to mediate the impacts of the accident and could help negate impacts of restart. Although the situation at TMI has played a minor role in shaping people's lives, it cannot be labeled as a pivotal point in the social history of the region.

The impacts of the restart of the undamaged reactor at TMI can only be estimated in a manner bound by the limits of prediction in the behavioral sciences. Those limits do not allow precise estimates of effects. The remaining question concerning what will happen is essentially an empirical one. The ultimate answer will only be achievable through monitoring and analysis, which may never be realized, not because the answers would be particularly damaging to the agencies and the decisions at hand, rather, because it was more expedient to ignore the issue unless mandated by the legal system. TMI restart offers a unique opportunity for the government to make significant progress towards sorting out the relationship between hazardous technologies and social well-being. The Supreme Court decision did not negate the relevancy of this category of impacts. Indeed, different wording of the contention in which the impacts resulted from the activities of restart rather than the risk of an accident may have led to a different ruling by the court. The decision, as a result, protects the interests of agencies from what they perceived to be an undue burden. Those perceptions are somewhat inaccurate, but establishing when psycho-social impacts are important and when they are not is possible. In fact, in situations like restart, it is in the best interest of both the agency and the public to address this impact category. As a result of the ruling, the opportunity to establish a scientific basis for evaluating psycho-social impacts has been diminished. The work done to date provides valuable insights into the issue, but still leaves future questions concerning psycho-social impacts of hazard open to considerable debate.

Appendix A

Survey Data Tables Used in Analysis

Table A-1. Correlation Matrix of Variables in the Model, Correlation Coefficients.

	NACDIST	SES	FLS	NUKEATT	TMIATT	SENSITIV	CONCERN	FEAR	DISTRESS	FAMILY	COMMUNITY
NACDIST	1.00000	-0.02809	0.06810	0.00927	-0.13949	-0.23760	0.23069	-0.10466	-0.08508	-0.31744	-0.12244
SES		1.00000	0.23743	-0.06895	0.04442	0.04800	0.00463	0.05986	-0.05210	0.15422	-0.06819
FLS			1.00000	-0.01635	0.03888	0.08340	-0.01396	0.09697	0.08914	0.13299	0.00608
NUKEATT				1.00000	0.14609	0.00000	-0.14609	0.12719	0.06993	0.10149	0.06173
TMIATT					1.00000	0.56455	-0.39885	0.54105	0.23464	0.44464	0.32867
SENSITIV						1.00000	-0.43429	0.65847	0.33070	0.61518	0.30415
CONCERN							1.00000	-0.37442	-0.21413	-0.39943	-0.24498
FEAR								1.00000	0.26721	0.46116	0.29406
DISTRESS									1.00000	0.31974	0.22368
FAMILY										1.00000	0.29714
COMMUNITY											1.00000

Table A-2. Coefficients for Reduced, Semi-Reduced, and Structural Equations.*

	SENS	SENS	CONC	CONC	FEAR	FEAR	FEAR	DISTR	DISTR	DISTR	FAM	FAM	FAM	FAM	COMM	COMM	COMM	COMM
NACDIST	-.17		.23	.14							-.33	-.19	-.17	-.17				
SES																		
FLS	.08										.16	.10	.10	.09				
NUKEATT	.05																	
TMIATT		.53			.54	.25	.23								.33	.24	.22	.19
SENSITIV				.40		.52	.50	.33	.29	.25		.56	.51	.47				
CONCERN							-.06		-.09	-.08			-.14	-.13				
FEAR										.08					.16	.14	.10	
DISTRESS														.11			.13	.11
FAMILY																		.13
R^2	.08	.35	.05	.21	.29	.48	.48	.11	.11	.12	.13	.43	.43	.45	.11	.13	.14	.16
adj. R^2	.08	.35	.05	.20	.29	.48	.48	.11	.12	.12	.12	.43	.43	.44	.11	.13	.14	.15

APPENDIX A

Table A-3. Risk Perceptions of the TMI-2 Accident.

a. Perception of threat during accident

Group	% responding to extreme levels of threat perception	
	Very serious threat	No threat
0-5 miles	50	14
5-10 miles	50	11
10-15 miles	47	11
15-25 miles	28	21
25-40 miles	18	24
40+ miles	20	42

Source: Flynn, 1979.

b. Perception of personal safety during accident

Group	% of respondents frightened for their safety		
	Yes, very frightened	Yes, somewhat frightened	No, not at all
0-5 miles	29	23	47
5-25 miles	21	29	49
Statewide	12	22	64

Source: Field Research, June 1980.

c. Perception of the outcome of the accident

Group	% of respondents confident they would come out "OK"		
	Yes, very confident	Yes, somewhat confident	Not at all
0-5 miles	36	29	33
5-10 miles	39	30	29
Statewide	47	30	19

Source: Field Research, June 1980.

d. Perceived exposure to risk

Group	% believing they received a dangerous dose of radiation from the accident		
	Yes	No	Don't know
0-5 miles	14	60	25
5-25 miles	8	72	19
Statewide	4	79	10

Source: Field Research, June 1980.

Table A-4. Attitudes toward Coping Ability.

a. Feelings of helplessness during accident

Group	% expressing helpless feeling		
	Very helpless	Somewhat helpless	Not at all
0-5 miles	46	27	27
5-25 miles	45	29	24
Statewide	42	31	25

Source: Field Research, June 1980.

b. Attitudes toward emergency response effort

Group	% feeling satisfied that everything possible was being done		
	Very satisfied	Somewhat satisfied	Not at all
0-5 miles	27	31	38
5-25 miles	28	32	35
Statewide	28	30	36

Source: Field Research, June 1980.

Table A-5. Coping by Evacuation.

Group	Evacuation behavior: % of people who evacuated				
	Individuals		Households		
	Household heads	Total Individuals	All of the household	Only part of the household	No one in household
0-5 miles	65.5	58.9	42.2	18.7	39.0
5-10 miles	49.1	44.5	29.2	11.3	59.5
10-15 miles	32.7	32.3	21.2	10.8	68.0
15-25 miles	11.7	11.4	2.5	0.8	96.6
25-40 miles	3.1	2.5	2.4	1.7	95.9
40+ miles	0.8	0.6			

Source: Flynn, 1979.

Table A-6. Evaluation of Information Sources.

	Judged usefulness of various information sources and channels				
	Extremely useful	Useful	Of some use	Totally useless	OK
Sources					
NRC	27	30	25	11	8
Pennsylvania Governor	21	36	27	13	4
State Emergency Agency	14	26	27	22	11
Local Emergency Agency	11	25	27	27	11
Metropolitan Edison	2	9	18	60	11
Channels					
Radio	34	33	20	7	7
Local TV	33	34	20	9	6
National TV	26	29	25	15	5
Newspaper	17	33	31	14	6
National News Magazines	6	20	20	24	30
Relatives	9	21	21	40	8
Friends	7	23	27	38	5

Source: Flynn, 1979.

Table A-7. Disruption to Households.

Group	Percent of households with disruption		
	High disruption	Some disruption	No disruption
0-5 miles	36	43	21
5-10 miles	29	46	25
10-15 miles	24	46	30
15-25 miles	11	36	53
25-40 miles	4	17	79
40+ miles	1	22	77

Source: Flynn, 1979.

Table A-8. Attitudes toward TMI Management.

a. Reliability of Metropolitan Edison officials

Group	% of respondents evaluating Metropolitan Edison officials' reliability as an information source		
	Very reliable	Somewhat reliable	Not too reliable
0-5 miles	8	36	51
5-25 miles	6	38	50

Source: Field Research, June 1980.

b. Believability of Metropolitan Edison information

Group	% of respondents evaluating degree of believability		
	Very believable	Somewhat believable	Not too believable
0-25 miles	5	30	58
Statewide	16	33	46

Source: Field Research, March 1981.

Table A-9. Attitudes toward Nuclear Power.

a. General attitudes

Group	Degree of support/opposition for increased use of nuclear power		
	% favoring	% opposing	No opinion
0-25 miles	53	47	0
Statewide	52	45	3

b. Specific attitudinal measures

Statements	% agreeing with statement			
	Group	Agree	Disagree	No opinion
We will have to rely on nuclear power as an important energy source for many years to come	0-5 miles 5-25 miles Statewide	62 66 69	35 30 28	3 4 8
The Three Mile Island events showed that even in a major accident the science and technology of nuclear power was adequate to cope with the problems that arose before anyone was hurt	0-5 miles 5-25 miles Statewide	49 48 53	46 47 39	5 5 8
All nuclear power plants in the country should be closed down until the federal government knows more about the safety risks involved in them	0-5 miles 5-25 miles Statewide	44 39 42	52 58 53	4 3 4
All nuclear power plants should be shut down permanently, and no more should be allowed to be built	0-5 miles 5-25 miles Statewide	28 24 20	66 72 74	6 4 6

Table A-10. Information Credibility—Degree of Reliability and Believability of Selected Information Sources.

Reliability[a]			Believability[b]		
Source (in rank order)	% of respondents evaluating source as very reliable		Source (in rank order)	% of respondents evaluating source as very believable	
	0-5 miles	Statewide		0-5 miles	Statewide
Scientists from nuclear power industry	44	51	Doctor who is a radiologist	54	57
Scientists from universities and national laboratories	39	48	Scientists from universities and national laboratories	49	50
Nuclear Regulatory Commission	31	31	Scientists from nuclear power industry	48	45
Environmental protection organizations	27	31	Nuclear Regulatory Commission	37	25
State/local agencies and officials	11	9	Environmental protection organizations	31	30
Babcock and Wilcox officials	11	18	"Union of Concerned Scientists"	26	34
TV news editorials	10	12	Chief nuclear engineer for GPU	25	20
Antinuclear groups	8	6	Local government officials	8	4
Metropolitan Edison officials	8	12	Pronuclear groups	8	11
Daily newspaper editorials	5	9	Officers of Metropolitan Edison	5	16

[a]Field Research, June 1980.
[b]Field Research, March 1981.

Table A-11. Knowledge about Nuclear Power/TMI.

Measure	Group	% answering		
		Correct	Incorrect	Don't know
Number of plants at TMI	0-25 miles	33	56	11
	Statewide	22	58	20
Operating status of the plants	0-25 miles	50	35	10
	Statewide	48	30	22
Number of plants damaged in accident	0-25 miles	86	3	11
	Statewide	70	8	22

Source: Field Research, March 1981.

Table A-12. Level of Sensitivity to a Nuclear Accident.

Statements	% of respondents agreeing with statements	
	0- to 25-mile group	Statewide group
Disadvantages of nuclear power include		
The possibility of an accident	35	29
Fear and anxiety for those living near the plant	7	10
Possibility of radiation leaks	9	22
What frightens people about TMI now includes		
The possibility of another accident	34	34
The possibility of radiation exposure	16	35
It might blow up	3	4

Source: Field Research, March 1981.

Table A-13. Coping Ability.

Measures	% of respondents	
	0- to 25-mile group	Statewide group
Feel helpless with current situation at TMI	63	64
Feel TMI-1 has not been allowed to restart because it is too difficult to evacuate area in case of another accident	54	65
Are aware of improved emergency notification procedures	56	33
Feel that since the accident Metropolitan Edison has demonstrated competence	38	49

Table A-14. Concern over Other Issues.

Most serious problems facing area		
	% of respondents	
Problem[a]	0- to 25-mile group	Statewide group
TMI-related problems	24	3
Unemployment	23	35
Inflation/cost of living	22	25
Crime/law enforcement	17	18
Taxes/government	11	17
Poor roads	4	10
Drug/alcohol use	3	5
Education/schools	3	4
No problems	6	4

Problem[b]	0- to 5-mile group	5- to 25-mile group	Statewide group
TMI danger	55	27	3
Inflation/cost of living	22	31	33
Unemployment	20	28	41
Taxes/government	10	11	15
Crime/law enforcement	8	12	13
Drugs/alcohol use	6	6	8
Poor roads	3	5	13
Education/schools	2	4	6
No problems	4	3	3

[a]Field Research, March 1981.

[b]Field Research, June 1980.

APPENDIX A

Table A-15. Perceived Risks of Restart.

a. Likelihood of radiation exposure

Group	Belief in the chance of getting a dangerous dose of radiation from TMI		
	Yes	No	Don't know
0-5 miles	49	32	19
5-25 miles	41	39	20
Statewide	29	55	17

Source: Field Research, June 1980.

b. Perceived safety of TMI-1

Statements	% of respondents in agreement	
	0- to 25-mile group	Statewide group
All studies conducted since the accident show that the undamaged plant can be operated safely	48	63
No matter what the government, scientists, and company executives say, restarting any unit at TMI would not be a safe thing	50	46

Source: Field Research, March 1981.

Table A-16.   Attitudes toward TMI Restart.

Group	Approve of Unit 1 restarting during cleanup of Unit 2[a]		
	% approve	% disapprove	% no opinion
0-5 miles	49	46	5
5-25 miles	53	41	6
Statewide	51	41	8

Group	Approve of Unit 2 restarting after it is cleaned up and repaired[a]		
	% approve	% disapprove	% no opinion
0-5 miles	51	43	6
5-25 miles	59	36	5
Statewide	63	30	7

Group	Should the undamaged plant be allowed to operate?[b]		
	% yes	% no	% no opinion
0-25 miles	56	40	4
Statewide	47	40	13

[a]Source: Field Research, June 1980.
[b]Source: Field Research, March 1981.

Appendix B

Profiles of Functional Social Groups

Table B-1. Farmers—West.

Group characteristics	Changes after accident	Baseline	Restart	No restart	Mitigation
• In Newberry Township (30-35 farmers) and in Fairview Township in 5-mile radius (~15 of ~30 total working farms within 5-mile radius)	• Two-year effect on farmers market because of reluctance to consume local produce/livestock; however, intensity not severe	• Continued decline in political base due to increased residential/industrial development	• Increase in industrial growth takes more agricultural land, reducing % of population that farm	• Less growth because power not available; therefore, farmer % of population not reduced as much	• Preserving agricultural land most suited for farming[a,d]
• Mostly small farms (4-10 acres) raising crops and livestock for feed or dairy purposes (~15-30 head)	• Accident made them aware of nuclear power and what it entails	• Those favoring see this as retarding development	• Raise property values over time	• Political base not lessened as much	• Energy conservation credits to protect from rate effects[a,c,d]
• Marginal income because land not very productive and small size of farms	• Worry about waste from TMI-1; consider themselves "stewards of the earth"; also concerned about chemical leaks/hazardous material transportation	• Those against think health and safety most important but see rate effect on local businesses	• Lessened political base due to above	• More effort to conserve energy and to develop alternative energy source because of less power/rate increases	• Favorable home improvement loans to reduce potential property value damage due to reduced rehab[a,d]
• Farmers cautious; honest, conservative, caring, and close-knit community; white; own land and pass down through generations; not very vocal; tolerant of others' views	• Cost of power not the big issue — safety is, particularly with regard to wastes	• Continued rate increases affect consumer spending, layoffs, repossessions of homes	• Beneficial tax situation	• Movement toward custom cultivation (renting out farms) slower	• Prepare the media with formal discussions with affected parties[a,c]
• Social organizations include Farmers Union, Grange, FFA, 4-H Clubs, Farm Womens Club, Farm Show	• Possible effect on animals of particular concern — suspect higher number of abortions may be due to accident		• Less effort to conserve energy because of slower increase in power rates	• Farmers who operate smaller farms/dairying/other livestock generally favor no restart	• Clean up of TMI-2[a,b,c]
• Other social contact through direct visitation, local churches, government programs, local restaurants; "good neighbor" policy in times of need			• Not likely to out-migrate		
			• Most won't demonstrate but tolerate divergent views		

[a] Restart mitigation action.
[b] No Restart mitigation action.
[c] Suggested by interviewees.
[d] Suggested by interviewers.

Tables B-2. Retirees—West.

Group characteristics	Changes after accident	Baseline	Restart	No restart	Mitigation
• Predominantly native to the area	• Rate increases affected lifestyles by cutting off some recreation, clothing, and food purchases	• Few will leave the area	• Some may leave, most likely those who converted seasonal homes to permanent structures/have less family ties to area/live closest to TMI	• No reason to out-migrate	• Set up information process to provide undistorted flow of information[a,c]
• Many originally farmers; others industrial workers from when communities were more prosperous/more diverse than at present; some white-collar professionals who started settling in area through purchase of seasonal homes	• Tolerate different viewpoints	• Continued rate increases burden to those on a fixed income; use of conservation measures and cut off of nonessentials	• If industrial development broadens tax base, tax benefits to homeowners affect this group	• Taxes would be higher due to slower rate of industrial development	• Energy conservation credits to help those on fixed incomes[a,d]
• Proportion of retirees in population within 5-mile radius on west side ~10% and decreasing	• Some no longer use the Goldsboro recreational facilities	• Some believe any decision better than no decision	• Generally indifferent or slightly against restart	• Property values would be less, and less home repair likely	• Some subsidy for home repair through grants/loans[b,c]
• Most own homes and some also own other property investments	• Minority group favoring restart believed Denton giving straight story but not Metropolitan Edison, rest of NRC, or the media		• Lack of faith in Metropolitan Edison's ability to run TMI		• Current state tax credits for real estate taxes could be expanded[b,c]
• Social interactions through senior center, churches, direct visitation			• Of those most negative, safety and health primary concern/tend to live closest to plant/generally were evacuated during accident		• Short-term relocation assistance[a,c]
• Political involvement less than representative proportion of population			• Heightened sense of anxiety over unscheduled events and alerts		• Revision of emergency evacuation plan[a,c]
• Size of group decreasing due to attrition and more newcomers moving in			• Minority group favors restart/did not evacuate/view media as culprit but question credibility of Metropolitan Edison and NRC		• Improve warning system for alerts[a,c]
					• Cleanup of TMI-2[a,b,c]

[a] Restart mitigation action.
[b] No restart mitigation action.
[c] Suggested by interviewees.
[d] Suggested by interviewers.

Tables B-3. Other Long-Time Residents—West.

Group characteristics
- Largest group in 5-mile radius (~40% of population)
- Over 1/2 born in the area
- Head of households aged 30s to 60s, with most 50-60
- Family size 2-3 children, most now high school age or beyond
- White collar professionals in local, state, and federal government, local business people, blue-collar workers for industries and utilities; middle to upper middle-income brackets
- Most own homes and many own businesses
- Extensive family ties; church activities, fire company activities, Lions Club, Womens Club, special community events, direct visitation via dinner parties
- Almost 2/3 actively involved in community politics and have been in control both at the township and borough levels for many years

Changes after accident
- Goldsboro developed a negative image (media-generated)
- Believe media has sensationalized the accident and subsequent incidents
- Most did not evacuate during accident

Baseline
- Goldsboro residents may out-migrate due to declining business, negative image, and conditions
- Some concern about letting TMI-1 sit and then restart; see this as increasing chance of accident due to corrosive agents in piping
- Continued rate increases, industrial development, and real estate value increases

Restart
- Substantial support
- This group because of their involvement in politics are more likely to place their faith in any decision government makes
- Would not out-migrate, but but still concerned about evacuation plans
- Believe that if TMI-1 restarted, it will be one of the safest plants in operation thereafter
- Feel a reliable power source is essential to industrial development
- Expect favorable result on electric rates
- Some of group opposed; fear repeat of accident/ little confidence in Metropolitan Edison/most concerned about safety
- Increased industrial development, jobs, tax base, and property values very beneficial to this group
- Some negative impact on Goldsboro businesses (?)

No restart
- Continued increase in values and real estate values
- Less positive effects on local business people
- Less negative effects on Goldsboro businesses (?)
- Higher taxes paid by homeowners

Mitigation
- Increasing type and amount of energy conservation credits?
- Preparing the media with formal discussions between Goldsboro residents, Metropolitan Edison, and the press?
- Development of a local chamber of commerce to promote area to industry?
- Liberalization of tax credits at state level?
- Revise emergency evacuation plan?
- Improve the warning system for alerts?
- Public education programs on nuclear power?
- Raise operation standards for TMI?
- Provide for public participation?
- Job placement services for TMI workers?
- Clean up of TMI-2?

[a] Restart mitigation action.
[b] No restart mitigation action.
[c] Suggested by interviewees.
[d] Suggested by interviewers.

Table B-4. Newcomers, Harrisburg Suburbanites—West.

Group characteristics	Changes after accident	Baseline	Restart	No restart	Mitigation
Immigration from Harrisburg to northern Newberry Township (some in Fairview)	Tighten bonds between these groups/more group cohesion	No decision would be viewed by the extremely opposed as a symbolic victory	Some with young children and no extended family ties to area will out-migrate from the 5-mile radius zone	No need for out-migration	Short-term relocation assistance.
Higher-status residential areas with housing units varying from $50,000 to $175,000	People become more politically active/attendance at public meetings increased as did voter turnout	Political involvement would continue to decline, with corresponding decrease in social cohesion	Increased political activity, demonstrating, signing petitions, protest meetings, in the short run	Slower growth in real estate values, industrial development, fewer jobs, reduced property values, less tax base diffusion	Improvements in energy conservation credit programs.
In 30-55 age group, with majority in 30s	Newberry Township [TMI] Steering Committee formed to disseminate information and to study effects of accident on residents		Short-term negative impact on real estate values		Subsidization of home improvement programs to help stabilize property values.
Almost all homeowners, many first-time, with small families (2 or less children of pre-school or primary school age)	Increase in number of domestic incidents that have required a police call (connected?)		Higher property values in new developments in the long run		Effort to liberalize tax credits for homeowners by the state.
White collar professionals employed in Harrisburg area with federal and state governments (often major industries (often high technology); high degree of job mobility due to job transfers	Were generally indifferent to nuclear power before accident and accepted that nuclear power basically beneficial		Range of opinions from moderately in favor to extreme opposition		Revise emergency evacuation plan.
No extensive family ties in area for most	Some evacuated during accident		Those opposed concerned about health and safety/erosion of public trust in Metropolitan Edison, and government/have young children, knowledge of available job opportunities outside area, no family ties to area/generally want TMI-2 cleaned up before TMI-1 is considered for restart/generally believe the media before government/Metropolitan Edison		Revise school evacuation plan.
Social participation centered on family-oriented activities such as PTO, kids sports, neighborhood parties, organizations such as Golf Club, Women's Club, Community Associations	Find the siren system and method of alerting people obnoxious; keeps people in constant fear because sirens used for fire alarms a lot		More moderately opposed think restart would have long-term positive effects on industrial development provided period of safe operation/do not trust or believe Metropolitan Edison would not evacuate because of family ties to area		Prepare the media with formal discussions with affected parties.
No extensive family ties in area for most	A fear of evacuation is common regardless of where the people stand on the restart issue		Those in favor concerned more with economics/believe restart will increase industrial development and hold down rate increases/concerned about Metropolitan Edison's ability to provide dependable information/feel government has the ability to make decision about TMI-1/condemn the media coverage of the accident and subsequent events		Clean up of TMI-2.
Churches do not play prominent role; most residents go to church outside the area					New management for TMI.
Political participation not very high; most vote but not very active, particularly the younger group members					Raise operation standards at TMI.
					Job placement services for TMI workers.
					Retrofit TMI unit for other energy source.
					Provide for public participation.
					Establish clear decision-making lines for authority.

'Restart Mitigation Action.
'No Restart Mitigation Action.
'Suggested by interviewees.
'Suggested by interviewers.

Table B-5. Other Newcomers—West.

Group characteristics	Changes after accident	Baseline	Restart	No restart	Mitigation
• This group 18-20% of total population in 5-mile radius. More highly concentrated in Lewisberry (25% of total pop.) and new-development areas located in southern Newberry Township. Also live in the boroughs of York Haven and in mobile home parks distributed within a 10-mile radius of TMI	• TMI first issue for many in which organization was formed to actively oppose something, decreasing over time as apathy toward TMI has set in • Increased already high voter turnout • No substantial out-migration	• Political participation would decline • Rate increases would continue to conserve and efforts made to conserve and cut back on nonessentials • Real estate values likely to increase some • Continuation of industrial development — more jobs, bigger tax base	• Range from moderately favorable to moderately unfavorable • Those in favor think industrial development will proceed without it but will be enhanced with it/think rate increases will slow down/do not see any real estate effects attributable to TMI/believe Metropolitan Edison can improve its severely damaged credibility with better information, public relations and a period of safe operation/maintain faith in government authorities (trusted NRC during accident)	• Continual decline in political participation • Rates and real estate same as no decision • Industrial development slower than no decision or restart: less jobs, less new residential development, lower property values, and no increased tax benefits	• Revise emergency evacuation plan, including schools' evacuation plans • Improve warning system for alerts • Home improvement loans • Job placement services for TMI workers • Provide for public participation • Clean up of TMI-2 • New management for TMI
• 50% are blue-collar who work in the York areas, some for utility companies and some in clerical jobs, some own small businesses in the boroughs, some white-collar positions as teachers, ministers, local civil servants	• Those in favor see media coverage as aggravating the various responses made by those indifferent or opposed		• Those indifferent somewhat same as above plus concern over the workability of evacuation plan and some concern over the effects of low-level radiation on human health		
• Incomes range from lower middle to upper middle income bracket					
• Most own homes, whether house or mobile home					

Table B-5 (continued).

Group characteristics	Changes after accident	Baseline	Restart	No restart	Mitigation
• Generally have lived in areas 5-14 years, more stable in community in terms of job (not transferred as other newcomers)			• Those opposed most concerned about health and safety, particularly health effects on their children/unconvinced about safe operating conditions of TMI-1/constant reminders of Metropolitan Edison handling of unscheduled events and alerts, many afflicted with "flight" syndrome/presence of growing children deterring migration		
• Family size 0-5 children (average:2), most under 14 years of age (age group 5-11 largest proportion)					
• Extensive family ties in area not common for this group, moved here for slow pace and friendly neighborhood atmosphere			• Increased political involvement largely limited to signing petitions and attending meetings		
• Several interactions through churches, school activities/sports activities for youngsters, bars, and fire company activities for blue-collar group/political and community meetings for the white-collar group			• Rates would likely decrease or at least stabilize		
• Favorable attitude toward growth			• Industrial expansion more rapid, more jobs, more residential development, higher property values and more tax benefits		
• Voter participation high but not too actively involved in community affairs					

[a] Restart mitigation action.
[b] No restart mitigation action.
[c] Suggested by interviewees.
[d] Suggested by interviewers.

Table B-6. Transients—West.

Group characteristics	Changes after accident	Baseline	Restart	No restart	Mitigation
• Group makes up less than 4% of population in the 10-mile-radius. Most live in boroughs of Goldsboro and York Haven and a few in the mobile home parks	• Most of the people not in the area at time of accident	• Overwhelming response of this group would be a lack of response	• Rate relief might provide more income for social activities	• Some would increase level of political participation to promote a restart/voting and signing petitions	• Some short-term relocation assistance[a,d]
• In lowest income strata — 70-80% are unemployed or on relief, other 20-30% work in low-paying blue-collar jobs that are seasonal or part-time	• Rate increases affect their income and social opportunities	• Increasing industrial development could impact this group if a movement of blue-collar industry into area occurs by increased job opportunities	• Increased industrial development offers increased job opportunities, which, in turn, could lead to changes in lifestyle regarding livelihood, property ownership, etc.	• Slower industrial growth and thus less job opportunities, increasing their transiency	• Expand job training programs in area[a,d]
• Age group mostly 20-30s, with larger family sizes (2-4 children)	• Largely indifferent to TMI		• Short-term political participation by transients opposed to restart; however, restricted to few with young children who have lived in area for several years		• Clean up of TMI-2[a,b,c]
• Almost all rent homes	• Those who did evacuate had young children		• With rising property values and faster residential development, more displacement of transients would occur due to rising rents and conversion to owner-occupied dwellings		
• Family ties in area are not extensive					
• Social activities: meeting at local drinking establishments, the post office to pick up mail, and direct visitation with immediate neighbors, parties — some through church and school PTOs					
• Group as whole not politically active but recently had 1 member on borough council in Goldsboro and some involvement with the planning commission					
• Turnover averages between 6 months and 1 year					
• Viewed in negative terms by members of other groups in some community: as troublemakers, poor rental prospects, criminal element					
• Indifferent attitude toward growth					

[a] Restart mitigation action.
[b] No restart mitigation action.
[c] Suggested by interviewees.
[d] Suggested by interviewers.

Table B-7. Old Middletowners—East.

Group characteristics	Changes after accident	Baseline	Restart	No restart	Mitigation
• This group of about 4300 comprised of professionals, white-collar and blue-collar workers – professionals include doctors, lawyers, accountants, school teachers/administrators (most live in the second ward). About 300 family businesses in area. Blue-collar workers work in nearby industries.	• No known residents moved as result of accident	• Out-migration highly improbable	• Out-migration highly un-likely even for those opposed to restart due to strong family and economic ties	• Less income for businesses as spending patterns likely to become more conservative	• Stress management training given to community leaders and other interested citizens.¹
• Have lived in community all their lives, have strong commitment to the town and value its heritage/conservative Republicans who hold traditional beliefs in free market and family values/provide jobs, goods, and services to local residents	• Some indicate no change after accident	• Current growth patterns will continue	• One group strongly believes the accident occurring without anyone injured indicates there is nothing to fear in restart/have low sensitivity to a second accident at TMI/distrust the NRC and the government's handling of post-accident events, but believe that Metropolitan Edison can operate the plant satisfactorily/some belong to F&F	• Borough of Middletown may face serious economic effects if a no-restart decision forces Metropolitan Edison into bankruptcy...taxes raised to maintain municipal services because of losses when town loses much reduced power price from Metropolitan Edison/electric rates would also rise	• Improve communications between group and NRC and Metropolitan Edison, particularly on emergency preparedness.¹
• Traditionally have participated greatly in borough political and social affairs/wealthiest members of community in this social group/social interaction, function of family and school ties, location, and class/social organizations include Elks, Rotary, Lions, Women's Club, and Civic Club	• Of those who changed social and political patterns of interaction, some helped organize either PANE (People Against Nuclear Power) or F&F (Friends and Family for TMI)	• No change in level of political activity – however, will lose some political power to newer members of community	• Second group strongly fears nuclear power and TMI as dangerous to health and oppose restart/highly distrust both NRC and Metropolitan Edison and feel Metropolitan Edison is not capable of operating TMI-1 safely/some belong to PANE/demonstrations likely from this group	• F&F is likely to petition the borough council to ask for reconsideration and to file litigation against NRC for reconsideration	• Police forces given positive crowd management training.¹
• Own their homes, some also own businesses and/or rental property			• Third group thinks TMI-1 should restart, but only after cleanup of TMI-2 facility/believe power is needed/distrust Metropolitan Edison and its ability to operate safely and think cleanup would demonstrate that Metropolitan Edison is trustworthy and capable of successful operation		• Assist elderly residents in applying state tax assistance act.²
• Age distribution in Old Middletown somewhat older than rest of Midtown			• PANE will likely file litigation for reconsideration of decision		• Middletown Chamber of Commerce and other business interests assisted in promoting economic development opportunities and attracting new industries.¹
• Were supportive of nuclear facilities on TMI, particularly since directly affected by emissions from coal-fired plant replaced			• Rate of economic growth greater – business owners more likely to profit. High and middle income residents, whose property appreciates, be impacted positively		• Relocation and job training assistance for unemployed TMI workers.¹
					• Assistance to senior citizens in selling homes to move into retirement homes.¹
					• Prepare media with formal discussions with affected parties.²
					• Public education programs on nuclear power.¹
					• Improve the warning system for alerts.²
					• Crowd management training.²

¹Restart mitigation action.
²No restart mitigation action.
ᵇSuggested by interviewees.
ᶜSuggested by interviewers.

Table B-8. Black Population—East.

Group characteristics	Changes after accident	Baseline	No restart	Restart	Mitigation
• Most of the blacks in the study area live in Middletown's first ward (a black single-family-dwelling neighborhood or Genesis Court housing complex (1000 blacks in Middletown)) • White-collar workers with state government in Harrisburg, federal government, or with local school system. Blue-collar workers at steel plant in Section or by federal and state government. Women work as domestics throughout area. Few blacks employed at either nuclear plant • 50 of blacks in single-family units own home. Genesis Court provides federally subsidized housing for poor community members, primarily female single parents who are welfare recipients • Though family ties are strong, those bonds tend not to cross the boundary between the 2 economic subgroups (middle class and poor). Middle class bond through participation in church activities, marriages, and common school activities. Genesis Court blacks tend not to participate in church or other group activities • Political power traditionally limited to voting, but black candidate for mayor in last election • TMI is not the most important public policy issue for blacks — by far more important are the health of the economy and employment opportunities	• Before accident, blacks not concerned with nuclear power or TMI. Now express deep concern for health and safety and fear home and property may be destroyed by a second accident			• Strong opposition to restart, particularly hostile are Genesis Court blacks (no jobs to lose since they have no jobs) • High sensitivity to another accident — highly concerned with adequacy of community's and school system's emergency evacuation plan if plan revised shortly after restart decision, political involvement likely to be temporary • Participation in protest activities likely	• Revise emergency evacuation plans for community and schools with participation from this group. Pay particular attention to adequate transportation since high percentage of blacks without private transportation.[a] • Public education programs by organizations other than NRC and Metropolitan Edison/retaining black scientists and leaders to participate to help ease fear[b] • Short-term relocation assistance.[c] • Improve the warning system for alerts.[c] • Expand job training programs.[c] • Retrofit TMI for other energy sources.[c] • Clean up of TMI-2.[c,d] • New management for TMI.[c]

[a]Restart mitigation actions.
[b]No restart mitigation actions.
[c]Suggested by interviewees.
[d]Suggested by interviewees.

Table B-9. Londonderry Township Long-Time Residents—East.

Group characteristics	Changes after accident	Baseline	Restart	No restart	Mitigation
• Approximately 1600 born and raised in Londonderry Township living throughout township	• No out-migration after accident	• No out-migration expected	• One group would like TMI-1 decommissioned and TMI-2 cleaned up immediately, view TMI-1 as threat to health and safety. Believe property values adversely affected. High level of sensitivity to second accident. Think Metropolitan Edison misrepresented safety and economy of nuclear power. Few of group belong to PANE or are otherwise politically active	• Few in group expected to participate in protest of no restart	• Housing relocation for few who leave[a]
• Most blue-collar workers in construction, large area industries (candy, steel, etc.) and small businesses in Middletown	• Shift in political power from newer residents of moderate or liberal views to long-time residents of more conservative views may or may not be associated with the accident			• Economic growth likely to be slower. Property values may decline or rise slowly	• Assistance to senior citizens in applying state tax assistance act[c]
• All white, most own homes and some own small number of businesses			• Second group for restart and some members of F&F, but believe restart only after TMI-2 cleaned up. Not sure Metropolitan Edison is capable of safe operation. Clean up would demonstrate that Metropolitan Edison is capable	• Less in-migration of newcomers will help maintain political balance for long-time residents	• Improved communications between group and NRC and Metropolitan Edison to reduce tensions, with particular attention to nuclear radiation effects on health[c]
• Strong values on rights of private property ownership					• Public education program on risks -- benefits of nuclear power[c]
• Very religious, many attend Geyer's Church. Strongly value traditional, family-centered relationships. Substantial intermarriage strengthens family ties			• Third group largely indifferent but would probably vote to close TMI-1 if proposition up for vote		• Additional law enforcement services[c]
					• Assist local Chambers of Commerce and other business interests promote area and attract new industries[c]
• Social interaction through family, church, youth-oriented activities, social and civic groups			• Highly improbable that even those opposed would out-migrate		• Relocation assistance and job training for dis- located TMI employees[c]
			• Those opposed unlikely to participate in protest demonstrations. Since TMI located in Londonderry Township, any demonstrations that do occur will probably take place in the township		• Comprehensive land-use planning[c]
• Not as politically active as the farmers but have substantial input into political decisions. Well informed on township policy issues					• Crowd management training[c]
			• In-migration likely to be accelerated, with more political power lost to new comers		• Clean up of TMI-2[a]
			• Restart likely to result in higher property values, more services causing higher taxes. Business owners profit as will high and middle income residents		• New management for TMI[a]
					• Provide for public participation[c]

[a] Restart mitigation action.
[b] No restart mitigation action.
[c] Suggested by interviewers.
[d] Suggested by interviewers.

Table B-10. Royalton—East.

Group characteristics	Changes after accident	Baseline	Restart	No restart	Mitigation
• Total population about 1000, primarily blue-collar workers at steel mill or army depot in New Cumberland. 20% elderly and retired on fixed income – most low-income	• Residents not concerned with nuclear power or TMI before accident and still not major issues in community	• Changes due to extension of water and sewer service rather than accident. Community leaders hope to encourage younger families with good income to settle there	• Some express desire to see TMI-1 closed but do not particiapte in PANE or participate in public meetings. Unlikely to participate in protests	• Relatively little effect – very few white-collar TMI employees in Royalton and the few blue-collar TMI workers would probably remain	• School evacuation plan can be revised to incorporate the concerns of some residents[a,c]
• Most all lifelong residents – many own homes			• Some employed at TMI (or have relatives or friends employed there)/have positive attitudes		• Revise general emergency evacuation plan
• Traditionally strong beliefs in rights of private property owners. Strong opposition to zoning, land use planning			• Some expressed concern over the adequacy of the school evacuation plan, particularly since school children must now leave the community to attend school		• Improve the warning system for alerts[a,c] • Expand job training programs[b,c] • Job placement services for TMI workers[b,c]
• Grocery store center for social exchange, as was school before it completely closed in 1981. Extended family ties and visitation with immediate neighbors			• Unlikely that the economic benefits from restart will significantly effect Royalton		• Crowd management training[a,c] • Retrofit TMI unit for other energy sources[b,c] • Provide for public participation[b,c]
• Political participation extremely low. The 8 Borough Council members and the mayor are Republican					• Clean up of TMI-2[a,b,c] • New management for TMI[a,c]

[a] Restart mitigation action.
[b] No restart mitigation action.
[c] Suggested by interviewees.
[d] Suggested by interviewers.

Table B-11. Farmers—East.

Group characteristics	Changes after accident	Baseline	Restart	No restart	Mitigation
• About 100 farms east of the river, primarily in Londonderry Township — 30 full-time farms (average 150 acres, mostly dairy, major crops corn and soybeans for livestock feed). 70 other farms provide supplemental income (less than 5 of which are owned by exurbanites who wanted to "go back to the land") • Full-time farmers all white and natives of township — part-time farmers also white but not all natives of township • Strong value is preservation of farm land • Native farmers highly cohesive social group with economic, political, and social interactions. Intermarriage and the sharing of educational experiences strengthens bonds • Prior to 1970s, farmers were the dominant political force in the township and controlled the board of supervisors. In-migration changed the balance of power but they remain a major political force in the township	• None are preoccupied with either TMI plant • Generally low level of sensitivity to another accident at TMI • Still maintain faith in government and nuclear power experts • Cost of power main issue, not health or safety		• Those with large farms regard nuclear power as relatively safe energy source • A few "back to the land" farmers have joined PANE and likely to participate in demonstrations • Both groups have ambivalent feelings toward Metropolitan Edison's management of TMI • Believe will minimize rate increases — chiefly concerned with costs of power • Increased industrial and residential development • Increasing farmland values may force marginal farmers out of business, concentrating ownership of agricultural lands in the hands of a few farmers • Increasing in-migration affects farmers' political influence more than baseline or no restart	• Retard in-migration • Property value may, in the short term, decline or remain stable • Slower industrial development	• Tax assessments based on present or best use rather than highest value would help ensure that productive farmland not lost to development[a,d] • County-wide comprehensive land use planning to reduce conflicts between competing interests[a,b,c] • Information on the radiation effects on agriculture and livestock from sources other than NRC or Metropolitan Edison[a,c] • Model energy conservation program on newer, more efficient agricultural practices[b,d] • Clean up of TMI[a,c,b,c] • New management for TMI[b,c] • Provide for public participation[a,b,c]

[a] Restart mitigation action.
[b] No restart mitigation action.
[c] Suggested by interviewees.
[d] Suggested by interviewers.

Table B-12. Residents of Newer Development—East.

Group characteristics	Changes after accident	Baseline	Restart	No restart	Mitigation
• The 5000 persons residing in the newer developments are a diverse group but share important socio-economic characteristics: live-in housing built after World War II, those desiring urban suburban setting settled in northern part of Middletown (third ward), those desiring rural setting chose Londonderry Township • Both white-collar (Penn. State University facility members, state government employees, teachers, professionals, Metropolitan Edison managers, small business owners) and blue-collar workers (AMP, Inc., steel mill in Steelton, in construction, candy factories in Hershey) • Majority commute to jobs • More likely to be Democrats than are the other groups • High level of political activity and geographic concentration has given this group representation on Middletown's borough council and on Londonderry Township's board of supervisors • Exhibit strong concern for environmental protection, growth management, and land use planning • Level of group cohesiveness has traditionally been low • Social interactions within group around child-centered activities such as PTO and other youth activities. Level of social interaction less for this group than others	• Formation of 2 organizations — one pro (Friends and Family of TMI-F&F) one con (People Against Nuclear Energy-PANE) and considerable hostility apparent between the groups • Increased social cohesion, even though around more than one viewpoint • Increased political activity • Provoked wide range of opinion as evidenced under Restart-No Restart	• No out-migration expected • Participation rates in political and interest groups continue to decline, barring unusual events • Current pattern of economic growth continues • TMI operators may leave	• PANE group convinced nuclear power is unsafe and resultant radiation will cause long-term health problems • F&F group convinced it is safe and they are more likely to benefit economically because family's major breadwinner is more likely to be a TMI employee • Majority of this group belong to neither organization. Residents on both sides of these issues: safety of TMI-1, adequacy of both NRC and Metropolitan Edison's operations of plant, cost of power, perceived inadequacy of community evacuation plans, flight syndrome, alert sirens, mistrust in government, restart after cleanup of TMI-2 • Social interaction between subgroups will again become hostile and protests and/or violence may erupt • Some out-migration expected • Property values will rise in long run, further residential development and increased demand for community services • Potential political strength of group will rise	• When TMI-1 employees lose jobs, violence could erupt • Some blue-collar workers may find work decommissioning plant • This group not expected to join in protest demonstrations, except for TMI-1 employees and their families • Both PANE and F&F likely to remain organized until TMI-2 cleanup complete • Retard economic growth in area • Borough of Middletown may face serious economic effects if no-restart decision forces Metropolitan Edison into bankruptcy, taxes raised to maintain municipal services because of losses when town loses much reduced power price from Metropolitan Edison, electric rates would also rise	• Substantial revision of both the community and school evacuation plans with community participation.[a] • Encourage state and local governments to retain outside authorities to provide public education on health effects and benefits, risks of nuclear power.[a] • A central information facility to provide information to both citizens and news media.[a] • Job training and relocation assistance for displaced TMI-1 workers.[b] • All levels of government should intensify efforts to attract new industries.[b] • Short-term relocation assistance.[c] • Improve the warning system for alerts.[c] • Comprehensive land-use planning.[c,d] • Raise operation standards at TMI.[d] • Retrofit TMI unit for other energy sources.[d] • Clean up of TMI-2.[d] • New management for TMI.[d] • Establish clear decision-making lines for authority.[d]

[a] Restart mitigation action.
[b] No restart mitigation action.
[c] Suggested by interviewees.
[d] Suggested by interviewees.

Appendix C

Love Canal, Wilsonville, and TMI Comparisons

Table C-1.   Summary of Analogous Elements in Three Unique Situations.

	Love Canal	Wilsonville	TMI-1*
Type and Timing of Public Involvement			
Began when —	Physical signs of chemicals in yards, air (odor, irritant), and possible physiological damages were noted	Proposal to bring in PCBs from cleanup of sites outside state	TMI-2 accident, resulting in releases to environment
Prior public response —	No public problems, general acceptance of irritant, used to chemicals, general knowledge that area was used as a dump earlier	Opened and operated with public participating in the permitting process	Two units opened and operated with public participation in the licensing process; minimal problems or controversy
Ultimate response —	Major chemical emergency situation without accident or known casualties, high visibility resulted in national disaster, a first for this type of situation	Site closed down after legally permitted without proof of significant environmental or health damage	Restart of adjacent facility after serious accident considered
Major Concerns			
	Possible health effects from chemical pollution	Possible health effects from chemical pollution	Possible health effects from radiation
	Satisfaction with home/neighborhood gone	Irritation of trucks through town, eyesore	Satisfaction with home/neighborhood affected

Table C-1 (continued).

Love Canal	Wilsonville	TMI-1*
Major Concerns (cont'd)		
Housing values severely affected in center, not as serious at some distance		Fear that housing values would be affected
Economic issues — Many work with chemical industry; important to region's economy	Citizens did not perceive any economic benefit to individuals or community	Issues include the rising cost of power, less attractive to industry overall, important to region's economy
Institutional issues — Who's responsible — federal, state, local, and corporate	Became political issue on local and state level, "not in my backyard" syndrome	Who's in charge and who's responsible equally important
Role of Information		
Access to information random and convoluted	Access to some information by court order only; no large-scale public understanding and acceptance program as part of siting process	Information not given to affected residents first; not given full story*
Credibility of information, particularly on health effects, wildy conflicting, even from the official stances taken at various times by local, state, and federal government sources; major factor contributing to the escalation of this situation to crisis proportions	Did not believe the technical experts and overturned the permit in the courts on basis of this information's credibility	Local, state or federal officials in the area of nuclear power not trusted; may be the <u>key</u> element in successful restart

Table C-1 (continued).

Love Canal	Wilsonville	TMI-1*
Role of Information (cont'd)		
Feedback/communication minimal and resulted in confrontation tactics	More feedback/communication at siting stage might have prevented this situation, either by getting citizen support or not allowing the operation at all	Important in implementing restart
Mitigation and/or Closure		
Health testing		Health testing*
Environmental monitoring of chemical contamination	Environmental monitoring of chemical contamination	Monitoring of radiation levels*
Evacuate (most-affected only)		
Buy houses (most-affected only)		
Leveling/closing site	Closing site/exhuming wastes	Cleanup of TMI-2 accident
Civil suits regarding health and property issues	Civil suit to close site and exhume wastes	
More information still needed on health, final disposition of site, cleaner definition of warnings, emergency plans, and who's responsible for what	Same as Love Canal	Same as others with focus on TMI-2 accident*

*TMI-2 accident response (taken into consideration in TMI-1 restart).

Bibliography

Adams, B. 1964. Structural Factors Affecting Parental Aid to Married Children. *Journal of Marriage and the Family* 26:327–332.

Adams, B. 1968. *Kinship in an Urban Setting*. Chicago: Markham.

Aharoni, Y. 1981. *The No-Risk Society*. Chatham, N.J.: Chatham House Publishers.

Aiken, M. and D. Goldberg. 1969. Social Mobility and Kinship: A Reexamination of the Hypothesis. *American Anthropologist* 71 (April): 261–270.

Aldous, J. 1967. Intergenerational Visiting Patterns: Variation in Boundary Maintenance as an Explanation. *Family Process* 6:235–251.

Allport, F. 1955. *Theories of Perception and the Concept of Structure*. New York: Wiley.

Alwin, D. and R. Hanser. 1975. "The Decomposition of Effects in Path Analysis," *American Sociological Review* 40:37–47.

Anderson, J. 1968. Cultural Adaptations to Threatened Disaster. *Human Organization* 27/4 (Winter): 298–307.

Anderson, W. 1969. Disaster Warning and Communication Processes in Two Communities. *The Journal of Communication* 19/2:92–104.

Andrews, F. and R. Inglehart. 1979. The Structure of Subjective Well-Being in Nine Western Societies. *Social Indicators Research* 6 (1):73–90.

Andrews, F. and S. Withey. 1976. *Social Indicators of Well-Being: Americans Perceptions of Life Quality*. New York: Plenum Press.

Angell, R. 1936. *The Family Encounters the Depression*. New York: Scribner.

Aronson, E. 1972. *The Social Animal*. San Francisco: W.H. Freeman and Company.

Aschenbrenner, J. 1975. *Lifelines: Black Families in Chicago*. New York: Holt, Rinehart, and Winston.

Atkinson, T. 1982. The Stability and Validity of Quality of Life Measures. *Social Indicators Research* 10:113–132.

Babchuck, N. 1971. Primary Extended Kin Relations of Negro Couples. *The Sociological Quarterly* 12 (Winter): 69–77.

Baker, E. 1977. Public Attitudes toward Hazard Zone Controls. *Journal American Institute Planners* 43:401–408.

Bakke, E. 1949. *Citizens without Work*. New Haven, CT: Yale University Press.

Barton, A. 1970. *Communities in Disaster*. Garden City, NY: Doubleday and Company.

Bates, F., C. Fogelman, V. Parenton, R. Pittman, and G. Tracy. 1963. The Social and Psychological Consequences of a Natural Disaster: A Longitudinal Study of Hurricane Audrey. *National Hurricane Research Council Disaster Research Group* 18, Publication No. 1081. Washington, DC: National Academy of Science.

Battisti, F. 1978. Some Conditions for the Social Perception of Pollution in Environmental Disasters. *Mass Emergencies* 3(4):201–207.

Baum, A. and L. Davidson. 1985. A Suggested Framework for Studying Factors That Contribute to Trauma in Disaster." pp. 29–40 in B. Sowder, (ed)., *Disasters and Mental Health: Selected Contemporary Perspectives*. NIMH: DHHS Publication No. 85–1421.

Baum, A., R. Gatchel, and M. Schaeffer. 1983. Emotional, Behavioral, and Physiological Effects of Chronic Stress at Three Mile Island. *Journal Consulting Clinical Psychology* 51:565–572.

Baum, A., R. Fleming, and J. Singer. 1982. Stress at Three Mile Island: Applying Psychological Impact Analysis. In L. Bickman (ed.), *Applied Social Psychological Annual*, pp. 217–248. Beverly Hills, CA: Sage.

Baum, A., R. Gatchel, S. Streufert, C. Baum, R. Fleming, and J. Singer. 1980. *Psychological Stress for Alternatives of Decontamination of TMI–2 Reactor Building Atmosphere*. NUREG/CR–1584, Human Design Group for Division of Engineering, Office of Nuclear Reactor Regulation, U.S. Nuclear Regulatory Commission, Washington, DC.

Baumann, D. and J. Sims. 1978. Flood Insurance: Some Determinants of Adoption. *Economic Geography* 54/3:189–196.

Bell, B. 1978. Disaster Impact and Response: Overcoming the Thousand Natural Shocks. *The Gerontologist* 18:531–540.

Bell, C. and H. Newby. 1971. *Communities*. London: Praeger.

Berardo, F. 1967. Kinship Interaction and Communication among Space-Age Migrants. *Journal of Marriage and the Family* 29 (August):541–554.

Blaufarb, H. and J. Levine. 1972. Crisis Intervention in an Earthquake. *Social Work* 17:16–19.

Blundell, W. E. 1981. Firms Seek to Avert Boomtown Problems by Providing Services. *The Wall Street Journal*, August 12, 1981.

Bochner, A. 1976. Conceptual Frontiers in the Study of Communications in Families. *Human Communication Research* 2:381–397.

Bolch, B, R. Harbison, E. Hargrove, and B.Walter. 1978. *Hazardous Waste Management: Recommendations to the Commonwealth of Kentucky.* Nashville, TN: Vanderbilt University.

Bolin, R. 1976. Family Recovery from Natural Disasters: A Preliminary Model. *Mass Emergencies* 1:267–277.

Bolin, R. 1982. *Long-Term Family Recovery From Disaster.* Family Recovery Project, Final Report. NSF Grant No. PFR–8020231. Department of Sociology and Anthropology; New Mexico State University; Las Cruces, NM.

Bolin, R. 1985. Disaster Characteristics and Psychosocial Impacts, pp.3–28 in B. Sowder (ed.), *Disasters and Mental Health: Selected Contemporary Perspectives.* NIMH: DHHS Publication No. 85–1421.

Bolin, R. and P. Bolton. Forthcoming. *Race and Ethnicity in Disaster Recovery.* Institute of Behavioral Science Monograph. University of Colorado, Boulder.

Bolin, R. and P. Bolton. 1983. Recovery in Nicaragua and the U.S.A. *International Journal of Mass Emergencies and Disasters* 1:125–144.

Bolin, R. and D. Klenow 1983. Response of the Elderly to Disaster: An Age-Stratified Analysis. *International Journal of Aging and Human Development.* 16, No. 4:283–296.

Bolin, R. and D. Klenow. 1981. Response of the Elderly to Disaster: An Age-Stratified Analysis. Paper presented at the Meeting of the Midwest Sociological Society; Minneapolis, MN. April 1981.

Bolin, R. and P. Trainer. 1978. Modes of Family Recovery following Disaster: A Cross National Study. In E. Quarantelli (ed.), *Disaster: Theory and Research*, pp. 231–247. London: Sage.

Bossard, J. and E. Boll. 1946. The Immediate Family and the Kinship Group: A Research Report. *Social Forces* 24(4):379–384.

Bott, E. 1971. *Family and Social Networks.* New York: The Free Press.

Boyle, R. 1967. Path Analysis and Ordinal Data. *American Journal of Sociology* 75:461–480.

Bromet, E. 1980. *Three Mile Island: Mental Health Findings.* Pittsburgh: Western Psychiatric Institute and Clinic.

Brown, M. 1979. Love Canal and the Poisoning of America. *Atlantic Monthly* 244:33–47.

Burgess, E. 1926. The Family as a Unity of Interacting Personalities. *The Family* 7:3–9.

Burr, W. 1973. *Theory Construction and the Sociology of the Family*. New York: Wiley.

Burton, I. 1972. Cultural and Personality Variables in the Perception of Natural Hazard. In J. W. Wohwill and D. H. Carson (eds.), *Environment and the Social Sciences*, pp. 184–195. Washington, DC: American Psychiatric Association.

Burton, I. and R. Kates. 1964. The Perception of Natural Hazards in Resource Management. *Natural Resources Journal* 3:412–441.

Burton, I., R. Kates, and G. White. 1978. *The Environment as Hazard*. New York: Oxford University Press.

Burton, I. *et al.* 1965. The Shores of Megalopolis: Coastal Occupance and Human Adjustment to Flood Hazard. *Climatology* 18/3. Elmer, NJ: C. W. Thortwaite Associates.

Campbell, A., P. Converse, and W. Rodgers. 1976. *The Quality of American Life*. New York: Russell Sage.

Campbell, D. 1969. Reforms as Experiments. *American Psychologist* 24:409–429.

Campbell, R. and D. Fiske. 1959. Convergent and Discriminant Validation by Multitrait-Multimethod Matrix. *Psychological Bulletin* 58:81–105.

Cantor, M. 1979. Neighbors and Friends. *Research on Aging* 1:434–463.

Cantril, Hadley. 1963. A Study of Aspirations. *Scientific American* 208:41–45.

Carle, Remy. 1981. Why France Went Nuclear. *Public Power*, July-August: 58–60, 82, 85.

Carnes, S. A., et. al., 1985. *Preliminary Assessment of the Health and Environmental Impacts of Transporting M55 Rockets From Lexington-Bluegrass Depot Activity, Anniston Army Depot, and Umatilla Depot Activity to Alternative Disposal Sites*. ORNL–6198. Oak Ridge, TN: Oak Ridge National Laboratory.

Carnes, S., E. Copenhaver, J. Sorensen, E. Soderstrom, R. Reed, D. Bjornstad, and E. Peelle. 1983. Incentives and Nuclear Waste Siting: Prospects and Constraints. *Energy Systems and Policy* 7(4):323–351.

Carnes, S., M. Schweitzer, and B. Bronfman. 1982. *Community-Based Assessment and Planning of Energy Futures: Final Report of the Decentralized Solar Energy Technology Assessment Program*, ORNL–5879. Oak Ridge, TN: Oak Ridge National Laboratory. June.

Carver, C. 1966. Self-Awareness, Perception of Threat and the Expression of Reactions through Attitude Change. In R. Lazarus (ed.), *Psychological Stress and the Coping Process*, pp. 501–512. New York: McGraw- Hill.

Cavan, R. and K. Ranck. 1938. *The Family and the Depression*. Chicago: University of Chicago Press.

Chamberlin, B. 1980. Mayo Seminars in Psychiatry: The Psychological Aftermath of Disaster. *Journal of Clinical Psychiatry* 41 (July):238–244.

Church, J. 1974. The Buffalo Creek Disaster: Extent and Range of Emotional and/or Behavioral Problems. *Omega: Journal of Death and Dying* 5:61–63.

City of New York v. United States Department of Transportation, 715 F2d 732 (CA2, 1983), cert den 79 L Ed 2d 730, 104 S Ct 1403 (1984).

Clifford, R. 1956. The Rio Grande Flood: A Comparative Study of Border Communities in Disaster. *National Research Council Committee on Disaster Studies*. No. 7, Publication No. 458. Washington, D.C.: National Academy of Science.

Cobb, S. 1976. Social Support as a Moderator of Life Stress. *Psychosomatic Medicine* 5:300–314.

Cochran, N. 1979. On the Limiting Properties of Social Indicators. *Evaluation and Program Planning* 2:1–4.

Cohen, E. and S. Poulshock. 1977. Societal Response to Mass Dislocation of the Elderly: Implications for Area Agencies on Aging. *The Gerontologist* 17:262–268.

Coleman, J. 1957. *Community Conflict*. Glencoe, IL: The Free Press.

Cook, J. and D. Campbell. 1979. *Quasi-Experimentation: Design and Analysis for Field Settings*. Chicago: Rand McNally.

Copenhaver, E., J. Sorensen, and M. Adler. 1985. Organizational interactions in emergency planning for nuclear power plants. *Nuclear Safety* 26(3):273–285.

Copenhaver, E., S. Carnes, E. Soderstrom, J. Sorensen, E. Peelle, and D. Bjornstad. 1984. Review of Institutional and Socioeconomic Issues for Radioactive Waste Repository Siting. In P. L. Hofman (ed.), *The Technology of High-Level Nuclear Waste Disposal. Advances in the Science and Technology of the Management of High-Level Nuclear Waste*, Office of Nuclear Waste Isolation, Battelle; Columbus, OH; DOE/TIC–4621, Vol. 2.

Council on Environmental Quality. 1985. Amendment to 40 CFR, Part 1502 *Federal Register* 15618–15626 (April 25, 1986).

Council on Environmental Quality. 1978. *Regulations for Implementing the Procedural Provisions of NEPA*. 40 CFR Parts 1500–1508, November 29, 1978.

Crain, R., E. Katz, and D. Rosenthal. 1969. *The Politics of Community Conflict: The Fluoridation Decision*. Indianapolis: Bobbs-Merrill Company.

Cronbach, L. 1975. Beyond the Two Disciplines of Scientific Psychology. *American Psychologist* 30:116–127.

Cutter, S. and K. Barnes. 1982. Evacuation Behavior and Three Mile Island. *Disasters* 6:116–124.

Dacy, D. and H. Kunreuther. 1969. *The Economics of Natural Disasters*. New York: The Free Press.

Danzig, E., P. Thayer, and L. Galanter. 1958. *The Effects of a Threatening Rumor on a Disaster-Stricken Community*. Washington, DC: National Academy of Science.

Diggory, J. 1955. Some Consequences of Proximity to a Disease Threat. *Sociometry*. 19:47–53.

Dintzer, L. and E. Soderstrom. 1978. Making a Case for an Introduction between Quasi-Experimental Design and Social Impact Analyses. *Evaluation and Program Planning* 1:309–318.

Drabek, T. 1968. *Disaster In Isle 13*. Columbus, OH: Disaster Research Center, Ohio State University.

Drabek, T. 1969. Social Processes in Disaster: Family Evacuation, *Social Problems* 16(3):336–349.

Drabek, T. 1981. Commentary. In *Social Science and Natural Hazards*, J. D. Wright and P. H. Rossi (eds.), pp. 160–170. Cambridge, MA: Abt Books.

Drabek, T. and K. Boggs. 1968. Families in Disaster: Reactions and Relatives. *Journal of Marriage and the Family* 30 (August):443–451.

Drabek, T. and W. Key. 1984. *Conquering Disaster: Family Recovery and Long-Term Consequences*. New York: Irvington.

Drabek, T. and J. Stephenson. 1971. When Disaster Strikes. *Journal of Applied Social Psychology* 1:187–302.

Ducan,G. and J. Morgan. 1975. *Five Thousand American Families: Patterns of Economic Progress*. Ann Arbor, MI: Institute for Social Research.

Dupree, H. and W. Roder. 1974. Coping with Drought in a Preindustrial, Preliterate Farming Society. In G. White (ed.), *Natural Hazards: Local, National, Global*. New York: Oxford University Press, pp. 115–119.

Dynes, R. 1970. *Organized Behavior in Disaster*. Lexington, MA: Heath and Company.

Dynes, R. and D. Wenger. 1971. Factors in the Community Perception of Water Resources Problems. *Water Resources Bulletin* 7(4):644–651.

Eisner, R. and R. Strotz. 1961. Flight Insurance and the Theory of Choice. *Journal of Political Economy* 80:623–648.

Economic Adjustment Committee. 1981. *Community Impact Assistance Study*.

Washington, DC: Intergovernmental/Interagency Task Force on Community Assistance.

Elder, G. 1974. *Children of the Depression*. Chicago: University of Chicago Press.

Environment Reporter. 1978. Toxic Waste Landfill May Be Closed by Illinois County Court's Decision. In *Environment Reporter*, p. 696, August 25, 1978.

Erickson, P., T. Drabek, W. Key, and J. Crowe. 1976. Families in Disaster. *Mass Emergencies* 1:206–213.

Erikson, K. 1976. *Everything in its Path*. New York: Simon and Schuster.

Festinger, L. 1957. *A Theory of Cognitive Dissonance*. Palo Alto, CA: Stanford University Press.

Fiddle, S. 1979. Foundations for a Sociological Theory of Uncertainty. Paper presented at the Meetings of the Southwest Social Science Association.

Field Research. 1980. *Public Opinion in Pennsylvania toward the Accident at Three Mile Island and Its Aftermath*. San Francisco: Field Research.

Field Research. 1981. *Pennsylvania Public Opinion Relating to the Situation at Three Mile Island*. San Francisco: Field Research.

Fisher, D. 1981. Planning for Large Scale Accidents: Learning from TMI. *Energy* 6:93–108.

Fischhoff, B., S. Lichtenstein, P. Slovic, R. Keeney, and S. Derby. 1980. *Approaches to Acceptable Risk: A Critical Guide*. ORNL/Sub–7656/1, Oak Ridge, TN: Oak Ridge National Laboratory.

Fischhoff, B., P. Slovic, and S. Lichtenstein. 1981. Lay Foibles and Expert Fables in Judgments about Risks. In T. O'Riordan and R. Turner (eds.), *Progress in Resource Management and Environmental Planning*, Vol. 3. Chichester, England: John Wiley and Sons.

Flynn, C. 1979. *Three Mile Island Telephone Survey: Preliminary Report on Procedures and Findings*. Report presented to the U.S. Nuclear Regulatory Commission. Seattle, WA: Social Impact Research, Inc.

Flynn, C. and J. Chalmers. 1980. *The Social and Economic Effects of the Accident at Three Mile Island*. Springfield, VA: National Technical Information Service.

Flynn, C. *et al.* 1982. Socioeconomic Impacts of Nuclear Generating Stations. Three Mile Island Study. Prepared as part of Nuclear Regulatory Commission Post-Licensing Study. Seattle, WA: Mountain West Research, Inc., with Social Impact Research, Inc.; February.

Frederick, C. 1980. Effects of Natural vs. Human-Induced Violence upon Victims. *Evaluation and Change*, 71–75.

Fried, M. 1966. Grieving for a Lost Home. In J. Wilson (ed.), *Urban Renewal,* pp. 359–379. Cambridge, MA: Massachusetts Institute of Technology Press.

Friedsam, H. 1961. Reactions of Older Persons to Disaster-Caused Losses. *The Gerontologist* 1:34–37.

Friedsam, H. 1962. Older Persons in Disaster. In Baker and Chapman (eds.), *Man and Society in Disaster*, pp. 151–184. New York: Basic Books.

Friesema, H. and P. Culhane. 1976. Social Impacts, Politics and the Environmental Impact Statement Process. *Journal Natural Resources* 16:339–356.

Friesema, P., J. Caporaso, G. Goldstein, R. Lineberry, and R. McCleary. 1979. *Aftermath: Communities after Natural Disaster.* Beverly Hills, CA: Sage.

Fritz, C. 1957. Disasters Compared in Six American Communities. *Human Organizations* 16 (Summer):6–9.

Fritz, C. 1961. Disaster. In R. Merton and R. Nisbet (eds.), *Contemporary Social Problems*, pp. 651–694. New York: Harcourt.

Fritz, C. and J. Mathewson. 1957. Convergence Behavior in Disasters: A Problem in Social Control. *National Research Council Committee on Disaster Studies* No. 9, Publication No. 476.

Galvin, K. and B. Brommel. 1982. *Family Communication.* Glenview, IL: Scott-Forseman.

Gamble, H. and R. Downing. 1981. *Effects of the Accident at Three Mile Island on Residential Property Values and Sales.* Washington, DC: U.S. Nuclear Regulatory Commission. January.

Gamson, W. 1966. Rancorous Conflict in Community Politics. *American Sociological Review* 31:71–81.

Gamson, W. 1975. *The Strategies of Social Protest.* Hamewood, IL: The Dorsey Press.

Gillespie, D., R. Perry, and D. Mileti. 1974. Collective Stress and Community Transformation. *Human Relations* 27/5:767–778.

Gleser, G. C., B. Green, and C. Winget. 1981. *Prolonged Psychological Effects of Disaster: A Study of Buffalo Creek.* New York: Academic Press.

Golant, S. and A. McCutcheon. 1980. Objective Quality of Life Indicators and the External Validity of Community Research Findings. *Social Indicators Research* 7:207–235.

Goldhaber, M., P. Houts, and R. Sabella. 1981. *Mobility of the Population within 5 Miles of Three Mile Island during Period from August 1979 through July 1980.* Harrisburg, PA: Pennsylvania Department of Health.

Goldstein, R. and J. Schorr. 1982. The Long-Term Impact of a Man-Made Disaster. *Disasters* 6:50–59.

Gray, M. and I. Rosen. 1982. *The Warning.* New York: Norton.

Greer, S. 1962. *The Emerging City.* New York: The Free Press.

Gricar, B. and A. Baratta. 1983. Bridging the Information Gap at Three Mile Island: Radiation Monitoring by Citizens. *Journal Applied Behavioral Science* 19:35–49.

Gross, J. and S. Raynor, 1985. *Measuring Culture.* New York: Columbia University Press.

Grosser, G., H. Wechsler, and M. Greenblatt (eds). 1964. *The Threat of Impending Disaster.* Cambridge, MA: Massachusetts Institute of Technology Press.

Gruntfest, E. 1977. *What People Did During the Big Thompson Flood.* University of Colorado, Institute of Behavioral Science, Natural Hazards Working Paper No. 32. Boulder: University of Colorado.

Gump, P. 1968. Persons, Settings, and Larger Contexts. In B. Indik and F. Berrien (eds.), *People, Groups, and Organizations.* New York: Teachers College Press.

Haas, J. and T. Drabek. 1970. Community Disaster and System Stress: A Sociological Perspective. In J. E. McGrath (ed.), *Social and Psychological Factors in Stress*, pp. 264–286. New York: Holt, Rinehart and Winston.

Haas, J. and T. Drabek. 1973. *Complex Organizations: A Sociological Perspective.* New York: Macmillan.

Haas, J., W. Kates, and M. Bowden (eds.). 1977. *Reconstruction Following Disaster.* Cambridge, MA: Massachusetts Institute of Technology Press.

Hall, P. and P. Landreth. 1974. Assessing a Natural Disaster's Long-Term Impact on a Community and Selected Victims from Routinely Collected Data. Rapid City, SD: Western Health Systems, Inc. (mimeographed).

Hannigans, J. and R. Kueneman. 1978. Anticipating Flood Emergencies: A Case Study of Canadian Disaster Subcultures. In E. Quarantelli (ed.), *Disasters, Theory and Research.* Beverly Hills, CA: Sage.

Hansen, D. and R. Hill. 1964. Families under Stress. In H. Christensen (ed.), *Handbook of Marriage and the Family*, pp. 782–822. Chicago: Rand McNally.

Hansen, D. and V. Johnson. 1979. Rethinking Family Stress Theory: Definitional Aspects. In W. Burr, R. Hill, I. Reiss, and I. Nye (eds.), *Contemporary Theories about Family.* Vol. 1:582–608. New York: The Free Press.

Hansson, R., R. Henze, M. Langenheim, and A. Filipovitch. 1979. Threat, Knowledge, and Support for a Collective Response to Urban Flooding. *Journal of Applied Social Psychology* 9(5):413–425.

Hartsough, D. 1982. Planning for Disaster: A New Community Outreach Program for Mental Health Centers. *Journal of Community Psychology* 10:255–264.

Hartsough, D. and J. Savitsky 1984. Three Mile Island: Psychology and Environmental Policy at a Crossroads. *American Psychologist* 39(10):1113–1122.

Hewitt, K. and I. Burton. 1971. *The Hazardousness of a Place.* Toronto: University of Toronto Press.

Hill, R. 1949. *Families under Stress.* New York: Harper.

Hill, R. 1958. Sociology of Marriage and Family Behavior 1945–1956: A Trend Report and Bibliography. *Current Sociology* 7:1–98.

Hill, R. 1970. *Family Development in Three Generations.* Cambridge, MA: Schenkman Publishing Company.

Hill, R. and D. Hansen. 1962. Families in Disaster. In G. Baker and D. Chapman (eds.), *Man and Society in Disaster*, pp. 185–221. New York: Basic Books.

Hocking, F. 1965. Human Reactions to Extreme Environmental Stress. *Medical Journal of Australia* 2:477–482.

Hocking, F. 1970. Psychiatric Aspects of Extreme Environmental Stress. *Diseases of the Nervous System* 31:542–545.

Holden, C. 1980. Love Canal Residents under Stress. *Science* 208:1242–1244.

Holden, C. 1982. Potassium Iodide and Nuclear Accidents. *Science* 215:1495.

Holdren, J. 1982. Energy Hazards: What to Measure, What to Compare. *Technology Review* 85(3):32–38.

Holmes, T. and R. Rahe. 1967. The Social Readjustment Rating Scale. *Journal of Psychosomatic Research* 11:213–218.

Houts, P., R. Miller, G. Tokuhata, and K. Ham. 1980a. *Health-Related Behavioral Impact of the Three Mile Island Nuclear Incident. Part I.* Harrisburg, PA: Pennsylvania Department of Health.

Houts, P., R. Miller, G. Tokuhata, and K. Ham. 1980b. *Health-Related Behavioral Impact of the Three Mile Island Nuclear Incident. Part II.* Harrisburg, PA: Pennsylvania Department of Health.

Howard, S. 1980. Children and the San Fernando Earthquake. *Earthquake Information Bulletin* 12:190–192.

Huerta, F. and R. Horton. 1978. Coping Behavior of Elderly Flood Victims. *The Gerontologist* 18:541–546.

Hufnagel, R. and R. Perry. 1982. Collective Behavior: Implications for Disaster Planning. Paper presented at the Pacific Sociological Association Meetings. San Diego, CA.

Hunter, F. 1963. *Community Power Structure*. Chapel Hill, NC: University of North Carolina Press.

Hunter, A. 1974. *Symbolic Communities*. Chicago: University of Chicago Press.

Hunter A. 1975. The Loss of Community: An Empirical Test Through Replication. *American Sociological Review* 40:537–552.

Hutton, J. and D. Mileti. 1979. *Analysis of Adoption and Implementation of Community Land Use Regulations for Floodplains*. San Francisco: Woodward-Clyde.

Hutton, J., J. Sorensen, and D. Mileti. 1981. Earthquake Prediction and Public Reaction. In T. Rikitake (ed.), *Current Research In Earthquake Prediction*, pp. 129–166. Tokyo: Center for Academic Publications and D. Reidel Publishing.

Indik, B. and F. Berrien (eds.). 1968. *People, Groups, and Organizations*. New York: Teachers College Press.

Instituut Voor Sociaal Onderzoek Van Het Nederlandse Volk Amsterdam. 1955. *Studies in Holland Flood Disaster 1953*. Committee on Disaster Studies of the National Academy of Sciences/National Research Council, Vol. I–IV. Washington: National Academy of Sciences.

Jackson, E. 1981. Response to Earthquake Hazard. *Environment and Behavior* 13(4):387–416.

Janerich, D., W. Burnett, G. Feck, M. Hoff, P. Nasca, A. Polednak, P. Greenwald, and N. Vianna. 1981. Cancer Incidence in the Love Canal Area. *Science* 212:1404–1407.

Janis, I. L. 1951. *Air War and Emotional Stress: Psychological Studies of Bombing and Civilian Defense*. New York: McGraw-Hill.

Johnson, D. 1981. *Sociological Theory*. New York: Wiley.

Johnson, J. and D. Ziegler. 1983. Distinguishing Human Responses to Radiological Emergencies. *Economic Geography* 59:386–402.

Johnston, D. 1970. Forecasting Methods in the Social Sciences. *Technological Forecasting and Social Change* 2:173–187.

Kantor, D. and W. Lehr. 1975. *Inside the Family: Toward a Theory of Family Process*. San Francisco: Jossey-Bass.

Kasperson, R. 1980. The Dark Side of the Radioactive Waste Problem. In T. O'Riordan and R. Turner (eds.), *Progress in Resource Management and Environmental Planning*. Chichester, England: John Wiley and Sons.

Kates, R. 1962. *Hazard and Choice Perception in Floodplain Management*. Department of Geography Research Paper No. 78. Chicago, IL: University of Chicago Press.

Kates, R. 1971. Natural Hazards in Human Ecological Perspective: Hypotheses and Models. *Economic Geography* 47:438–451.

Kates, R. 1977. Experiencing the Environment as Hazard. In S. Wapner, S. Cohen, and B. Kaplan (eds.), *Experiencing the Environment*, pp. 133–156. New York: Plenum Press.

Kates, R. 1978. *Risk Assessment of Environment Hazard*. New York: Wiley.

Katz, A. 1970. Self Help Organizations and Volunteer Participation in Social Welfare. *Social Work* 15 (January):51–60.

Kemeny, J. 1979. *Report of the President's Commission on the Accident at Three Mile Island*. Washington, DC: U. S. Government Printing Office.

Kerlinger, F. 1973. *Foundations of Behavioral Research*. New York: Holt, Rinehart, and Winston.

Kessler, R. 1979a. A Strategy for Studying Differential Vulnerability to the Psychological Consequences of Stress. *Journal of Health and Social Behavior* 20:100–108.

Kessler, R. 1979b. Stress, Social Status, and Psychological Distress. *Journal of Health and Social Behavior* 20:259–272.

Key, W. 1983. Comments on Gricar and Baratta. *Journal of Applied Behavioral Science* 19:49–53.

Kiecolt, K. and J. Nigg. 1982. Mobility and Perceptions of a Hazardous Environment. *Environment and Behavior* 14(2):131–154.

Kilpatrick, F. 1947. Problems of Perception in Extreme Situations. *Human Organization* 16:10–22.

Kilijanek, T. and T. Drabek. 1979. Assessing Long-Term Impacts of a Natural Disaster: A Focus on the Elderly. *The Gerontologist* 19:555–566.

Kim, J. 1975. Multivariate Analysis for Ordinal Variables. *American Journal of Sociology* 88:262–298.

Kinlin, L. and R. Doll. 1981. Fluoridation of Water Supplies and Cancer Mortality. *Journal of Epidemiology and Community Health* 35:239–244.

Kinston, W. and R. Rosser. 1974. Effects on Mental and Physical State. *Journal of Psychosomatic Research* 18:437–456.

Klein, L. R. 1970. *An Essay on the Economic Theory of Prediction*. Chicago, IL: Markham.

Komarovsky, M. 1940. *The Unemployed Man and His Family*. New York: Dryden Press.

Koss, E. 1946. *Families in Trouble*. Morningside Heights, NY: Kings Crown Press.

Kovak, N. 1982. Department of Environmental Conservation, New York State, Personal communication, May 5, 1982.

Kroder, L. 1970. Environmental Threat and Social Organization. *The Annals* 389 (May):11–26.

Kropotkin, P. 1914. *Mutual Aid: A Factor of Evolution*. Boston: Extending Horizons Books.

Kunreuther, H. 1974. Economic Analysis of Natural Hazards: An Ordered Choice Approach, pp. 206–214. In G. White (ed.), *Natural Hazards: Local, National, Global*. New York: Oxford University Press.

Kunreuther, H. 1978. *Disaster Insurance Protection: Public Policy Lessons*. New York: Wiley.

Lachman, R. and W. Bonk. 1960. Behavior and Beliefs during the Recent Volcanic Eruption at Kapoho, Hawaii. *Science* 13:1095–1096.

Lachman, R., M. Tatsuoka, and W. Bonk. 1961. *Human Behavior During* the Tsunami of May 1960. *Science* 133:1405–1409.

Laing, R. 1972. *The Politics of the Family*. New York: Vintage Books.

Lang, K. and G. Lang. 1964. Collective Responses to the Threat of Disaster. In G. Grosser, H. Wechsler, and M. Greenblatt (eds.), *The Threat of Impending Disaster*. Cambridge, MA: Massachusetts Institute of Technology Press.

LaRossa, R. 1977. *Conflict and Power in Marriage*. Beverly Hills, CA: Sage.

Lazarus, R. 1966. *Psychological Stress and the Coping Process*. New York: McGraw-Hill.

Lazarus, R. and J. Cohen. 1977. Environmental Stress. In I. Altman and J. Wohlwill (eds.), *Human Behavior and the Environment*, vol. 2. New York: Plenum Press.

Lee, G. 1977. *Family Structure and Interaction: A Comparative Analysis*. Philadelphia, PA: B. Lippincott.

Lee, G. 1980. Kinship in the Seventies: A Decade Review of Research and Theory. *Journal of Marriage and the Family* 42(4):923–934.

Leik, R., J. Clark, and M. Carter. 1981. *Community Response to Natural Hazard Warnings*. Minneapolis, MN: University of Minnesota.

Leik, R., S. Leik, K. Ekker, and G. Gifford. 1982. *Under the Threat of Mt. St. Helens: A Study of Chronic Family Stress*. Washington, DC: Federal Emergency Management Agency.

LeMasters, E. 1974. *Parents in Modern America*. Homewood, Ill: The Dorsey Press.

Levine, A. 1981. Love Canal. Paper presented at the Meetings of the Eastern Sociological Society, New York, March.

Levine, A. 1982. *Love Canal: Science, Politics, and People*. Lexington, MA: Lexington Books, Heath and Company.

Lifton, R. and E. Olson. 1976. The Human Meaning of Total Disaster. *Psychiatry* 39:1–18.

Lin, N., W. Ensel, R. Simeone, and W. Kuo. 1979. Social Support, Stressful Life Events and Illness: A Model and an Empirical Test. *Journal of Health and Social Behavior* 20 (June):108–119.

Lindy, J. and M. Grace. 1985. The Recovery Environment: Continuing Stressor vs. a Healing Psychosocial Environment, pp 137–149 in. B. Sowder (ed.), *Disasters and Mental Health: Selected Contemporary Perspectives*, NIMH: DHHS publication No. 85–1421.

Lindell, M., T. Earle, J. Hebert, and R. Perry. 1978. *Radioactive Wastes: Public Attitudes toward Disposal Facilities, B-HARC–411–004.* Seattle, WA: Battelle Human Affairs Research Center.

Linderman, M. 1980. Community Decision Making in the Future, pp. 403–407, in *Through the '80s. Thinking Globally, Acting Locally,* Frank Feather (ed.), Washington, DC: World Future Society.

Littlejohn, S. 1978. *Theories of Human Communication.* Columbus, OH: Charles Merrill.

Litwak, E. 1960a. The Use of Extended Family Groups in the Achievement of Social Goals. *Social Problems* 7 (1959–1960):177–187.

Litwak, E. 1960b. Occupational Mobility and Extended Family Cohesion. *American Sociological Review* 25:9–14.

Litwak, E. and I. Szeleny. 1969. Primary Group Structures and Their Functions: Kin, Neighborhoods, and Friends. *American Sociological Review* 34 (August):475–481.

Litwak, E. *et al.* 1974. Theories of Linkage between Bureaucracies and Community Primary Groups—Education, Health, and Political Action as Empirical Cases in Point. Paper presented at the 1974 Meetings of the American Sociological Association, Montreal, Quebec.

Liu, B. 1975. *Quality of Life Indicators in U.S. Metropolitan Areas, 1970.* Washington, DC: U.S. Environmental Protection Agency.

Logue, J. N. 1980. Mental Health Aspects of Disasters. Presented at the Natural Hazards Research Applications Workshop, July 20–23. Boulder, CO: University of Colorado.

Logue, J., M. Melich, and H. Hansen. 1981. Research Issues and Directions in the Epidemiology of Health Effects of Disasters. *Epidemiological Review* 3:140–162.

Lucas, R. 1966. The Influence of Kinship upon Perception of an Ambiguous Stimulus. *American Sociological Review* 31:227–236.

Lucas, R. 1969. *Men in Crisis: A Study of a Mine Disaster.* New York: Basic Books.

MacLeod, G. 1981. Some Public Health Lessons from Three Mile Island: A Case Study in Chaos. *Ambio* 10(1):18–23.

McCombs, M. and D. Shaw. 1972. The Agenda-Setting Function of Mass Media. *Public Opinion Quarterly* 36:176–187.

McCubbin, H. 1979. Integrating Coping Behavior in Family Stress Theory. *Journal of Marriage and the Family* 41:237–244.

McCubbin, H., C. Joy, A. Cauble, J. Comeau, J. Patterson, and R. Needle. 1980. Family Stress and Coping: A Decade Review. *Journal of Marriage and the Family* 42(4):855–871.

McCubbin, H. and D. Olson. 1980. Beyond Family Crisis: Family Adaptation. Paper presented at the XVIII Internationl Seminar of the Committee on Family Research. Family and Disaster. Rosersberg Castle, Sweden.

McGrath, J. 1970. *Social and Psychological Factors in Stress.* New York: Holt, Rinehart, and Winston.

McLuckie, B. 1970. A Study of Functional Response to Stress in Three Societies. Unpublished doctoral dissertation. Departments of Sociology and Anthropology. Columbus, OH: Ohio State University.

Mack, R. and G. Baker. 1961. *The Occasion Instant.* National Academy of Sciences/National Research Council Disaster Study No. 15. Washington, DC: National Academy of Sciences.

Mandelker, D. 1984. *NEPA Law and Litigation.* Wilmette, IL: Callaghan.

Manderscheid, D. 1981. Stress and Coping: A Biopsychosocial Perspective on Alienation. In R. Geyer and D. Schweitzer (eds.), *Alienation: Problems of Theory Meaning and Method.* London: Routledge and Kegan.

Manderthaner, R., G. Guttmann, E. Swaton, and H. J. Otway. 1978. Effect of Distance upon Risk Perception. *Journal of Applied Psychology* 63(3):380–382.

Marshall, E. 1979a. NAS Study on Radiation Takes the Middle Road. *Science* 204:711–714.

Marshall, E. 1979b. A Preliminary Report on Three Mile Island. *Science* 204:280–281.

Marshall, E. 1981. New A-Bomb Data Shown to Radiation Experts. *Science* 212, 19 June.

Marshall, E. 1982. NRC Reviews Brittle Reactor Hazard. *Science* 15:1596–1597.

Martin, E. and J. Martin. 1978. *The Black Extended Family.* Chicago, IL: University of Chicago Press.

Marx, J. 1979. Low-Level Radiation. Just How Bad Is It? *Science* 204:160–164.

Mazur, A. 1975. Opposition to Technological Innovation. *Minerva*, pp. 58–81.

Meidinger, E. 1977. *Projecting Secondary jobs: An Empirical Examination and Epistemological Critique.* Paper presented at the Annual meeting of the American Sociological Association; Chicago, IL; September.

Melick, M. 1978. Life Change and Illness: Illness Behaviors of Males in the Recovery Period of a Natural Disaster. *Journal of Health and Social Behavior* 19:335–342.

Meltzer, B., J. Petras, and L. Reynolds. 1975. *Symbolic Interactionism: Genesis, Varieties and Criticism.* Boston: Routledge.

Menninger, W. 1952. Psychological Reactions in an Emergency. *American Journal of Psychiatry* 109 (August): 128–130.

Metropolitan Edison Co. v. People Against Nuclear Energy, 75 L. Ed. 2d 534.

Michael, D. 1978. An Aesthetic for Technology Assessment. *Alternative Futures* 1:19–28.

Michelson, W. 1977. *Environmental Choice, Human Behavior, and Residential Satisfaction.* New York: Oxford University Press.

Milburn, T. 1977. The Nature of Threat. *Journal of Social Issues* 22(1):126–139.

Mileti, D. 1974. A Normative Causal Model Analysis of Disaster Warning Response. Ph.D. dissertation. Boulder, CO: University of Colorado.

Mileti,D. 1975. *Natural Hazard Warning Systems in the United States.* Boulder,CO: Institute of Behavioral Science, Monograph 13.

Mileti, D. 1980. Human Adjustment to the Risk of Environmental Extremes. *Sociology and Social Research* 64(3):328–347.

Mileti, D., T. Drabek, and J. Haas. 1975. *Human Systems in Extreme Environments: A Sociological Perspective.* Monograph 21, Institute of Behavioral Sciences. Boulder, CO: University of Colorado.

Mileti, D., D. Hartsough, and P. Madson. 1982. *The Three Mile Island Incident: A Study of Behavioral Indicators of Human Stress.* Prepared for Shaw, Pittman, Potts, and Trowbridge, Washington, DC., Legal Council to General Public Utilities, March.

Mileti, D., J. Hutton, and J. Sorensen. 1981. *Earthquake Prediction Response and Options for Public Policy.* Boulder, CO: University of Colorado, Institute of Behavioral Science.

Miller, D. 1977. Methods for Estimating Societal Futures, pp. 202–210. In K. Finsterbusch and C. Wolf (eds.), *Methodology of Social Impact Assessment.* Straudsburg, PA: Dowden, Hutchinson, and Ross.

Miller, J. 1964. A Theoretical Review of Individual and Group Psychological Reactions to Stress, pp. 11–33. In G. Grosser, H. Wechsler, and M. Greenblatt (eds.), *The Threat of Impending Disaster.* Cambridge, MA: Massachusetts Institute of Technology Press.

Miller, S. and F. Reisman. 1961. The Working Class Subculture: A New View. *Social Problems* 9 (Summer):86–97.

Milne, G. 1977. Cyclone Tracy: Some Consequences on the Evacuation for Adult Victims. *Australian Psychologist*. 12:39–54.

Mitchell, G. 1969. The Concept and Use of Social Networks. In G. Mitchell (ed.) *Social Networks in Urban Situations*. Manchester, England: University Press.

Mitchell, J. 1974. *Community Response to Coastal Erosion*. Chicago, IL: University of Chicago, Department of Geography.

Mitchell J., K. Barnes, J. Brosius, and S. Cutter. 1979. *Responses of Impacted Populations to the Three Mile Island Nuclear Reactor Accident: An Initial Assessment*. Unpublished paper in Rutgers Geography Discussion Paper Series, Department of Environmental Resources, Rutgers University, Rutgers, NJ.

Molotch, H. 1970. Oil in Santa Barbara and Power in America. *Sociological Inquiry* 40:131–144.

Moore, H. 1958. *Tornadoes over Texas*. Austin, TX: University of Texas Press.

Moore, H., F. Bates, M. Layman, and V. Parenton. 1963. *Before the Wind: A Study of Response to Hurricane Carla*. Washington, DC: National Academy of Sciences.

Moore, H. and H. Friedsam. 1959. Reported Emotional Stress Following a Disaster. *Social Forces* 38 (December):135–140.

Morgan, W. 1939. *The Family Meets the Depression*. Minneapolis, MN: University of Minnesota Press.

Murdock, S. and F. Leistritz. 1979. *Energy Development in the Western United States: Impacts on Rural Areas*. New York: Praeger.

National Research Council, Panel of Social and Economic Aspects of Radioactive Waste Management, Board of Radioactive Waste Management, Commission on Physical Sciences, Mathematics, and Resources, 1984. *Social and Economic Aspects of Radioactive Waste Disposal. Considerations for Institutional Management*. Washington, DC: National Academy Press.

Nelkin, D. 1981. Some Social and Political Dimensions of Nuclear Power: Examples from Three Mile Island. *American Political Science Review* 75:132–140.

Netter, J. and W. Waserman. 1974. *Applied Linear Statistical Models*. Homewood, ILL: Richard Irwin.

Newman, C. 1978. Children of Disaster: Clinical Observations at Buffalo Creek. *American Journal of Psychiatry* 133:306–312.

222   BIBLIOGRAPHY

New York Department of Environmental Conservation. 1982. Private com-
    munication, May 5.

Nilson, D. 1981. Seismic Safety and Public Policy Process. Presented at Natural
    Hazards Research and Applications Workshop, Boulder, CO, July 19–
    22.

Olson, D., D. Sprenkle, and C. Russell. 1979. Circumplex Model of Marital
    and Family Systems: Cohesion and Adaptability Dimensions, Family
    Types, and Clinical Applications. *Family Process* 18:3–28.

Palm, R. 1981. *Real Estate Agents and Special Studies Zones Disclosure: The
    Response of California Home Buyers to Earthquake Hazards Information.*
    Boulder, CO: The University of Colorado, Institute of Behavioral
    Science.

Palm, R. 1982. Special Studies Zones and Home Mortgage Lending Policies.
    Paper presented at the Association of American Geographers, San An-
    tonio, TX, April 25–28.

Parr, A. 1969. Flood Preparation—1969. Observations Concerning the Southern
    Manitoba Spring Flood Preparations. *EMO National Digest* (June–July):
    25–27.

Parsons, T. 1943. The Kinship System of the Contemporary United States.
    American Anthropologist 45:22–38.

Parsons, T. 1949. The Social Structure of the Family. In R. Anshen (ed.), *The
    Family: Its Function and Destiny*. New York: Harper.

Parsons, T. 1959. The Principal Structures of Community: A Sociological View.
    In C. J. Friedrich (ed.), *Community*. New York: The Liberal Arts Press.

Pearlin, L. and C. Schooler. 1978. The Structure of Coping. *Journal of Health
    and Social Behavior* 16:2–21.

Penick, E., B. Powell, and W. Sieck. 1976. Mental Health Problems and Natural
    Disaster: Tornado Victims. *Journal of Community Psychology* 4:64–67.

Pennsylvania Department of Health. 1981. *The Three Mile Island Population
    Registry. Report One: A General Description*. Harrisburg, PA: Pennsyl-
    vania Department of Health, Division of Epidemiological Research.

People Against Nuclear Energy v. United States Nuclear Regulatory Commis-
    sion, 673 F. 2nd 552 (D. C. Cir. 1982) (order vacating NRC decision);
    678 F. 2nd 222, 235 (D. C. Cir. Filed April 2, 1982) (amended interim
    order); 678 F. 2nd 222, 228 (D. C. Cir. 1982) (Wilkey dissenting in part).

Perrow, C. 1984. *Normal Accidents*. New York: Basic Books.

Perrow, C. 1979. The Sixtees Observed, pp. 192–211. In M. Zald and D.
    McCarthy (eds.), *The Dynamics of Social Movements*. Cambridge, MA:
    Winthrop.

Perry, R. 1983. Environmental Hazards and Psychopathology: Linking Natural Disaster with Mental Health. *Environmental Management* 7:543–552.

Perry, R. and M. Greene. 1982. *Citizens Response to Volcanic Eruptions*, New York: Irvington.

Perry, R. and M. Lindell. 1978. The Psychological Consequences of Natural Disaster. *Mass Emergencies* 3:105–117.

Perry, R. 1981. *Citizen Evacuation in Response to Nuclear and Nonnuclear Threats.* Seattle WA: Battelle HARC.

Perry, R., M. Lindell, and M. Greene. 1980. *Evacuation Decision-Making and Emergency Planning.* Seattle, WA: Battelle HARC.

Perry, R., M. Lindell, and M. Greene. 1981. *Evacuation Planning in Emergency Management.* Lexington, MA.: Heath and Company.

Perry, H. and S. Perry. 1959. *The Schoolhouse Disasters: Family and Community as Determinants of the Child's Response to Disaster.* Washington, DC: National Academy of Sciences.

Perry, S., E. Silber, and D. Bloch. 1956. The Child and His Family in Disaster: A Study of the 1953 Vicksburg Tornado. *National Research Council Commitee on Disaster Studies.* 5, Publication No. 394. Washington, DC: National Academy of Sciences.

Petersen, W. 1969. Kin Network Research: A Plea for Comparability. *Journal of Marriage and the Family* 31 (March):270–279.

Peterson, Bruce. 1982. A Review of Effects of the Accident at Three Mile Island on Residential Property Values and Sales. Unpublished draft. Oak Ridge, TN: Oak Ridge National Laboratory.

Polyani, M. 1966. *The Tacit Dimension.* Garden City, NJ: Anchor Books.

Popper, K. 1973. *Objective Knowledge.* London: Oxford University Press.

Poulshock, W. and E. Cohen. 1975. The Elderly in the Aftermath of Disaster. *The Gerontologist* 15 (August):357–361.

Prasad, J. 1935. The Psychology of Rumour: A Study Relating to the Great Indian Earthquake of 1934. *British Journal of Psychology* XXVI (July):129–144.

Quarantelli, E. 1970. Emergent Accommodation Groups: Beyond Current Collective Behavior Typologies, pp. 111–123. In T. Shibutani (ed.), *Human Nature and Collective Behavior: Paper in Honor of Hubert Blumer.* Englewood Cliffs, NJ: Prentice Hall.

Quarantelli, E. 1978. *Disasters, Theory and Research.* Beverly Hills, CA: Sage.

Quarantelli, E. 1979. *The Consequences of Disasters for Mental Health: Conflicting Views.* Monograph No. 62. Columbus, OH: Ohio State University, The Disaster Research Center.

Quarantelli, E. and R. Dynes. 1972. Response to Social Crisis and Disaster. *Annual Review of Sociology* 3:23–49.

Quarantelli, E. and R. Dynes. 1976. Community Conflict: Its Absence and Its Presence in Natural Disasters. *Mass Emergencies* 1:139–152.

Rangell, L. 1976. Discussion of the Buffalo Creek Disaster: The Course of Psychic Trauma. *American Journal of Psychiatry.* 133 (March):313–316.

Reed, J. and J. Wilkes. 1981. Technical Nuclear Knowledge and Attitudes Toward Nuclear Power Before and After TMI. Presented at Annual Meeting of the Society for the Social Study of Science, Atlanta, GA, November 5.

Roder, W. 1961. Attitudes and Knowledge on the Topeka Floodplain. In G. F. White (ed.), *Papers on Flood Problems.* Department of Geography Research Paper No. 70. Chicago, IL: University of Chicago Press.

Rossers, C. and Harris. 1965. *The Family and Social Change.* London: Routledge, Paul and Keegan.

Rossi, P. 1955. *Why People Move.* New York: The Free Press.

Rossi, P. and J. Wright. 1981. *Social Science and Natural Hazards.* Boston: Abt Books.

Schelling, T. 1978. *Micromotives and Macrobehavior.* New York: Norton.

Schiff, M. 1977. Hazard Adjustment, Locus of Control and Sensation Seeking: Some Null Findings. *Environment and Behavior* 9:233–254.

Schneider, D. 1957. Typhoons on Yap. *Human Organization* 16 (Summer):10–15.

Schneider, M. 1975. The Quality of Life in Large American Cities: Objective and Subjective Social Indicators. *Social Indicators Research* 1:495–509.

Schorr, J. and R. Goldsteen. 1980. Public Response to a Nuclear Reactor Accident: The Case of TMI. Paper presented at Annual Meeting of the Southern Sociological Society. Knoxville, TN. March.

Schwebel, M. and B. Schwebel. 1981. Children's Reactions to the Threat of Nuclear Plant Accidents. *American Journal of Orthopsychiatry* 51(2) April:327–347.

Seligman, D. 1981. A Toxic Turnaround. *Fortune* 104 (July 27):30–31.

Seligman, M. 1975. *Helplessness: On Depression, Development, and Death.* San Francisco, CA: Freeman.

Selye, H. 1956. *The Stress of Life.* New York: MfcGraw-Hill.

Shearer, D. 1980. *Three Mile Island Nuclear Accident Community Impact Study on Real Estate.* Harrisburg, PA: Greater Harrisburg Board of Realtors. March.

Shiff, M. 1977. Hazard Adjustment, Locus of Control, and Sensation Seeking: Some Null Findings. *Environment and Behavior* 9:233–254.

Sills, D., C. P. Wolf, and V. Shelanshi (eds). 1982. *Accident at Three Mile Island: The Human Dimensions.* Boulder, CO: Westview Press.

Simon, H. 1956. Rational Choice and the Structure of the Environment. *Psychological Review* 63:129–138.

Sims, J. and D. Baumann. 1972. The Tornado Threat: Coping Styles of the North and South. *Science* 176:1386–1392.

Sinha, D. 1952. Behavior in Catastrophic Situations: A Psychological Study of Reports and Rumors. *British Journal of Psychology* 43:200–209.

Slovic, P., B. Fischoff, and S. Lichtenstein. 1979. Rating the Risks. *Environment* 21(3):14–39.

Slovic, P., B. Fischoff, and S. Lichtenstein. 1982. Perceived Risk: Psychological Factors and Social Implications. In F. Warner and D. Slater (eds.), *The Assessment and Perception of Risk.* London: The Royal Society.

Slovic, P., H. Kunreuther, and G. White. 1974. Decision Processes, Rationality, and Adjustment to Natural Hazards, pp. 187–204. In G. White (ed.), *Natural Hazards: Local, National, Global.* New York: Oxford University Press.

Smelser, N. 1963. *Theory of Collective Behavior.* New York: The Free Press.

Smith, D. 1973. *The Geography of Social Well-Being in the United States.* New York: McGraw Hill.

Smith, R. 1982a. The Risks of Living near Love Canal, 217 *Science* 4562:808–811 (August 27).

Smith, R. 1982b. Love Canal Study Attracts Criticism, 217 *Science* 4561:714–715 (August 20).

Social Impact Research. 1982. *Three Mile Island: Community Stress Impact Assessment, Final Report.* Seattle, WA: Social Impact Research, Inc.,

Soderstrom, E. 1981. *Social Impact Assessment, Experimental Methods and Approaches.* New York: Praeger.

Soderstrom, E., J. Sorensen, E. Copenhaver, and S. Carnes. 1984. Risk Perception in an Interest Group Context: An Examination of the TMI Restart Issue. *Risk Analysis* 4(3):231–244.

Solid Waste Management. 1979. U.S. Disaster Agency Cuts Off Funding to Love Canal Area. *Solid Wastes Management/RRJ*, p. 12, March.

Solomon, S. 1985. Enhancing Social Support for Disaster Victims, pp. 107–121 in B. Sowder (ed.), Disasters and Mental Health: Selected Contemporary Perspectives. NIMH:DHHS Publication No. 85–1421.

Sorensen, J. 1981. *Emergency Response to Mount St. Helens' Eruption: March*

20 to April 10, 1980. Boulder, CO: University of Colorado, Institute of Behavioral Science.

Sorensen, J. 1983. Knowing How to Behave Under the Threat of Disaster: Can It Be Explained? *Environment and Behavior*, 15:438–457.

Sorensen, J. and J. Hutton. 1979. Equity and Earthquake Warnings. San Francisco: Woodward Clyde Consultants.

Sorensen, J. and G. White. 1980. Natural Hazards: A Cross-Cultural Perspective. In I. Altman, A. Papaport, and J. Wohwill (eds.), *Human Behavior and the Environment.* New York: Plenum Press.

Sorensen, J., E. Soderstrom, E. Copenhaver, and S. Carnes. 1983. Social and Psychological Impacts of Restarting TMI Unit One. Draft Report for the Nuclear Regulatory Commission. Oak Ridge, TN: Oak Ridge National Laboratory.

Speare, A., S. Goldstein, and W. Prey. 1972. *Residential Mobility, Migration, and Metropolitan Change.* Cambridge: Ballinger.

Srole, L. 1956. Social Integration and Certain Corollaries: An Explanatory Study. *American Sociological Review* 21:709–716.

Srole, L., T. Langner, S. Michael, M. Opler, and T. Rennie. 1962. *Mental Health in the Metropolis: The Midtown Manhattan Study.* Vol. 1. New York: McGraw-Hill.

Starr, C. 1969. Social Benefit Versus Technological Risk. *Science* 165:1232–38.

Starr, C. 1980. Risk Criteria for Nuclear Power Plants: A Pragmatic Proposal. Paper presented at the ANS/ENS International Conference, Washington, DC. November 16–20.

Sterling, J., T. Drabek, and W. Key. 1977. The Long-Term Impacts of Disasters on the Health Self-Perceptions of Victims. Paper read at meetings of the American Sociological Association. Chicago, IL.

Stephens, M. 1981. *Three Mile Island.* New York: Random House.

Sussman, M. 1953. Parental Participation in Mate Selection and Its Effect upon Family Continuity. *Social Forces* 32:76–81.

Sussman, M. 1954. Family Continuity: Selective Factors which Affect Relationship between Families at Generational Levels. *Marriage and Family Living* 16 (March):112–120.

Sussman, M. and L. Burchinal. 1962. Kin Family Networks: Unheralded Structure in Current Conceptualizations of Family Functioning. *Marriage and Family Living* 24:231–240.

Suttles, G. 1972. *Social Construction of Communities.* Chicago, IL: University of Chicago Press.

Taylor, J., L. Zurcher, and W. Key. 1970. *Tornado: A Community Responds to Disaster.* Seattle, WA: University of Washington Press.

Taylor, V. 1976. *Delivery of Mental Health Services in Disasters*. Columbus, OH: Ohio State University, Disaster Research Center.

Tennessee Valley Authority. 1980. *Hartsville Nuclear Plants Socioeconomic Monitoring and Mitigation Reports*. Knoxville, TN: Tennessee Valley Authority.

Tichener, J. and F. Kapp. 1976. Family and Character Change at Buffalo Creek. *American Journal of Psychiatry*. 133:295–299.

Tichener, J., F. Kapp, and C. Winget. 1976. The Buffalo Creek Syndrome: Symptoms and Character Change after a Major Disaster. In H. J. Parad, H. L. P. Reznik, and L. G. Parad (eds.), *Emergency and Disaster Management: A Mental Health Source Book*. Bowie, MD: Charles Press.

Tierney, K. and B. Blaisden. 1979. *Crisis Intervention Programs for Disaster Victims*. Rockville, MD: U.S. Public Health Service.

Trainer, P. and R. Bolin. 1976. Persistent Effects of Disasters on Daily Activities: A Cross-Cultural Comparison. *Mass Emergencies* 1:279–290.

Turner, R. 1979. The Mass Media and Preparation for Natural Disaster, pp. 281–292. In *Disasters and the Mass Media*. Committee on Disasters and the Mass Media Workshop. Washington, DC: National Academy of Science.

Turner, R. and L. Killian. 1972. *Collective Behavior* (2nd Ed.). Englewood Cliffs, NJ: Prentice-Hall.

Turner, R., J. Nigg, D. Paz, and B. Young. 1979. *Earthquake Threat: The Human Response in Southern California*. Los Angeles: University of California, Institute for Social Science Research.

Tversky, A. and D. Kahneman. 1974. Judgment Under Uncertainty: Heuristics and Biases. *Science* 185:1124–1131.

Tyhurst, J. 1951. Individual Reactions to Community Disaster. *American Journal of Psychiatry* 107:764–769.

U.S. Atomic Energy Commission. 1972. *Final Environmental Statement, Three Mile Island Nuclear Station, Units 1 and 2*. Washington, DC: Directorate of Licensing, December.

U.S. Department of Energy. 1981a. *Final Environmental Impact Statement, Solvent Refined Coal-I Demonstration Project, DOE/EIS–0073*. Washington, DC: U.S. Department of Energy, July 1981.

U.S. Department of Energy. 1981b. *Final Environmental Impact Statement, Solvent Refined Coal-II Demonstration Project*, DOE/EIS–0069/V1. Washington, D.C.: U.S. Department of Energy, January.

U.S. Nuclear Regulatory Commission. 1976a. *Final Supplement to the Final Environmental Statement, Three Mile Island Nuclear Station, Unit 2,*

NUREG- 0112. Washington, DC: U.S. Nuclear Regulatory Commission Office of Nuclear Reactor Regulation, December.

U.S. Nuclear Regulatory Commission. 1976b. *Draft Supplement to the Final Environmental Statement, Three Mile Island Nuclear Station, Unit 2, NUREG- 0066.* Washington, DC: U.S. Nuclear Regulatory Commission Office of Nuclear Reactor Regulation, July.

U.S. Nuclear Regulatory Commission. 1979. *Final Environmental Statement, Greene County Nuclear Power Plant, NUREG–0512.* Washington, DC: U.S. Nuclear Regulatory Commission, Office of Nuclear Reactor Regulation, January.

U.S. Nuclear Regulatory Commission. 1982. Personal communication, Michael Kaltman, April 30.

VanAarsdol, M., G. Sabagh, and F. Alexander. 1964. Reality and the Perception of Environmental Hazards. *Journal of Health and Human Behavior* 5:144–155.

Vlek, C. and P. Stallen. 1980. Rational and Personal Aspects of Risk. *Acta Psychologica* 45(1–3):273–300.

Vosburg, R. 1971. Disaster Alert and the Community Mental Health Center. *Community Mental Health Journal* 7:24–28.

Walker, P., W. Fraize, J. Gordon, and R. Johnson. 1982. *Workshop on Psychological Stress Associated with the Proposed Restart of Three Mile Island Unit 1, NUREG/CP–0026,* Washington, DC: U.S. Nuclear Regulatory Commission.

Wallace, A. 1956. Tornado in Worcester: An Exploratory Study of Individual and Community Behavior in an Extreme Situation. *National Research Council Committee on Disaster Studies.* 3, Publication No. 392. Washington, DC: National Academy of Science.

Walsh, E. 1981. Resource Mobilization and Citizen Protest in Communities around Three Mile Island. *Social Problems* 29(1):1–21.

Warren, R. 1972. *The Community in America* (2nd Ed.). Chicago, IL: Rand McNally.

Wasserman, I. and L. Chua. 1980. Objective and Subjective Social Indicators of the Quality of Life in American SMSAs. A Reanalysis. *Social Indicators Research.* 8:305–381.

Waterstone, M. 1978. *Hazard Mitigation Behavior of Urban Floodplain Residents.* University of Colorado, Institute of Behavioral Science, Natural Hazards Working Paper No. 35. Boulder, CO: University of Colorado.

Watzlawick, P., J. Beavin, and D. Jackson. 1967. *Pragmatics of Human Communication.* New York: W. W. Norton and Co.

Webb, E., D. Campbell, R. Schwartz, and L. Sechrest. 1966. *Unobtrusive*

Measures: Nonreactive Research in the Social Sciences. Chicago, IL: Rand McNally.

Weber, M. 1947. *The Theory of Social and Economic Organizations*. Translated by A. M. Henderson and T. Parsons. New York: The Free Press.

Weinberg, A. *et al*. 1984. *The Second Nuclear Era*. Oak Ridge, TN: Institute for Energy Analysis, Oak Ridge Associated Universities.

Weller, J. and D. Wenger. 1973. Disaster Subcultures. The Cultural Residues of Community Disasters. Paper presented at the North Central Sociological Society Meetings. Cincinnati, OH.

Wellman, B. 1973. Community Ties and Support Systems. In Bourne (ed.), *The Form of Cities in Central Canada*. Toronto: University of Toronto Press.

White, G. 1945. *Human Adjustment to Floods*. Department of Geography, Research Paper No. 29. Chicago, IL: University of Chicago Press.

White G. 1964. *Choice of Adjustments to Floods*. University of Chicago, Department of Geography. Research Paper No. 93. Chicago, IL: University of Chicago Press.

White G. 1981. Commentary, pp. 171–177. In *Social Science and Natural Hazards*, J. D. Wright and P. H. Rossi (eds.). Cambridge, MA: Abt Books.

White G. (ed). 1974. *Natural Hazards: Local, National, Global*. New York: Oxford University Press.

White, G., D. Bradley, and A. White. 1972. *Drawers of Water*. Chicago, IL: University of Chicago Press.

White, G., and J. Haas. 1975. *Assessment of Research on Natural Hazards*. Cambridge, MA: Massachusetts Institute of Technology Press.

White, G. *et al*. 1958. *Changes in Urban Occupance of Floodplains in the United States*. Department of Geography Research Paper No. 57. Chicago, IL: University of Chicago Press.

Whyte, A. 1977. The Role of Information Flow in Controlling Industrial Lead Emissions. The Case of the Avonmouth Smelter. In *Proceedings of the International Conference on Heavy Metals*. Toronto: Institute for Environmental Studies.

Whyte, A. and I. Burton (eds.). 1980. *Environmental Risk Assessment*. New York: Wiley.

Wilmot, W. 1975. *Dyadic Communication: A Transactional Perspective*. Reading, MA: Addison-Wesley.

Wilson, T. 1962. Disaster and Mental Health, pp. 124–150. In Baker and Chapman (eds.), *Man and Society in Disaster*. New York: Basic Books.

Windham, G., E. Posey, P. Ross, and B. Spencer. 1977. *Reactions to Storm*

Threat During Hurricane Eloise. State College, Mississippi: Mississippi State University, Social Science Research Center Report 51.

Withey, S. 1962. Reaction to Uncertain Threat, pp. 93–123. In G. Baker and D. Chapman (eds.), *Man and Society in Disaster.* New York: Basic Books.

Withey, S. 1964. Sequential Accommodations to Threat, pp. 105–114. In G. Grosser, H. Wechsler, and M. Greenblatt (eds.), *The Threat of Impending Disaster.* Cambridge, MA: Massachusetts Institute of Technology Press.

Wolf, S. 1980. Public Opposition to Hazardous Waste Sites: The Self-Defeating Approach to National Hazardous Waste Control under Subtitle C of the Resource Conservation and Recovery Act of 1976. *Environmental Affairs* 8:463–540.

Wolfenstein, M. 1957. *Disaster: A Psychological Essay.* New York: Mac Millan.

Wolpert J. 1964. The Decision Process in Spatial Context. *Annals, Association of American Geographers.* 54:537–58.

Wolpert, J. 1965. Behavioral Aspects of the Decision to Migrate. *Papers and Proceedings, Regional Science Association.* 15:159–69.

Wolpert, J. 1966. Migration as an Adjustment to Environmental Stress. In R. W. Kates and J. F. Wohlwill (eds.). *Man's Response to the Physical Environment. Journal of Social Issues* 22:92–102.

Wortman, C. 1976. Causal Attribution and Personal Control. In J. Harvey, W. Ickers and R. Kidd (eds.), *New Directions in Attribution Research.* Hillsdale, NJ: Erlbaum.

Wright, J. and P. Rossi. 1981. The Politics of Natural Disaster: State and Local Elites, pp. 45–67. In J. D. Wright and P. H. Rossi (eds.), *Social Science and Natural Hazards.* Cambridge, MA: Abt Books.

Wright, J., P. Rossi, S. Wright, and E. Weber-Burdin. 1979. *After the Clean-Up: Long-Range Effects of Natural Disasters.* Beverly Hills, CA: Sage.

Young, M. 1954. The Role of the Extended Family in a Disaster. *Human Relations.* 7:383–391.

Zald, M. and J. McCarthy. 1979. *The Dynamics of Social Movements.* Cambridge, MA: Winthrop.

Zeigler, D., S. Brunn, and J. Johnson, Jr. 1981. Evacuation from a Nuclear Technological Disaster. *The Geographical Review* 71:1–16.

Index

231